DEFINING MOMENTS
WOODSTOCK

DEFINING MOMENTS
WOODSTOCK

Kevin Hillstrom and Laurie Collier Hillstrom

155 W. Congress, Suite 200
Detroit, MI 48226

Omnigraphics, Inc.

Kevin Hillstrom, *Series Editor*
Cherie D. Abbey, *Managing Editor*

Peter E. Ruffner, *Publisher*
Matthew P. Barbour, *Senior Vice President*

Elizabeth Collins, *Research and
Permissions Coordinator*
Kevin M. Hayes, *Operations Manager*

Mary Butler, *Researcher*
Shirley Amore, Joseph Harris, Martha Johns,
and Kirk Kauffmann, *Administrative Staff*

Library of Congress Cataloging-in-Publication Data

Hillstrom, Kevin, 1963-
  Woodstock / by Kevin Hillstrom and Laurie Collier Hillstrom.
    p. cm. — (Defining moments)
  Includes bibliographical references and index.
  Summary: "Provides a comprehensive account of the 1969 Woodstock Music and Art Fair. Places Woodstock within the context of the 1960s; describes the festival itself; details how Woodstock changed American popular music; and explores the festival's enduring significance. Includes a narrative overview, biographies, primary sources, chronology, glossary, bibliography, and index"—Provided by publisher.
  ISBN 978-0-7808-1284-0 (hardcover : alk. paper) 1. Woodstock Festival (1969 : Bethel, N.Y.) I. Title.
  ML38.B43W64 2012
  781.66078'74735--dc23   2012026921

TABLE OF CONTENTS

Primary Sources

PREFACE

Throughout the course of America's existence, its people, culture, and institutions have been periodically challenged—and in many cases transformed—by profound historical events. Some of these momentous events, such as women's suffrage, the civil rights movement, and U.S. involvement in World War II, invigorated the nation and strengthened American confidence and capabilities. Others, such as the Great Depression, the Vietnam War, and Watergate, have prompted troubled assessments and heated debates about the country's core beliefs and character.

Some of these defining moments in American history were years or even decades in the making. The Harlem Renaissance and the New Deal, for example, unfurled over the span of several years, while the American labor movement and the Cold War evolved over the course of decades. Other defining moments, such as the Cuban missile crisis and the Japanese attack on Pearl Harbor, transpired over a matter of days or weeks.

But although significant differences exist among these events in terms of their duration and their place in the timeline of American history, all share the same basic characteristic: they transformed the United States' political, cultural, and social landscape for future generations of Americans.

Taking heed of this fundamental reality, American citizens, schools, and other institutions are increasingly emphasizing the importance of understanding our nation's history. Omnigraphics' *Defining Moments* series was created for the express purpose of meeting this growing appetite for authoritative, useful historical resources. This series will be of enduring value to anyone interested in learning more about America's past—and in understanding how those historical events continue to reverberate in the twenty-first century.

Each individual volume of *Defining Moments* provides a valuable resource for readers interested in learning about the most profound events in our nation's history. Each volume is organized into three distinct sections—Narrative Overview, Biographies, and Primary Sources.

- The **Narrative Overview** provides readers with a detailed, factual account of the origins and progression of the "defining moment" being examined. It also explores the event's lasting impact on America's political and cultural landscape.

- The **Biographies** section provides valuable biographical background on leading figures associated with the event in question. Each biography concludes with a list of sources for further information on the profiled individual.

- The **Primary Sources** section collects a wide variety of pertinent primary source materials from the era under discussion, including official documents, papers and resolutions, letters, oral histories, memoirs, editorials, and other important works.

Individually, each of these sections is a rich resource for users. Together, they comprise an authoritative, balanced, and absorbing examination of some of the most significant events in U.S. history.

Other notable features contained within each volume in the series include a glossary of important individuals, places, and terms; a detailed chronology featuring page references to relevant sections of the narrative; an annotated bibliography of sources for further study; an extensive general bibliography that reflects the wide range of historical sources consulted by the author; and a subject index.

New Feature—Research Topics for Student Reports

Each volume in the *Defining Moments* series now includes a list of potential research topics for students. Students working on historical research and writing assignments will find this feature especially useful in assessing their options.

Information on the highlighted research topics can be found throughout the different sections of the book—and especially in the narrative overview, biography, and primary source sections. This wide coverage gives readers the flexibility to study the topic through multiple entry points.

Acknowledgements

This series was developed in consultation with a distinguished Advisory Board comprised of public librarians, school librarians, and educators. They evaluated the series as it developed, and their comments and suggestions were invaluable throughout the production process. Any errors in this and other volumes in the series are ours alone. Following is a list of board members who contributed to the *Defining Moments* series:

Comments and Suggestions

We welcome your comments on *Defining Moments: Woodstock* and suggestions for other events in U.S. history that warrant treatment in the *Defining Moments* series. Correspondence should be addressed to:

Editor, *Defining Moments*
Omnigraphics, Inc.
155 West Congress, Suite 200
Detroit, MI 48226

HOW TO USE THIS BOOK

Defining Moments: Woodstock provides users with a detailed and authoritative overview of this pivotal episode in U.S. cultural history. The preparation and arrangement of this volume—and all other books in the *Defining Moments* series—reflect an emphasis on providing a thorough and objective account of events that shaped our nation, presented in an easy-to-use reference work.

Woodstock is divided into three main sections. The first of these sections, **Narrative Overview**, provides a comprehensive account of the 1969 Woodstock Music and Art Fair, one of the seminal cultural events of the last half-century in America. Coverage begins with two chapters that put Woodstock within the larger context of the 1960s, a turbulent decade that brought wrenching change to American politics, culture, and music. The narrative overview then focuses in on the festival itself, with chapters devoted to the frantic preparations for the three-day concert, the music of Woodstock, and the experiences of the young men and women who attended the iconic show. This section concludes by examining the various ways in which Woodstock has changed the trajectory of American popular music—both as a business and as an art form—and exploring the festival's enduring symbolic significance.

The second section, **Biographies**, provides informative biographical profiles of individuals who played an important role at Woodstock or in the wider world of rock and roll in the 1960s. Biographies are provided for all four of the principal organizers of the festival (Michael Lang, Artie Kornfeld, John Roberts, and Joel Rosenman), leading musicians who performed at Woodstock (Joan Baez and Jimi Hendrix) and other individuals who helped shape the Zeitgeist of the festival (Woodstock host Max Yasgur) or the defiant music of the era (singer-songwriter Bob Dylan).

The third section, **Primary Sources**, collects essential and illuminating documents on Woodstock. Featured primary sources include Michael Lang's recollection of the mad scramble to find a site for the festival; an account of the concert experience from the drummer of a previously unknown band called Santana; a firsthand account of the making of the famous *Woodstock* film documentary; and diverse assessments of Woodstock's legacy, both from participants and from those who followed the weekend's events from afar.

Other valuable features in *Defining Moments: Woodstock* include the following:

- Attribution and referencing of primary sources and other quoted material to help guide users to other valuable historical research resources.

- Glossary of Important People, Places, and Terms.

- Detailed Chronology of events with a *see reference* feature. Under this arrangement, events listed in the chronology include a reference to page numbers within the Narrative Overview wherein users can find additional information on the event in question.

- Photographs of the leading figures and major events associated with the Woodstock Music and Art Fair and Sixties counterculture.

- Sources for Further Study, an annotated list of noteworthy works about Woodstock and the fast-changing world of rock and roll in the 1960s.

- Extensive Bibliography of works consulted in the creation of this book, including books, periodicals, and Internet sites.

- A Subject Index.

RESEARCH TOPICS FOR
DEFINING MOMENTS: WOODSTOCK

When students receive an assignment to produce a research paper on a historical event or topic, the first step in that process—settling on a subject for the paper—can also be one of the most vexing. In recognition of that reality, each book in the *Defining Moments* series now highlights research areas/topics that receive extensive coverage within that particular volume.

Potential research topics for students using *Defining Moments: Woodstock* include the following:

- Examine how important historical events like the Vietnam War and the civil rights movement inspired changes in the world of American popular music during the 1960s.

- Discuss the ways in which Woodstock symbolized the "hippie" countercultural lifestyle that became popular in the 1960s.

- Study the preparations undertaken by Woodstock's promoters and organizers for the festival and the differing reactions to the festival from Wallkill, opponents in Bethel, and Max Yasgur. Summarize their positions and explain which one would most closely approximate your own attitude if your community was asked to host a Woodstock-type festival.

- Explain the importance of the Woodstock film documentary and albums to the event's continued fame.

- Compare and contrast the events at Woodstock with those at Altamont. What factors contributed to the wildly different atmospheres at these two concert events? Which festival stands as a more accurate symbol of American society in the late 1960s?

- Examine the history of Woodstock anniversary concerts. In what ways were these events successful, and in what ways did they fall short? If a fiftieth anniversary Woodstock celebration was announced for 2019, would you support or oppose such a concert?

- Explore popular music trends during other turbulent periods of American history, such as the Civil War, the Great Depression, and World War II. How did the popular songs of these eras reflect or shape public attitudes? Who were the leading musical artists of these eras and why?

- Discuss the ways in which generational tensions contributed to the growth of rock and roll in the 1960s, and provide examples of ways in which these tensions are still present in popular music today.

- Document and explain the fascination that Woodstock continues to hold for many Americans today.

NARRATIVE OVERVIEW

PROLOGUE

The 1960s was a decade of alienation and rebellion for millions of American young people. All across the country, teenagers and young men and women expressed profound dissatisfaction with the society in which they had been raised. They condemned U.S. involvement in the war in the distant Asian land of Vietnam, despaired at the racism and poverty that afflicted the nation, criticized the materialism of American society, and adopted attitudes toward sex and drugs and popular music that shocked their parents and communities. Many of the young people who held these attitudes grew their hair long, wore colorful clothing, and adopted other behaviors with the conscious goal of setting themselves apart from mainstream American culture.

These same "hippies," as they came to be known, expressed a longing for a more peaceful and carefree world. By the late 1960s they had adopted "countercultural" lifestyles that orbited around recreational drug use, non-Western religions and cultures, sexual freedom, a closer relationship with Mother Earth, and "doing your own thing." Some hippies even moved into group living arrangements called communes, which they hoped would take them back to the innocence and peacefulness of the Biblical Garden of Eden.

For most of the 1960s, this American counterculture evolved without any real sense of its own size or strength. But in August 1969 an event took place that showed just how much the nation's young rebels were changing American society. The event was Woodstock, a three-day rock music festival that was held on the upstate New York property of dairy farmer Max Yasgur. To the disbelief of the concert organizers and America itself, the countercultural festival attracted as many as half a million people. And while the event itself was famously marred by rainstorms, bad drug trips, and musical performances that were pushed back into the middle of the night, it became even better known for the spirit of peace, love, and fellowship that prevailed on Yasgur's farm.

For many young Americans, the Woodstock Festival confirmed the legitimacy of countercultural beliefs and attitudes. Whether they attended the concert themselves, followed the weekend's events on television and radio, or learned about the event through the 1970 documentary film *Woodstock*, they came to see Woodstock as a powerful symbol of peace and brotherhood in a troubled world.

Certainly that's how singer-songwriter Joni Mitchell viewed the festival. Mitchell had been invited to perform at Woodstock, but her manager had convinced her to fulfill a scheduled television appearance instead. Mitchell came to greatly regret this decision when she watched footage of the concert on her hotel room television. This sense of loss intensified after musicians who had played at the festival, including her then-boyfriend Graham Nash, told her what a great experience it was.

Rather than mourn the missed opportunity, though, Mitchell decided to write a song about the event. Within a few days the song, called simply "Woodstock," was done, and a few months later it was formally released on Mitchell's album *Ladies of the Canyon*. People who were at Woodstock raved that Mitchell's lyrics perfectly captured the feeling of the festival, and it quickly became the concert's unofficial anthem:

> I came upon a child of God
> He was walking along the road
> And I asked him where are you going
> And this he told me
>
> I'm going on down to Yasgur's farm
> I'm going to join in a rock 'n' roll band
> I'm going to camp out on the land
> I'm going to try an' get my soul free
>
> We are stardust
> We are golden
> And we've got to get ourselves
> Back to the garden
>
> Then can I walk beside you
> I have come here to lose the smog
> And I feel to be a cog in something turning
> Well maybe it is just the time of year

Or maybe it's the time of man
I don't know who I am
But you know life is for learning

We are stardust
We are golden
And we've got to get ourselves
Back to the garden

By the time we got to Woodstock
We were half a million strong
And everywhere there was song and celebration
And I dreamed I saw the bombers
Riding shotgun in the sky
And they were turning into butterflies
Above our nation

We are stardust
Billion year old carbon
We are golden
Caught in the devil's bargain
And we've got to get ourselves
Back to the garden[1]

"Woodstock, for some reason, impressed me as being a modern miracle, like a modern day fishes-and-loaves story," Mitchell said years later. "For a herd of people that large to cooperate so well, it was pretty remarkable and there was tremendous optimism. So I wrote the song 'Woodstock' out of these feelings, and the first three times I performed it in public, I burst into tears, because it brought back the intensity of the experience and was so moving."[2]

More than four decades have passed since Mitchell wrote that tribute to the Woodstock Music and Art Fair. Yet the most famous rock-and-roll concert in U.S. history lives on in the memories of performers and attendees, in the expansive collection of photos and videos documenting the experience, and in the event's lasting influence on America's cultural landscape. Woodstock remains a potent symbol of the 1960s—or at least an idealized version of that era, when young people came together to celebrate the power of peace, love, and music over war, materialism, and racism.

Notes

[1] Mitchell, Joni. "Woodstock." Nashville, TN: Crazy Crow Music, 1969.
[2] Quoted in Zimmer, Dave. *Crosby, Stills & Nash: The Authorized Biography.* New York: St. Martin's Press, 1984, p. 111.

Chapter One

AMERICAN CULTURE IN THE 1960s

⊸⏤⫯⏤⊶

All political systems are on the way out.... We're finally gonna get to the point where there's no more bigotry or greed or war. Peace is the way.... People are simply gonna learn that they can get more by being groovy than greedy. And when they find out, it's gonna be the biggest surprise party of all time.

—Folksinger Arlo Guthrie in *Newsweek,* September 29, 1969

When World War II drew to a close in 1945, the United States strode out of the smoking rubble of that conflict with its stature enhanced and its confidence renewed. Before the war, the American people had been mired in the horrible economic collapse known as the Great Depression. But the immense wartime demand for jeeps, airplanes, rifles, uniforms, blankets, medical supplies, and all other manner of materials had set the U.S. economy back on its feet. Just as important, America's central role in defeating the so-called Axis Powers—Japan, Italy, and Adolf Hitler's Nazi Germany—filled the U.S. population with justifiable pride. After all, millions of American households had sacrificed to help the Allies win the war. Families had sent their fathers, husbands, sons, and brothers off to battle, kept factory assembly lines humming on the home front, and accepted years of shortages of basic goods like gasoline and sugar.

With the war behind them, though, Americans were able to enjoy the benefits of peacetime. Rapid economic growth gave the average American family a higher standard of living than ever before. Advances in technology, meanwhile, bestowed new comforts, conveniences, and recreational options. Televisions sprouted in living rooms all across the country, refrigerators and other handy appliances became standard kitchen items, and shiny new vacation campers traveled on the nation's fast-expanding network of highways. The sustained economic boom of the late 1940s and 1950s also enabled record numbers of Americans to purchase automobiles, buy homes in the suburbs, and send their kids to college.

The so-called Eisenhower Years—named for moderate president Dwight D. Eisenhower, who occupied the White House from 1953 to 1961—became synonymous with cultural and economic stability and health. Music and other forms of popular culture reflected the prosperity and conservative values of the times, too. Television shows like *Ozzie and Harriet,* for example, focused on the idyllic life of a white suburban American family.

Changes on the Horizon

Just beneath this placid and prosperous surface, however, the waters were much more turbulent. America's postwar rivalry with the Communist Soviet Union seemed to intensify with each passing month. As this "Cold War" with the world's other post-World War II superpower deepened, Americans expressed increasing anxieties about the possibility of nuclear annihilation. Many Americans also succumbed to overblown fears that their country was riddled with Communist agents and sympathizers. This phenomenon came to be known as McCarthyism, in dark tribute to U.S. senator Joe McCarthy, an irresponsible and bullying anti-Communist crusader. McCarthy's conspiracy theories and accusations convinced many Americans to regard one another with suspicion and accept greater government and corporate censorship of ideas and speech in American life.

Other signs of a gathering storm were present as well. Deep in the American South, an African-American civil rights movement was stirring to life. Inspired by the U.S. Supreme Court's unanimous *Brown v. Board of Education* (1954) ruling outlawing segregation in public schools, activists began using nonviolent protests to attack the racist society that whites had built and nurtured across the South. On the West and East coasts, meanwhile, a small but influential Beat Movement emerged and spread into the American heartland (see "The Beat Generation," p. 9). This literary and cultural movement, first given life by a group of restless young writers, condemned 1950s America as a wasteland of greedy materialism, blind conformity, and shallow self-involvement.

Most Americans were completely unaware that all of these trends and movements would soon converge to remake their country forever. Political advisor and scholar Arthur Schlesinger Jr., though, recognized that a certain restlessness had taken hold in America by the end of the 1950s. Writing in Janu-

The Beat Generation

The Beat Movement was developed and popularized by a group of American writers of the 1950s who came to be collectively known as the Beat Generation. Prominent writers in this movement included Jack Kerouac, William Burroughs, Allen Ginsberg, and Gary Snyder. Their writing focused on the quest for self-awareness and enlightenment in an American culture that, in their view, had become lifeless and materialistic. Many of their works reflected an intense interest in Buddhism and other spiritual belief systems.

Followers of the Beat Movement, known as beatniks, established thriving artistic enclaves in New York City, Los Angeles, and San Francisco. These communities were characterized by a rejection of "middle-class" values, a casual attitude toward illegal drug use and sexual activity, respect for the natural world and native cultures, a distrust of traditional figures and institutions of authority, and an emphasis on the importance of individuality. A decade later, all of these attitudes would become associated to one degree or another with the 1960s counterculture.

Sources:

Charters, Ann, ed. *Beat Down to Your Soul: What Was the Beat Generation?* London: Penguin, 1991.

Morgan, Bill. *The Typewriter Is Holy: The Complete, Uncensored History of the Beat Generation.* New York: Simon and Schuster, 2010.

ary 1960, he spoke of an emerging desire for "a new sense of national purpose" among the American people—and especially among the nation's youth (see "Historian Arthur Schlesinger Jr. Predicts the 'Mood' of the 1960s," p. 155). Schlesinger also made a bold forecast for the decade to come: "The '60s will probably be spirited, articulate, inventive, incoherent, turbulent, with energy shooting off wildly in all directions. Above all, there will be a sense of motion, of leadership, and of hope."[1]

The Civil Rights Movement

When John F. Kennedy was inaugurated as America's thirty-fifth president on January 20, 1961—becoming the youngest person ever to hold the nation's highest office—he tapped into that emerging American desire to seek out new

A peaceful protester is attacked by a police dog during a 1965 civil rights demonstration in Montgomery, Alabama.

challenges and make the world an even better place. "Let the word go forth, from this time and place, to friend and foe alike, that the torch has been passed to a new generation of Americans," he declared in his inaugural address.

These sentiments certainly applied in the American South, where a bold young African-American minister named Martin Luther King Jr. led legions of young students and activists in a movement for full racial equality in America. Young African Americans constituted the heart of the great civil rights organizations of the 1960s, including King's Southern Christian Leadership Conference (SCLC), the Student Nonviolent Coordinating Committee (SNCC), the National Association for the Advancement of Colored People (NAACP), and the Congress of Racial Equality (CORE). Many of these organizations, though, also included white activists from northern universities and the American Jewish community.

As the fight for civil rights unfolded across the Deep South and the wider United States, American television screens, newspapers, and magazines were filled with disturbing images and stories of racial hatred and appalling violence. Black activists—including women and children—were repeatedly and viciously attacked by white police and state troopers with clubs, high-pressure hoses, and attack dogs. Civil rights workers were murdered by white supremacists. Black and white activists who tried to integrate southern lunch counters and buses through nonviolent protests were subjected to ugly taunts, firebombings, and beatings.

As the months passed by, however, the courage, dignity, and determination of the civil rights activists also shone through in dozens of peaceful marches and protest events. The most famous of these gatherings was the August 28, 1963, March on Washington, in which more than 250,000 Americans of all races, ages, and backgrounds gathered together in support of equality. It was at this event that King issued his landmark "I Have a Dream" speech, which talked of a future America in which his children would be judged "not by the color of their skin, but by the content of their character."

Less than three months later, Kennedy was assassinated in Dallas, Texas. His violent murder shocked the nation, but new president Lyndon B. Johnson assured his fellow Americans that he intended to pursue Kennedy's policy priorities, which included expanded civil rights for minorities. In fact, Johnson declared less than a week after Kennedy's death that "no memorial or oration or eulogy could more eloquently honor President Kennedy's memory than the earliest possible passage of the civil rights bill for which he fought so long. We have talked long enough about equal rights in this country. We have talked for one hundred years or more. It is time now to write the next chapter and write it in the books of law."[2]

Congress heeded Johnson's call to action, passing both the Civil Rights Act of 1964 and the Voting Rights Act of 1965. These pieces of legislation, combined with dozens of lesser laws passed at the state and federal levels, affirmed that African Americans and other minorities were entitled to the same civil rights and liberties that white Americans had always received.

The Vietnam War

Johnson was immensely proud of the civil rights legislation that he signed into law. He saw these measures not only as a fulfillment of American ideals, but as part of a wider plan to build a "Great Society" that would end poverty and injustice across the nation. During the mid-1960s, though, a dark shadow fell across Johnson's ambitious plans. The name of this shadow was Vietnam, a small, war-torn country located half a world away from Washington, D.C.

Back in 1954 the Southeast Asian nation of Vietnam had gained its independence from France after years of armed struggle. However, this rebellion had been carried out under the leadership of Ho Chi Minh and other dedicated Communists. The United States and some of its allies around the world were frightened at the prospect of a Communist-ruled Vietnam. Most U.S. policy-makers subscribed to the so-called "domino theory"—a belief that when one nation converted to communism, neighboring countries were at higher risk of toppling into communism as well. Hoping to prevent the spread of communism throughout the region, the United States engineered a temporary partition of Vietnam into North Vietnam and South Vietnam. The government in North Vietnam was led by Ho Chi Minh, while the one in South Vietnam was filled with anti-Communist allies of America.

> *"Let the word go forth, from this time and place, to friend and foe alike, that the torch has been passed to a new generation of Americans,"* President John F. Kennedy declared in his 1961 inaugural address.

The temporary division of Vietnam was supposed to end in 1956, when the Vietnamese people were scheduled to elect a government to lead the reunified nation. When it became clear that Ho Chi Minh was going to win, however, the United States scrapped the elections so as to keep South Vietnam out of Communist hands. This development infuriated both North Vietnam and pro-Communist people living in South Vietnam. By the late 1950s the southern Communists, known as Viet Cong, had launched a ruthless guerrilla campaign to overthrow the pro-American regime in South Vietnam and put it under Ho Chi Minh's direction. This effort was strongly supported by North Vietnam, which funneled huge amounts of supplies and fighters to the south to help the Viet Cong.

During the late 1950s and early 1960s the United States only provided military advisors and financial assistance to help South Vietnam repel these threats. In the mid-1960s, however, the war in Vietnam became increasingly "Americanized." South Vietnam's politicians and military forces were so weak, ineffectual, and incompetent that the United States took on more and more of the burden of defending the country from the Communists. In early 1965 the United States launched a sustained campaign of bombing attacks against targets in North

Vietnam. The Johnson administration and its top military advisors also began sending American combat troops into Vietnam. These soldiers quickly became South Vietnam's main defense against the Viet Cong and North Vietnamese.

U.S. troop deployments steadily grew throughout 1966 and 1967, and by late 1967, 485,000 American soldiers were stationed across the country. This intervention kept South Vietnam alive, but it also became a political nightmare for Johnson back home. American military officials, administration officials, and the president himself kept reassuring the American public and Congress that victory was near. Media coverage of the war suggested, however, that the fighting and bloodshed was just getting worse, with no end in sight. Growing numbers of Americans condemned the war for its escalating toll on Vietnamese families caught in the middle of the conflict. As U.S. casualties mounted, critics of the war also noted that most of the young American men who were losing their lives or suffering horrible injuries in Vietnam were white, black, and Hispanic kids from poor or working-class communities. Since young men attending college could avoid being drafted into the military, America's primarily white middle-class and wealthy communities suffered comparatively few losses during the war.

The Antiwar Movement

By 1967 millions of Americans from all walks of life had become outspoken opponents of U.S. military involvement in Vietnam. Opposition to the war became particularly strong on America's college campuses. Students organized a wide range of marches, candlelight vigils, sit-ins, burnings of draft cards, and other protest actions to register their anger with the war. These "doves," as they came to be known, demanded an end to the military draft and the complete withdrawal of U.S. troops from Vietnam. Their protests, however, horrified supporters of the war effort in Vietnam. These "hawks" believed that America's future depended on stopping the spread of communism in Asia. Many supporters of the war thus came to feel that antiwar protestors were foolish at best—and unpatriotic cowards at worst.

This emotional divide in American society over the Vietnam War also had a strong generational element. Some older Americans opposed the war, just as some younger Americans (especially those who had friends or family members in the military) supported the U.S. presence in Vietnam. In general, however, older Americans who had lived through World War II and the McCarthy era were more supportive of the war. College students, meanwhile, remained the

More than 100,000 people expressed their opposition to U.S. involvement in the Vietnam War at the 1967 March on the Pentagon.

backbone of the antiwar movement. Some youthful antiwar activists embraced their leadership role, but others admitted that it sometimes felt strange to be at the forefront of the movement. Antiwar activist Carl Pope, who would later become executive director of the Sierra Club environmental organization, recalled reading a *New York Times* editorial about how the youth were going to save America from the war.

> I thought, "This is bizarre. I am young. I can't get a piece in *The New York Times*. Why am I supposed to save America from the war? Why aren't *you* guys saving America from the war?" There was this tremendous sense that the generation ahead of us had abdicated. I think they believed in social action. They just wanted someone else to do it. They were not unsupportive; they just wanted someone else to lead. And so the movement was led by kids, who are impulsive—not very strategic. It's ultimately unstable and volatile.... I think [older Americans] were deeply scarred by McCarthyism. They had learned not to stick their necks out. These people were socially engaged, but they were not willing to lead. They wanted to follow.[3]

Much of the antiwar movement's rhetoric focused on the moral failings of the "establishment"—lawmakers, judges, police officers, parents, and other authority figures in American society. Among activists, though, there was widespread disagreement about whether these people were hopelessly corrupt or just tragically mistaken in their beliefs. This debate reflected the movement's growing internal turmoil as the war dragged on. Millions of protestors were genuinely dedicated to the cause. They felt that the war was unjust, and they desperately wanted the bloodshed and carnage to end. But the movement also included radical elements that seemed more focused on taunting authorities and boosting their own fame than on ending the war. Some of their actions—such as mindless acts of vandalism, desecrations of the American flag, and calls for the overthrow of the U.S. government—hurt the antiwar cause. "The fringe of the antiwar movement engaging in violence attracted more attention than the hundreds of thousands of ordinary people who occasionally marched, went to vigils, or wrote members of Congress," wrote historian Robert D. Schulzinger. "The tumult within the antiwar movement turned away as many people as it recruited."[4]

The generational divide in attitudes about the war also extended to millions of individual families. One woman recalled that she became a dedicat-

A supporter of the women's liberation movement drops her bra in a trash can during a 1968 protest of the Miss America pageant.

ed antiwar activist during her freshman year at the University of Wisconsin. "I had violent arguments with my parents every time I went home that year," she recalled. "They were really disgusted with me, and they had no sympathy whatsoever. They thought I'd become a dupe of [been deceived by] Communist propaganda. I really became estranged from my parents at that time. After a while, my father and I couldn't even talk. It was an eye-opening time, and not only for the kids."[5]

A New World of Possibilities for Women

The 1960s also saw American women begin to demand more freedom, respect, and equality from their husbands, fathers, and employers. Historically, women in American society had always been conditioned to accept the roles of housewife, chief child caregiver, and supportive spouse to the "man of the house." Their career choices were overwhelming limited to professions like teaching and nursing, both of which had a traditional caregiving quality to them. Many men did not even believe that women were capable of becoming good lawyers, doctors, engineers, scientists, or architects.

In 1963, however, author Betty Friedan published a book called *The Feminine Mystique* that challenged women to question their confinement to the traditional roles of wife and mother in American society. Friedan believed that millions of women were secretly dissatisfied with their lives. American girls and women, she wrote, "were taught to pity the neurotic, unfeminine, unhappy women who wanted to be poets or physicists or presidents. They learned that truly feminine women do not want careers, higher education, political rights—the independence and the opportunities that the old-fashioned feminists [of the suffragist movement] fought for. Some women, in their forties and fifties, still remembered painfully giving up those dreams, but most of the younger women no longer even thought about them.... All they had to do was devote their lives from earliest girlhood to finding a husband and bearing children." According to Freidan, this state of affairs was a tragedy. "Our culture does not permit women to accept or gratify their basic need to grow and fulfill their potentialities as human beings,"[6] she said.

Friedan's book jolted a new feminist movement into being in American communities, households, and dormitories. This quest for women's liberation from outdated ideas and suffocating societal expectations gathered steam throughout the 1960s. Women of all ages began demanding equal employment opportunities, equal pay for equal work, and increased reproductive rights. Younger women in particular also set about exploring their sexuality in ways that angered and scandalized older generations. Meanwhile, new "women's lib" groups like the National Organization for Women-NOW (founded in 1966) condemned American beauty pageants and advertising campaigns for implying that the worth of a girl or woman depended on her physical appearance.

"Our culture does not permit women to accept or gratify their basic need to grow and fulfill their potentialities as human beings," feminist author Betty Friedan wrote in her 1963 book The Feminine Mystique.

Many Americans acknowledged that women had been treated as second-class citizens for too long. Some older women, though, insisted that they had always been perfectly content to devote their lives to marriage and motherhood. They sometimes interpreted the views of Friedan and other feminist leaders like Gloria Steinem as attacks on their own life choices. Tradition-minded men expressed hostility to women's liberation as well. Some of them disliked the prospect of losing their dominant position in their homes and workplaces. Others were genuinely fearful that women's liberation threatened the existence of marriage, family, and other traditional cornerstones of American life. By the close of the 1960s American media outlets were breathlessly reporting that yet another divisive and emotional struggle—this one a "battle of the sexes"—was underway in the United States.

The Rise of the Counterculture

As battles over civil rights, Vietnam, women's rights, and the values of modern America swirled across the nation's political and cultural landscape, growing numbers of young people decided to turn their backs on mainstream society altogether and "do their own thing." These hippies, as they came to be

Some young Americans reacted to the turmoil of the 1960s by embracing the hippie counterculture.

known, supported racial equality and opposed the war, but relatively few of them were active members of the civil rights or antiwar movements. Despite their enthusiasm for nature and "Mother Earth," they also were not strongly engaged in the environmental movement, which pushed a wide assortment of success-ful anti-pollution and wilderness preservation campaigns during the 1960s.

Instead, these young people decided to create their own "countercul-ture." Rejecting the middle-class and upper-middle-class lifestyles from which they mostly came, the hippies built lives that centered around poetry and rock and roll music, marijuana and harder drugs like LSD (lysergic acid diethy-lamide), sexual and artistic freedom, and the pursuit of "peace and love." They also adopted a distinctive look that set them apart from mainstream Amer-ica. Men and women alike wore colorful clothing, decorated themselves with flowers and beads, and wore their hair long.

The fashion trends of the counterculture filtered down to tens of thousands of young Americans who remained in the work force or in school. Older generations of Americans were puzzled and angered by this development, which struck them as yet another rejection of traditional values. "To many parents, the counterculture's style was as repugnant as its creed," explained one analysis. "California's governor [Ronald] Reagan summed up the opposition when he defined a hippie as someone who 'dresses like Tarzan, has hair like Jane, and smells like Cheetah [the chimpanzee].'"[7]

A Year of Rage and Pain

The turmoil of the 1960s reached its peak in 1968, a year in which the American people absorbed a series of crushing and disorienting blows. The first of these blows came on January 30, when the North Vietnamese Army and Viet Cong fighters launched the Tet Offensive, a massive surprise attack on cities, towns, and military bases all across South Vietnam. U.S. and South Vietnamese forces eventually beat back this Communist assault, and many military historians have said that the Tet Offensive actually amounted to a defeat for Ho Chi Minh. But the surprise attack sparked widespread disillusionment with the war in America.

For the previous few years, the Johnson administration and top military leaders had told the American public that they were on the verge of victory in Vietnam. These assurances had shored up support for the war even as the number of U.S. casualties soared. The scale of the Tet attacks, though, made it clear to everyone that the enemy remained formidable and that the war was a long way from being over. Large numbers of Americans concluded that when it came to assessing the strength and dedication of the enemy, their leaders were either liars or fools. Respected television newsman Walter Cronkite summarized the post-Tet attitude of Americans when he declared on nationwide television that "we have been too often disappointed by the optimism of the American leaders, both in Vietnam and Washington, to have faith any longer in the silver linings they find in the darkest clouds.... It seems now more certain than ever that the bloody experience of Vietnam is to end in a stalemate."[8]

On March 31 Johnson shocked the nation with a nationally televised speech announcing that he would not run for re-election later that year. A much bigger blow came on April 4, when Martin Luther King Jr. was murdered by a white gunman in Memphis, Tennessee. The news of King's assassination triggered violent race riots in more than 100 U.S. cities, many of which were already grappling with black militants who had come to believe that the best way to end poverty and powerlessness in the ghettos was through racial separatism and acts

The 1968 Democratic National Convention was marred by violent clashes between antiwar protesters and Chicago police.

of violence against white oppressors. By the time the riots ended, entire sections of urban ghettos lay in ruins, thirty-nine people were dead (thirty-four of them black), and racial tensions across America had reached a fever pitch.

On June 5 Americans were sent into mourning once again with the shooting of Senator Robert F. Kennedy, the younger brother of slain president John F. Kennedy. The death of Kennedy in the early morning hours of June 6 was a shattering event. Kennedy had been campaigning for the Democratic presidential nomination in Los Angeles when he was assassinated, and his campaign pledges to end the Vietnam War, protect the environment, and lift people out of poverty had inspired many young Americans.

Kennedy's murder cast a giant shadow over the quest for the Democratic presidential nomination. Johnson's vice president, Hubert Humphrey, eventually clinched the spot. But Humphrey's general election campaign never recovered from the chaotic Democratic National Convention in Chicago in late August. The convention was marred by violent, nationally televised clashes outside the convention center between youthful antiwar protestors and Chicago police. News accounts and film footage of these clashes indicated that many of the officers veered out of control in their zeal to punish the protestors. "The Chicago police department responded [to the protestors] in a way that could only be characterized as sanctioned mayhem," commented *Time* magazine. "With billy clubs, tear gas, and Mace, the blue-shirted, blue-helmeted cops violated the civil rights of countless innocent citizens and contravened every accepted code of professional police discipline."[9]

In November 1968 Republican nominee Richard M. Nixon defeated Humphrey to become the thirty-seventh president of the United States. When Nixon was sworn in on January 20, 1969, though, he took leadership of a nation that was angry, confused, and wracked with deep racial, generational, political, cultural, and economic divisions.

Notes

[1] Schlesinger, Arthur, Jr. "The New Mood in Politics" (1960). In *The Politics of Hope and the Bitter Heritage: American Liberalism in the 1960s*. Princeton, NJ: Princeton University Press, 2008, pp. 105-20.

[2] Johnson, Lyndon B. Address before a Joint Session of Congress, November 27, 1963. *Public Papers of the Presidents of the United States: Lyndon B. Johnson, 1963-64. Volume 1*. Washington, DC: Government Printing Office, pp. 8-10. Retrieved from www.lbjlib.utexas.edu/johnson/kennedy/Joint%20 Congress%20Speech/speech.htm.

[3] Quoted in Brokaw, Tom. *Boom: Voices of the Sixties, Personal Reflections on the '60s and Today.* New York: Random House, p. 415.

[4] Schulzinger, Robert D. *A Time for War: The United States and Vietnam, 1941-1975*. New York: Oxford University Press, 1997, p. 244.

[5] Quoted in Morrison, Joan, and Robert K. Morrison, eds. *From Camelot to Kent State: The Sixties Experience in the Words of Those Who Lived It.* New York: Times Books, 1987, p. 160.

[6] Friedan, Betty. *The Feminine Mystique*. 1963. New York: W.W. Norton, 2001, pp. 57, 133.

[7] Editors of Time-Life Books. *Turbulent Years: The 60s.* Alexandria, VA: Time-Life Books, 1998, p. 137.

[8] Cronkite, Walter. CBS Evening News television broadcast, February 27, 1968. *Reporting Vietnam: Part One: American Journalism 1959-1969.* New York: Library of America, 1988, pp. 581-82.

[9] "Dementia in the Second City." *Time,* September 6, 1968. Retrieved from www-cgi.cnn.com/ALLPOLITICS /1996/analysis/back.time/9609/06/.

Chapter Two

MUSIC DRIVES SOCIAL CHANGE

<hr>

I think we designed rock 'n' roll specifically for parents to hear what we had to say.

—Richie Havens in a 2007 interview with jambase.com

As American culture and politics became enveloped in turmoil and controversy during the 1960s, the nation's music underwent radical changes. Sometimes the new sounds and lyrics echoed the surging chaos and confusion in American society. Other times, the songs created by the era's leading musical artists and bands amplified the youthful discontent and disillusionment that seemed to be bursting out of every nook and cranny of America. And on a few memorable occasions, songs of the 1960s stood at the forefront of social protest. These songs did not just *react* to events, they actually *inspired* new actions and levels of participation in the antiwar and civil rights movements. During the 1960s, summarized scholar Les Cleveland, "contemporary popular music [became] related directly to the passions and anxieties of an entire generation of people."[1]

Early Days of Rock and Roll

The music that would come to be known by the all-encompassing name of rock and roll first stirred to life in the 1950s. During the course of that decade, white record producers, musicians, and singers built on (or stole from, according to some rock historians) the sturdy foundations of gospel and rhythm and blues, vital musical forms that had been honed into being over the previous few decades by African-American artists.

Elvis Presley was one of the biggest stars of the 1950s, during the early days of rock-and-roll music.

A few African-American musicians and singers rocketed to fame during this time. The energy, talent, and charisma of black artists like Chuck Berry, Ruth Brown, Fats Domino, Little Richard, Ray Charles, and Big Joe Turner enabled them to build thriving careers despite the ugly racial animosities of the era. American record companies, however, sensed that there were greater profits to be had by nurturing the careers of white musicians. Consequently, they began combing the country for brash and handsome young rock and rollers who could be marketed to white teenagers. The best of these artists—people like Elvis Presley, Jerry Lee Lewis, Buddy Holly, Carl Perkins, and the Everly Brothers—burned with passion for the blues and country music, the latter of which had been developed by both white and black artists during the pre-World War II era. Presley, Lewis, and other white artists released an avalanche of hit singles during the mid-1950s. Their songs of teenage romance, rebellion, and wild times were hugely popular with their target audience, but the sexually charged posturing and dancing of Presley and some of his peers scandalized older Americans—and especially parents.

In the late 1950s the young genre of rock and roll fell into a creative lull. This slump was partially attributed to the disappearance from the stage of Presley, Lewis, and Holly in quick succession. Presley began serving a two-year stint in the Army in 1958, the same year that the public learned that the twenty-three-year-old Lewis had married his thirteen-year-old cousin the year before. The scandal nearly ruined Lewis's career. He disappeared from radio air waves until the late 1960s, when he reinvented himself as a country artist. Holly, meanwhile, died in a tragic 1959 airplane crash that also took the lives of fellow rock and rollers Richie Valens and J.P. "Big Bopper" Richardson.

The biggest culprit in rock and roll's creative slump, though, was the music industry itself. Record producers and record companies had become so preoccupied with smoothing off the roughest edges of black rhythm-and-blues music for white mass consumption that they had robbed the music of all its vitality and energy. By the end of the 1950s the kings of the pop world were "safe," clean-cut, and uncontroversial singers like Bobby Vinton, Fabian, and Pat Boone. In addition, televised music shows like Dick Clark's *American Bandstand*, which had been created to capitalize on white teens' fascination with rock and roll, scrubbed the music of much of its controversial content.

The Age of Protest Music

In the early 1960s American popular music received a new injection of energy and creativity. The source was acoustic folk music, which during the 1930s and 1940s had been led by guitar-strumming social commentators like Woody Guthrie, Pete Seeger, and Seeger's band the Weavers. During the 1950s, however, folk songs that praised labor unions, promoted civil rights, and condemned class inequality aroused the suspicions of conservative McCarthyites. They claimed that artists like Seeger who sang of racial equality and workers' rights actually harbored secret Communist agendas. These charges, which were leveled at a time when Cold War fears were peaking, had a chilling effect on the careers of many folk artists. Seeger and the Weavers, for example, were blacklisted—banned—from American radio and television for many years.

The civil rights movement and the Cold War, though, proved to be irresistible subjects to a new generation of folksingers. These issues had been ricocheting around in the American consciousness since their childhoods. During the early 1960s, fears of nuclear annihilation, opposition to the Vietnam War, and stories of white racial hatred in the South seemed to be escalating with each passing week. Young troubadours spoke out on these and other social and political issues with voices that burned with conviction. Many artists contributed to this fast-rising wave of "protest music," including Joan Baez (see Baez biography, p. 115), Tom Paxton, and Phil Ochs. The undisputed king of the early 1960s folk revival, though, was a skinny, tousle-haired native of Minnesota known as Bob Dylan (see Dylan biography, p. 119).

In 1962 and 1963 Dylan composed, recorded, and performed a flurry of songs that became powerful anthems among civil rights activists and members of the peace movement. Some of his songs shone a spotlight on racial injustice and the bigotry of poor whites ("The Lonesome Death of Hattie Carroll," "Only a Pawn in Their Game," "Oxford Town") while others attacked McCarthyism and the Cold War arms race ("Masters of War," "Talkin' John Birch Society Blues," "With God On Our Side," "Talkin' World War III Blues").

Dylan's most enduring protest songs from this period, though, were not explicitly oriented toward specific events or controversies. Instead, songs like "A Hard Rain's A-Gonna Fall," "The Times They Are A-Changin'," "When the Ship Comes In," and "Blowin' in the Wind" used a powerful blend of inspirational and apocalyptic imagery to conjure up visions of an America that was on the verge of sweeping transformation. Fellow folksinger Dave Van Ronk recalled that when he heard "A Hard Rain's A-Gonna Fall" for the first time, "it absolutely stunned me…. I was acutely aware that it represented the beginning of an artistic revolution."[2] Songwriter and actor Kris Kristofferson offered a similar assessment. Dylan's songwriting "liberated me," he recalled. "It was like poetry. He elevated pop songs from 'That Doggie in the Window' to an art form. Something respectable."[3]

> *Bob Dylan's songwriting "was like poetry," recalled songwriter and actor Kris Kristofferson. "He elevated pop songs from 'That Doggie in the Window' to an art form. Something respectable."*

When the folk trio Peter, Paul, and Mary released a cover version of "Blowin' in the Wind" in 1963, it rocketed to the top of the charts. The song's popularity also sealed Dylan's reputation as the unofficial spokesman of an emerging generation of idealistic young Americans fighting against bigotry, poverty, and nuclear holocaust. This image was further burnished in March 1963, when he and Baez (with whom he had a brief but intense romantic relationship) performed together at the famous March on Washington for civil rights.

Dylan Goes Electric

By the close of 1963, though, Dylan showed growing signs of unhappiness with his status as America's leading chronicler of social problems. He was eager to explore more personal themes in his songs, and he resented pressure from fellow "folkies" and liberal political activists to keep shaping his work to meet their needs and expectations.

Over the next two years Dylan walked away from what he called his "finger-pointing songs," as well as the simple work clothes of his folksinging days. Instead, Dylan self-consciously adopted a mysterious and caustic hipster image, complete with sunglasses that he seemed to wear day and night. More importantly, he released three albums—*Bringing It All Back Home, Highway 61 Revis-*

Bob Dylan started a seismic shift in the American music scene when he "went electric" at the 1965 Newport Folk Festival.

ited, and *Blonde on Blonde*—of wildly inventive, angry, rebellious, and surreal songs backed with electric instrumentation. "It wasn't a rejection of protest music," said poet Allen Ginsberg, "because he continued writing music that was relevant in that way. But he didn't want to be limited, he didn't want to be stereo-

27

typed as the protest boy. Because he could expand much beyond that as a poet, and as a singer."[4] The lead single off *Highway 61 Revisited* was "Like a Rolling Stone," a raucous song of youthful alienation that clocked in at over six minutes, almost three times as long as most hit singles of the era. Today, rock historians continue to rank "Stone" as one of the most influential songs in rock-and-roll history.

Dylan's shifting musical vision was on vivid display at the 1965 Newport Folk Festival. The annual festival was the most prestigious concert event in the world of folk music, but it also emphasized traditional acoustic music. When Dylan defiantly played a blistering set of songs fueled by electric guitars and pounding percussion, folk purists like Seeger were furious. As it turned out, though, Dylan was carving out a new path for musicians and audiences alike. "Rock fans were accustomed to going to concerts to be near an idol, to jump up and down, perhaps to scream," wrote rock critic Robert Palmer. "What Dylan in 1965 managed to do was to blast himself free from the intellectual complacency of the folk scene while daring the rock fans to *listen* [to the lyrics]. ... It didn't take long for Dylan's new style to hit home. As the Beatles and every other rock musician with artistic pretensions understood immediately, it was the end of 'yeah yeah yeah' and the start of something else—a new kind of music, made for a new kind of listener."[5]

An Explosion of New Sounds

No band was changed as much by its exposure to Dylan as the Beatles. During the early 1960s the Beatles (John Lennon, Paul McCartney, George Harrison, and Ringo Starr) had perfected a brand of sunny and romantic pop that made them superstars in America as well as their native England. But Dylan's electric turn and his challenging lyrics fascinated Lennon and McCartney, who had only begun to tap their potential as songwriters. Dylan also introduced the Beatles to marijuana in an August 1964 meeting, and the drug was soon being regularly used by all four band members before, during, and after songwriting sessions.

In 1965-1966 the Beatles released two classic albums, *Rubber Soul* and *Revolver*, that displayed a new sense of musical adventure and lyrical richness. They also carried out a 1966 U.S. concert tour in support of *Revolver*, but sound-system technology of the era was so poor that they could not even hear themselves playing over the screams of their teenaged female fans. From this point forward

The Beatles, shown performing on television in 1964, created songs with more depth and relevance in the second half of the decade.

the band abandoned live touring and focused its energies on the recording studio. Over the next few years the Beatles produced several more albums (including *Sgt. Pepper's Lonely Hearts Club Band, Let It Be,* and *Abbey Road*) that vaulted them to a place among rock and roll's legendary bands. Years later, Lennon acknowledged that the band's ascent to stardom made for an exhilarating ride. "We were all on this ship in the sixties, our generation, a ship going to discover the New World," he said. "And the Beatles were in the crow's nest of that ship."[6]

Other exciting musical trends were in the air as well. Bands like the Roger McGuinn-led Byrds borrowed from Dylan and the Beatles to create a blend of acoustic and electric sound that came to be known as folk rock. The civil rights gains of the 1960s, meanwhile, opened the doors for African-American singers, musicians, and songwriters to become celebrities across *all* of American society, not just in its black communities. Motown Records in Detroit and the Memphis-based Stax/Volt label led the way in bringing "soul music"—a fusion of pop, blues, and gospel—to America, but the performers came from everywhere. Artists like Aretha Franklin, Otis Redding, Wilson Pickett, James Brown, Marvin Gaye, Diana Ross and the Supremes, the Temptations, Curtis Mayfield, and Sly and the Family Stone sang about everything from timeless subjects like love, jealousy, and self-respect to the need for greater peace and understanding in the world. Unlike previous generations of black performers, though, the music of these singers and bands of the Sixties could be heard coming out of millions of white-owned households and car radios.

> *"The fact that our generation owned the music was very important," confirmed one young music lover. "Our music was an essential part of our lives. It defined us as a movement, a unique culture that was for us and no one else. It was like a secret language, unbeknownst to the elders."*

The evolving world of rock music was also viewed as the unique property of a single generation of young people, which gave it additional symbolic value. "The fact that our generation owned the music was very important," confirmed one young music lover who ended up making the trek to Woodstock. "My parents had their old favorites, like wartime tunes and hymns, but that reflected a nostalgic past that was totally meaningless to me. *Our* music was an essential part of our lives. It defined us as a movement, a unique culture that was for us and no one else. It was like a secret language, unbeknownst to the elders."[7]

"The mid-sixties were a very fortunate period to be a part of," remembered musician Robbie Robertson of the well-known rock group The Band. "The Beatles were making very interesting records, there was a whole wave of amazing music coming from Motown and Stax, and Dylan was writing songs with much more depth than what had come along before. Everything was changing, all these doors were being opened, and it made you think, 'I could try *anything, right now.*' Revolutionary times are very healthy for experimenting and trying stuff—and for being fearless in what you try."[8]

Acid Rock and the Counterculture

Another major musical development of the 1960s was the emergence of acid rock, also known as psychedelic rock. This music blended core elements of folk rock, blues, and pop with heavy use of marijuana, LSD (or "acid"), and other hallucinogenic drugs. The final result was a multi-year stream of musical experimentation that hailed mind-altering substances and sexual freedom and urged young people to "do your own thing" and reject the conformity of mainstream America. Not surprisingly, the nation's growing hippie counterculture embraced many of the new acid-rock songs as anthems.

The Grateful Dead helped shape the psychedelic or acid rock music that became the soundtrack for the 1960s counterculture movement.

The roots of acid rock have frequently been traced back to the drug-fueled mid-Sixties output of Dylan and the Beatles (band members later referred to *Rubber Soul* as their "pot album" and *Revolver* as their "LSD album"). The musicians of the psychedelic-rock movement made a much more explicit linkage between their music and drug use, though. One of the earliest acid-rock hits, for example, was "Eight Miles High" (1966) by the Byrds. The lyrics were nominally about a plane flight to England, but the song was widely interpreted as a tale about getting high. "Did I think 'Eight Miles High' was a drug song?" said David Crosby of the Byrds (and later the folk-rock band Crosby, Stills, and Nash). "No, I *knew* it was. We denied it, of course. But we had a strong feeling about drugs, or rather, psychedelics and marijuana. We thought they would help us blast our generation loose from the fifties."[9]

By 1967 the West Coast in general—and San Francisco in particular—had emerged as the center of the acid-rock universe. Bay Area bands like the Grateful Dead, Jefferson Airplane, Big Brother and the Holding Company, Santana, and Moby Grape were hugely influential in shaping the psychedelic sound and sensibility of the late 1960s. Several prominent rock groups from the other side of the Atlantic also added to the acid rock scene to one degree or another, including the Yardbirds, the Rolling Stones, Pink Floyd, Cream, the Who, the Small Faces, and the Jimi Hendrix Experience. These bands formed the leading edge of yet another music industry phenomenon of the 1960s—the so-called "British Invasion" of bands from the United Kingdom onto American record store shelves and airwaves.

Through it all, San Francisco and its Haight-Ashbury district remained the home base and primary playground of the acid rock movement's foremost musical acts (Jefferson Airplane and the Grateful Dead) and most dedicated fans. "San Francisco bands had developed along with an audience that largely shared their backgrounds, their values, and their choice of chemical stimulation," wrote Palmer. "They played both for and with the dancers, and their song arrangements expanded (or exploded) according to the evolving dynamic of the city's unique dance-concerts, which took place weekly in old ballrooms like the Avalon and Fillmore, and frequent free concerts in the parks."[10] In essence, both the creators and consumers of psychedelic music had come to believe that when music and drugs were combined, they attained a power that neither could acquire in isolation.

As psychedelic rock gained steam it also adopted many of the symbols, fashions, and attitudes of the emerging American counterculture. The two movements, in fact, increasingly blurred together. Concert posters, album covers, "underground" comic books, alternative newspapers, and hippie clothing all incorporated swirling, kaleidoscopic, flowery imagery that was meant to suggest the altered consciousness that hallucinogenic drugs provided. Meanwhile, America's two most controversial advocates of LSD and other hallucinogenic drugs—novelist Ken Kesey and former Harvard professor Timothy Leary—became associated with musical artists ranging from the Grateful Dead to John Lennon.

The Summer of Love Brings a New Concert Experience

As the months of 1967 ticked by and countercultural messages of personal freedom, peace, justice, and ecological awareness grew louder, tens of thousands of restless young hippies joined together in cities across America. Gatherings occurred in New York, Seattle, Chicago, Los Angeles, Philadelphia, Seattle, and many other cities, but the largest of these massive celebrations occurred in San Francisco.

The epicenter of San Francisco's so-called "Summer of Love" was Haight-Ashbury. As youth flocked to the neighborhood in search of pleasure, enlightenment, or friendship, national media outlets followed close behind in order to tell mainstream America what was going on. "*Life, Time,* and the trendspotters of the evening news outdid themselves trumpeting the new youth culture," wrote media critic and former antiwar activist Todd Gitlin. "The cultural panic spread the news, the image of hippiehood. Alarmists and proselytizers [counterculture supporters] alike collaborated in the belief that American youth en masse were abandoning the stable routes of American society and striking out onto unprecedented trails (or into unprecedented thickets)."[11]

The most famous musical event of the Summer of Love was the Monterey Pop Festival, which was held outside of San Francisco at the Monterey County Fairgrounds from June 16 to June 18. The ambitious three-day concert was organized by record producer Lou Adler and Michelle and John Phillips of the Mamas and the Papas band. From the outset, the festival was intended as "a large-scale celebration of the music-led, flower-power philosophy that was spreading around the world."[12] One concertgoer explained her expectations for the show even more vividly in an interview with documentary filmmaker D. A. Pennebaker: "I think it's gonna be like Easter and Christmas and New Year's and your birthday all together, ya know?" she said. "The vibrations are just gonna be flowing everywhere!"[13]

Folksinger Joan Baez performs on the corner of Haight and Ashbury Streets in San Francisco during the 1967 Summer of Love.

The Monterey Pop Festival featured a wide range of famous and soon-to-be-famous acts, including the Byrds, the Who, Otis Redding, Jefferson Airplane, Ravi Shankar, the Mamas and the Papas, Big Brother and the Holding Company (headed by Janis Joplin), the Grateful Dead, Buffalo Springfield, the Steve Miller Band, Simon and Garfunkel, and Jimi Hendrix (see Hendrix biography, p. 124). The high visibility of Redding, Hendrix, and several other black performers was especially noteworthy because their inclusion did not prompt any protests from the mostly white crowd. To the contrary, the sets unleashed by Redding and Hendrix were among the highlights of the entire weekend.

When it was all over, the festival's promoters, musical acts, and concertgoers all agreed that the concert had been a huge success. The festival had attracted at least 50,000 people, the biggest crowd ever for a rock and roll concert at that time. Despite the size of the crowd, the concert unfolded smoothly and peacefully. In addition, several of the musicians who performed at Monterey (such as Redding, Hendrix, Joplin, and Miller) rose to new levels of stardom on the basis of their performances in Monterey (see "Janis Joplin Sings

Janis Joplin Sings the Blues

One of the breakout stars of the 1967 Monterey Pop Festival was Janis Joplin, the female lead singer of Big Brother and the Holding Company. Born in Port Arthur, Texas, on January 19, 1943, Joplin endured a difficult adolescence. The subject of relentless taunting for her appearance, she reportedly sought to dull this pain through heavy partying and fleeting sexual encounters. "By her senior year of high school," according to Biography.com, "Joplin had developed a persona of sorts—a ballsy, tough-talking girl who liked to drink and be outrageous."

During the early 1960s Joplin left Port Arthur and drifted across the country to pursue her dreams of being a blues singer. Over the next few years she displayed an incredible singing voice and a no-holds-barred performing style, but she also showed a weakness for excessive drinking and drug use. In 1966 she showed up in San Francisco to audition for Big Brother and the Holding Company, a blues and acid rock band that was seeking a new singer. Joplin got the job, which only required her to sing on a few songs and play the tambourine. As the months passed by, however, her vocal gifts became impossible to ignore. She became the band's lead singer, and before long Big Brother had become one of the most popular bands on the San Francisco scene.

the Blues," p. 34). The festival had also showcased the growing sophistication of concert lighting and sound systems. Monterey Pop, in other words, had proven that it was possible to pull off huge, multi-day concerts with some of the biggest names in rock and roll as headliners.

Growing Anger and Alienation

The festivities of the Summer of Love reflected one side of the world of popular music during the late 1960s. Songs like "Let's Get Together" (by Jefferson Airplane) and "Everyday People" (Sly and the Family Stone) were joyful and upbeat, and they called on listeners to love one another and build a better world. The Top 40 music charts also continued to feature a heavy mix of songs like "Since You've Been Gone" by Aretha Franklin and "Good Vibrations"

In June 1967 Joplin's performance at the Monterey Pop Festival in California instantly made her one of America's most famous rock-and-roll voices. Her fearless, anguished vocals on songs like the blues classic "Ball and Chain" stunned concertgoers, critics, and fellow musicians alike. "It wasn't only her voice that thrilled, with its amazing range and strength and awesome wails," wrote biography Myra Friedman. "To see her was to be sucked into a maelstrom of feeling that words can barely suggest."

In 1968 Big Brother released *Cheap Thrills*, which was a big hit. By this time, though, Joplin's fame was creating hard feelings with other band members. Joplin decided to strike out on her own in December 1968. Her first solo album, *I've Got Dem Ol' Kozmic Blues Again Mama!*, appeared in 1969. Later that year Joplin was one of the headliners at the famous Woodstock Music Festival. On October 4, 1970, though, she was found dead of a heroin overdose in a Hollywood hotel room. A short time later a final Joplin album of previously recorded songs, called *Pearl*, was released. The album, which included the smash hit single "Me and Bobby McGee," was one of the most popular albums of 1971.

Sources:

Friedman, Myra. *Buried Alive: The Biography of Janis Joplin.* New York: Morrow, 1973.

"Janis Joplin," Biography.com. Retrieved from http://www.biography.com/people/janis-joplin-9357941?page=1.

by the Beach Boys—tunes that swirled around the timeless subjects of romantic love and regret.

On the flip side, though, late-1960s popular music also featured a growing element of disillusionment and alienation. Some of these songs, like Simon and Garfunkel's "Mrs. Robinson," mourned an America that had lost its bearings. Others, like "Fortunate Son" by Creedence Clearwater Revival and "War" by Edwin Starr, railed against the Vietnam War with new levels of ferocity.

Some of the most popular and influential rock-and-roll groups of the late 1960s, though, showed little interest in identifying or fixing social problems. Groups like the Doors, the Velvet Underground, and the Rolling Stones all offered up a steady diet of songs that provided dark and sometimes menacing perspectives on American society and even life itself. The Stones, led by vocalist Mick Jagger and guitarist Keith Richards, became particularly famous for crafting propulsive electric blues songs that sometimes seemed to glorify violence and celebrate the pursuit of earthly pleasures. Songs like "Sympathy for the Devil," "Gimme Shelter," "Street Fighting Man," and "Midnight Rambler" crackled with imagery and statements that alarmed and offended many Americans.

The songs offered up by the Stones and their less-famous brethren reflected an understanding that by the late 1960s, there were a lot of record buyers out there who had become disillusioned and hardened by the continued bloodshed in Vietnam, the assassinations of Martin Luther King Jr. and Robert F. Kennedy, and the recurring outbursts of rioting in America's inner cities. These record buyers were in an angry mood, and they were thirsty for music that reflected that anger. But while the music of the Stones, the Doors, and others was shaped in part by the desire to sell records, it also tapped into a genuine sense that the modern world had become a diseased and broken thing. "At the time, people thought the Velvet Underground was being very negative and bleak and dark," recalled Lou Reed, the band's lead singer. "Whereas I thought we were an accurate reflection of things that were happening, and were going to happen on a larger scale."[14]

Notes

[1] Cleveland Les. *Dark Laughter: War in Song and Popular Culture.* Westport, CT: Praeger, 1994.

[2] Quoted in Spitz, *Bob. Dylan: A Biography.* New York: McGraw-Hill, 1989, p. 205.

[3] Quoted in Brokaw, Tom. *Boom! Voices of the Sixties, Personal Reflections on the '60s and Today.* New York: Random House, 2007, pp. 264-66.

[4] Quoted in Palmer, Robert. *Rock and Roll: An Unruly History.* New York: Harmony Books, 1995, p. 102.

[5] Miller, James. *Flowers in the Dustbin: The Rise of Rock and Roll, 1947-1977.* New York: Simon and Schuster, 1999, pp. 223, 225.

[6] Quoted in Miles, Barry. *The British Invasion: The Music, the Times, the Era.* New York: Sterling, 2009, p. 298.

[7] Northlake, John. "I *Had* to Go," *Woodstock Revisited.* Edited by Susan Orleans. Avon, MA: Adams, 2009, p. 80.

[8] Quoted in Palmer, pp. 110-11.

[9] Quoted in Palmer, p. 166.

[10] Palmer, p. 168.

[11] Gitlin, Todd. *The Sixties: Years of Hope, Days of Rage.* New York: Bantam, 1987, p. 205.

[12] Evans, Mike, and Paul Kingsbury, eds. *Woodstock: Three Days that Rocked the World.* New York: Sterling, 2009, p. 30.

[13] Quoted in White, Armond. "Monterey Pop: People in Motion." *Current,* November 11, 2002. Retrieved from www.criterion.com/current/posts/235-monterey-pop-people-in-motion.

[14] Quoted in Palmer, p. 175.

Chapter Three

PLANNING FOR AN EPIC CONCERT

I envisioned the festival as a gathering of the tribes, a haven for like-minded people.

—Woodstock promoter Michael Lang
in *The Road to Woodstock*, 2009

The Woodstock Music Festival was in many ways a natural outgrowth of the social turbulence and musical creativity of the Sixties. The concert's slogan, which promised attendees "three days of peace and music," sent a clear message: This was an event for young people who opposed the Vietnam War and believed in Martin Luther King Jr.'s dream of universal brotherhood. Most of all, though, Woodstock called out to a younger generation that was excited about the phenomenon of rock and roll—and the rebellious, countercultural lifestyle that many top rock stars were living and singing about.

An Idea Takes Shape

The creators of the Woodstock concept were two young men who had each carved out careers in the world of rock and roll. Michael Lang was one of the country's best-known young concert promoters (see Lang biography, p. 131). Fresh off his successful staging of the Miami Pop Festival in May 1968, Lang traveled to New York City in an effort to get a record contract for a rock band that he had agreed to manage. He went to the offices of Capitol Records, where he met with young record executive Artie Kornfeld (see Kornfeld biography, p. 128).

Kornfeld was not impressed with Lang's band, but the two men nonetheless struck up a friendship, in part because they had both grown up around the

Michael Lang (left) and Artie Kornfeld dreamed up the original idea for the Woodstock Music and Art Fair.

same time in Bensonhurst, a neighborhood in Queens, New York. Before long the two young men were regularly hanging out together and sharing their hopes and dreams for the future. "Over time, Michael ended up staying at my place with me and my wife, Linda, and we'd spend nights talking and rambling until morning,"[1] recalled Kornfeld.

During the course of these late night sessions the two men frequently talked about opening their own recording studio. Neither of them had the money to build such a facility, but they kicked around the idea of obtaining the necessary funds through a series of rock concerts. As the weeks passed, these discussions evolved into conversations about the "perfect concert." They compiled lists of the bands they would invite to this fantasy event and debated the benefits and drawbacks of potential concert venues.

One of the places that Lang mentioned again and again was Woodstock, a small town in New York State where he and his girlfriend owned some property. Woodstock had attracted painters, musicians, and playwrights since the late nineteenth century, and its reputation as a popular artists' colony was still alive and well in the late 1960s. "People like Paul Butterfield, Bob Dylan, the Band, and Richie Havens were [all] living there, and it had really become the 'in' place," said Kornfeld. "We talked endlessly about putting on this show and hoped that maybe 100,000 people would show up, or at least 50,000.... I would say we dreamt about this for months and figured it would stay just that—a dream."[2]

In early 1969, though, a friend of Lang's put him and Kornfeld in touch with two young men, John Roberts and Joel Rosenman, who were interested in investing in unusual new business ideas (see Roberts biography, p. 135, and Rosenman biography, p. 142). Roberts and Rosenman were actually seeking script ideas for a television show about two young rich guys seeking their fortunes in the business world. After they heard the pitch from Lang and Kornfeld about building a recording studio and organizing a big concert, though, Roberts and Rosenman became intrigued by the idea of forming a genuine business partnership with them. This was a big development. Roberts had recently received a huge inheritance from his family's pharmaceutical business, so he could provide the initial funding for the studio and concert. Rosenman's background in law, meanwhile, would give the group someone who could draw up and review contracts and make sure all other legal affairs were in order.

Most important of all, Lang and Kornfeld felt comfortable going into business with Roberts and Rosenman. "We both liked them," recalled Lang, "and the thought of working with a couple of guys our age appealed to us.... After a few additional meetings, John agreed to finance the festival and the studio. We would become partners, and because the projects were based in Woodstock, we decided to call our company Woodstock Ventures."[3]

Planning for Three Days of Peace and Music

As the months rolled by, the recording studio idea gradually fell by the wayside, in large part because the partners of Woodstock Ventures put most of their time and energy into the music festival idea. Roberts handed over nearly $500,000 in initial financing, and he and Rosenman began putting together the festival's financial and ticketing operations from rented offices in New York City. Lang and Kornfeld turned their attention to lining up bands and hiring staff for the festival, which was scheduled for the long weekend of August 15-17.

The four partners also worked together to build a thematic name and concept for the festival, the plans for which grew more ambitious with each passing day. They eventually decided to call it "An Aquarian Exposition: The Woodstock Music and Art Fair," with a subtitle that described the event as "Three Days of Peace and Music." "We were setting out to create a new paradigm in festival events," explained Lang.

> There had been so much conflict over the past year, with violent confrontations occurring on college campuses, in urban ghettos, and at demonstrations across the country. At Woodstock we would focus our energy on peace, setting aside the onstage discussion of political issues to just groove on what might be possible. It was a chance to see if we could create the kind of world for which we'd been striving throughout the sixties. That would be our political statement—proving that peace and understanding were possible and creating a testament to the value of the counterculture.[4]

Securing big-name musical acts for the concert was a daunting challenge, but both Lang and Kornfeld possessed contacts throughout the rock music industry. Even more importantly, Roberts's money gave Woodstock Ventures instant credibility with top musicians and their agents and managers. Lang and John Morris, who also played a pivotal role in lining up the early acts, had the ability to offer paydays that were twice the size of usual concert payments to a targeted group of bands, including Jefferson Airplane, Creedence Clearwater Revival, and Canned Heat. By the end of April 1969, all of these bands had agreed to play at Woodstock. Their participation elevated Woodstock's reputation with other bands in the world of rock and roll. When musicians and bands began clamoring to be included in the suddenly "hot" event, the organizers were able to reduce some of the fees they paid out. Some acts, however, such as Jimi Hendrix and the Who, still negotiated huge paychecks for themselves.

Woodstock's organizers were thrilled with the growing lineup, despite the fact that none of rock-and-roll's "big three"—Bob Dylan, the Beatles, and the Rolling Stones—would be performing. The angry, confrontational music of the Stones was seen as a poor fit with the "peace and love" ethos of the festival, and the Beatles had stopped touring and were on the verge of breaking up. Dylan toyed with the idea of showing up and performing as an unannounced guest, but he eventually declined.

As all of these band negotiations were going on, Lang took the lead in assembling a production team capable of putting on a huge multi-day music festival. "My philosophy in all areas of festival staffing was to get the very best people available on our team," wrote Lang. "I looked for those with the most expertise in their field and, whenever possible, people who understood what we were trying to do."[5] He quickly secured the services of Stanley Goldstein, a veteran concert organizer who had worked with Lang on the 1968 Miami Pop Festival. Goldstein agreed to help Lang build a top-level staff and work on preliminary site plans. A short time later, Mel Lawrence came on board as Woodstock's director of operations, a position that gave him responsibility for overall site layout and landscaping, including the design and construction of the stage and associated lighting and sound systems.

Woodstock organizers used various methods to promote the concert, including radio stations, newspapers, and this famous poster.

Other key hires during the spring of 1969 included production stage manager Steve Cohen; technical director Chris Langhart; lighting director Chip Monck; sound engineer Bill Hanley; chief of security Wes Pomeroy; concessions director Peter Goodrich; production coordinator John Morris; and community relations director Don Ganoung. Woodstock Ventures also hired publicist Jane Friedman and her company, the Wartoke Concern, to handle public relations for the show. "The staff that I put together was really what made Woodstock work," Lang later said. "A lot of people thought it was overstaffed or top-heavy, but that's the reason we managed to get through in one piece, because these people were just the best at what they did, and they gave everything they had.... That initial group, that core group, was a really miraculous group of people."[6]

Getting the Word Out

By early summer the festival's executive staff was in place and the lineup was coming into focus. Around this same time, Woodstock Ventures began selling tickets to the show. The promoters set up a mail-order operation to process ticket orders from across the country. In addition, record stores and head shops (stores that specialize in selling pipes and other paraphernalia for drug use) all across the Northeast were recruited to sell tickets. The first advance tickets were priced at $6 each, but the promoters later changed the advance ticket system so that fans could buy a one-day ticket for $7, a two-day ticket for $13, and a ticket for all three days of the festival for $18.

Publicizing the concert was a significant challenge in the 1960s, long before Facebook, Twitter, and the Internet existed. In order to sell tickets, the Woodstock organizers first had to make rock fans aware that an epic music festival was being put together. Friedman spearheaded this effort. She organized a three-month blitz of letters and phone calls to commercial and college radio stations, mainstream newspapers and magazines, and members of the nation's "underground" press and radio—small, independent newspapers and radio stations with strong countercultural orientations. "We had developed an incredible list of underground press," she remembered.

> In those days, there was very little daily coverage of pop music, very few music magazines. We kept pummeling them and sending out the same kind of information day after day, always with something new but the same old stuff included, so that it would start to resonate. And we covered radio too, all over the world.... Suddenly we had people from across the nation wanting to come: college newspaper editors, student body presidents, student activities organizers, daily newspaper columnists, music writers, people interested in rock and roll, underground newspaper writers and editors, politically involved people.[7]

By July, thousands of tickets to Woodstock were being sold every week, and the organizers' dreams of attracting 200,000 fans suddenly seemed within reach. Lang, Kornfeld, Roberts, and Rosenman were thrilled at the growing excitement surrounding the festival. By this time, however, they also were engaged in a desperate race against the clock to find and prepare a concert site in time for the mid-August show.

The Desperate Search for a Festival Site

The hunt for a festival site had begun in early 1969. The partners in Woodstock Ventures wanted to lease rural property that was meadow-like in character, close to major roadways, and large enough to accommodate as many as

200,000 music lovers. After rejecting a few possible sites right around Woodstock, Lang and Kornfeld found a 700-acre site in nearby Saugerties. Negotiations with the landowner to lease his property got off to a promising start, but in late March the owner decided not to rent his property. The promoters later speculated that objections to the festival from town and county officials probably accounted for the landowner's change of heart.

When the Saugerties site was scratched, Lang admitted that "we started to get concerned. We had booked talent, we were hiring staff, and we had no place for the festival. We began searching areas farther afield from Woodstock, surveying properties via helicopter, and driving to check out possible sites."[8] Rosenman and Roberts quickly located an alternative 300-acre site in Wallkill, a town about 35 miles south of Woodstock. The site was not particularly attractive—it was a mostly flat and treeless tract of undeveloped industrial park land—but the organizers knew that they needed to get a site lined up so that they could start building the stage and preparing the festival grounds. They also consoled themselves by noting that the site, called the Mills Industrial Park, was easily accessible and already had water and electricity.

> *When the Woodstock promoters ran into local opposition to their concert plans, "we started to get concerned," Michael Lang admitted. "We had booked talent, we were hiring staff, and we had no place for the festival."*

Woodstock Ventures secured a rental agreement from the owner of the park, and the festival staff and their employees quickly began readying the grounds for the show. The promoters, however, still needed to get permits from the township to hold the festival. This proved to be a hurdle that was too great to overcome, even though Rosenman and Roberts downplayed the size and rock-and-roll nature of the festival to Wallkill officials. According to Goldstein, in fact, "John and Joel ... misrepresented the festival to the town: There wasn't going to be any loud music, there were going to be 50,000 people or less, and it was going to be a nice quiet country and folk festival without a lot of noise and tumult. There was no discussion of camping."[9]

Wallkill residents were not fooled. They had seen and heard the Woodstock advertisements themselves, and many of them feared that hosting the festival meant an invasion of dirty, long-haired hippies with loose morals and horrible drug habits. A Concerned Citizens' Committee was quickly established to urge the Wallkill Zoning Board to turn down the permit request—and thus prevent the festival from taking place in the town. Several meetings were held to try to address the township's concerns, but nothing worked. "It was like being discriminated against," said Lawrence. "They didn't want to hear from the music aspect of it, or this is what's going on for people right now. They just didn't want it in their place."[10]

According to Roberts, the townspeople developed a grudging respect for Lawrence and Goldstein and their knowledge of the various elements of festival site preparation, including campgrounds, food concessions, parking and traffic routing, sanitation, security, sewage disposal, and stage construction. "People who went and listened to [our] presentation usually came away impressed. 'Well, these guys know what they're doing.' [But other] people who walked into the room with that kind of unreasoning feeling about young people, long hair, rock music, and all that implied to them, wouldn't listen to anything that was being said.... There was an us-versus-them feeling there."[11]

In early July the town leaders passed a law requiring a permit for any gathering of more than 5,000 people. This was a severe blow to Woodstock Ventures, which also still needed to obtain approvals from the county health department, state police and transportation departments, and town sanitary and health officials, among others. By July 15, 1969, when the Wallkill Zoning Board of Appeals finally killed the festival with an official rejection of Woodstock Ventures' permit application, the promoters knew that they were in big trouble. They had already spent about $750,000, and if they had to cancel the show they would have to refund another $600,000 worth of tickets. "We had to find a new location for the festival—and fast,"[12] said Lang (see "Michael Lang Recalls the Frantic Search for a New Concert Site," p. 162).

Finding a Home on a Dairy Farm in Bethel

One day after the Wallkill plan fell apart, Woodstock Ventures received a promising phone call. The caller was Elliot Tiber, a young man who helped manage his family's motel in White Lake, a small town in Bethel Township in upstate New York. Tiber offered to host the concert on his family's property, so Lang, Lawrence, and Goldstein drove over to check it out. The Tiber property was immediately rejected as too small and swampy. Lang, however, decided that as long as he was in the area he might as well take a ride around Bethel with a local real estate agent known to Tiber.

It was during this somewhat aimless drive through the countryside that Lang and the realtor drove past a broad expanse of beautiful, rolling pastureland. Lang immediately recognized that the land would be perfect for the con-

Max Yasgur's dairy farm in Bethel, New York, provided an idyllic setting for the Woodstock festival.

cert. Under intense questioning from Lang, the realtor said that the property belonged to Max and Miriam Yasgur, who owned the largest dairy farm operation in the county. The realtor made a quick phone call to Max Yasgur, who invited them over to his house (see Yasgur biography, p. 149).

Yasgur knew that Lang was part of the group that had been kicked out of Wallkill, but he assured the young promoter that he was open to leasing some of his property for Woodstock. Yasgur, Lang, and the realtor then drove over to a huge open field on his property that was shaped like a vast green bowl—an ideal spot for the concert stage. Lang and Yasgur began negotiating a deal on the spot, and over the next few days Woodstock Ventures and the dairy farmer hammered out a rental agreement for about 700 acres.

Everyone involved agreed that Yasgur negotiated a financially lucrative deal for himself. But they also emphasize that since the promoters had no other sites in mind and the concert was less than a month away, Yasgur could have been much more ruthless. "Max was a businessman and Max made a good deal and Max got his dollars and so on and so forth. But the real telling thing with Max was that he felt ... that in fact we had been mistreated [in Wallkill]," said Goldstein. "[He felt] that there was nothing that we were doing that was un-American and not right, that people deserved to have their say and their moment, that we were entitled to that as folks. And, by God, he was going to see that we had our chance."[13]

Getting the Town on Their Side

Once word got out that the Woodstock festival was coming to Bethel, some residents of the township and the village of White Lake became very upset. Lang and the other promoters were greatly troubled when conservative White Lake residents began expressing sentiments similar to the ones that had chased them out of Wallkill. Nearby summer camp owners claimed that the festival would be a disruption, and people around town described Woodstock as a public nuisance and health menace. Some residents even claimed that Yasgur had betrayed them. One of his neighbors erected a big sign by the road that read STOP MAX'S HIPPIE MUSIC FESTIVAL. NO 150,000 HIPPIES HERE. BUY NO MILK.

"They're pretty good kids, and I welcome them," dairy farmer Max Yasgur said in defense of the Woodstock promoters. "Just because a boy wears long hair doesn't mean he's going to break the law. I don't buy that nonsense. This is going to be something different, but I don't have any fears at all."

If these sorts of statements were meant to pressure Yasgur into withdrawing his hospitality, they had the opposite effect. The dairy farmer became more determined than ever to support the festival and the men and women who were working so hard to make it happen. "They're pretty good kids, and I welcome them," he told one newspaper reporter. "Just because a boy wears long hair doesn't mean he's going to break the law. I don't buy that nonsense. This is going to be something different, but I don't have any fears at all."[14]

Partly because of Yasgur's stand, opposition to the concert in White Lake never coalesced beyond scattered grumbling. The other factor that reduced hostility to the festival was the fact that Woodstock Ventures was pouring so much money into the local economy. "The more money we spent,

Woodstock organizers and crew members scrambled to construct the stage, lighting, and sound system for the massive concert event.

the better we were treated by the community," said Lang. "We were buying materials locally and hiring residents, and as that happened, it changed some of the negative attitudes in town and began to endear us to them. More and more White Lake residents got into the Woodstock spirit. They became supporters because they liked what we were doing, and they saw everybody working hard."[15]

A Race Against Time

On July 21 the Bethel Town Board and the Bethel Zoning Board formally approved all the permits needed by Woodstock Ventures to hold the festival on Yasgur's farm. The relieved promoters and the festival staff immediately turned their attention to readying the property for what was shaping up to be a massive crowd of at least 200,000 people. By early August more than 120,000 tickets had already been sold, and the buzz about the festival from mainstream news outlets, rock radio stations, and the underground press was growing with each passing day.

"There was an enormous amount to be done in a very short period of time," recalled Roberts. "The major hassle, of course, was building the site, building the stage, getting the lights and the sound system up, the fences, and, of course, we were in the last throes of contracting with food concessionaires, with the small concessionaires who were going to be putting together the shops and the booths."[16]

Yasgur's farm became a beehive of activity with hundreds of carpenters, electricians, plumbing contractors, and other workers scrambling around under Lawrence's supervision. "There were guys cutting down trees so that we could build the food stands, guys building the stage, guys building the pathways through the woods," recalled Lawrence. "Everybody was pulling together."[17] As the days ticked down, sound engineer Bill Hanley also put together a sound system capable of pouring quality music out to hundreds of thousands of sets of ears (see "The Hanley Sound at Woodstock," p. 49). Many observers never quite figured out how Hanley managed to accomplish this task, which was essential to the festival's ultimate success. "[Bill's] equipment was falling apart around you," recalled Goldstein. "It was simply lashed together.... He was in a lot of ways very innovative, very creative, and very sloppy. His equipment didn't get the maintenance that it required. But Bill was extraordinary.... There were other people who claimed that they could [put together a Woodstock-sized sound system], but there was no one else."[18]

Meanwhile, the partners in Woodstock Ventures had their own to-do lists to complete. They reached agreement with a hippie commune known as the Hog Farm to build trails, organize the campground, and set up a free kitchen for the festival. They also hired filmmaker Michael Wadleigh to make a documentary of the upcoming event (see Wadleigh biography, p. 145).

Another priority was festival safety and security. The Woodstock organizers reached deals with radical political groups and individuals to keep them from causing trouble at the concert. The organizers also carefully selected 350 New York police officers to provide security for the three-day festival during their off-duty hours. The officers would be unarmed and wear "Peace Service Corps" uniforms consisting of jeans and red t-shirts with PEACE on the front and Woodstock's dove and guitar logo on the back. A few days before the show, however, New York's police commissioner threatened to fire any officers who worked the concert. Some officers still showed up under false names (for twice the previ-

The Hanley Sound at Woodstock

Preparations for Woodstock were frantic and confused in the days leading up to the famous concert, and the sound system was no exception. The man responsible for this vital element of the festival was a thirty-two-year-old sound engineer named Bill Hanley, who was known in the music industry for his capacity to quickly build terrific concert sound systems from scratch.

A native of Medford, Massachusetts, Hanley had been fascinated by electronics in general—and amplifiers, speakers, and other audio components in particular—since childhood. By the late 1950s he was scratching out a living as a "soundman," putting together sound systems for jazz concerts and festivals up and down the East Coast. Hanley's work became so well known during the 1960s that pop and rock bands like the Beach Boys, the Beatles, and Buffalo Springfield all hired him at one time or another.

When Michael Lang hired Hanley to be the sound engineer for the Woodstock festival, he emphasized the massive scale of the job. Hanley was unfazed, though, even after the late switch in venue from Wallkill to Bethel. He assembled all the necessary speakers, amplifiers, and other components, orchestrated their positioning for maximum sonic effect, and operated the system through all three days of the show. According to singer-songwriter Richie Havens, who opened the concert on Friday afternoon, Hanley's technological wizardry was one of the unappreciated keys to Woodstock's success. "The best sound that I have ever played on outdoors to date happened at Woodstock," Havens said in a 1989 interview. "As a matter of fact, they said they heard it ten miles away in every direction, because they put those towers up there, and it bounced through those mountains. We not only did it for the crowd there, we did it for the whole countryside at that point."

Lang also cited Hanley's audio work as one of the elements that made Woodstock work. "I thought the sound was great, and everyone I talked to thought the sound was great," he said. "Everyone could hear, nothing blew up, and it all hung together perfectly. And it was all mostly on Bill's instincts."

Sources:

Havens, Ritchie. Interview in Makower, Joel, ed. *Woodstock: The Oral History.* New York: Doubleday, 1989, pp. 185-190.

"Parnelli Innovator Honoree, Father of Festival Sound." FOH Online, September 2006. Retrieved from http://www.fohonline.com/index.php?option=com_content&task=view&id=579&Itemid=1.

ously agreed-upon price), but the commissioner's move forced the promoters to look elsewhere to meet most of the festival's crowd control needs.

With few last-minute options to choose from, security was added to the duties of the Hog Farm. The notion of serving as a security presence greatly amused Hog Farm leader Wavy Gravy (actual name Hugh Romney), who announced that their "Please Force" intended to use cream pies and seltzer water for crowd control (see Romney biography, p. 138). According to Rosenman, though, putting security in the commune's hands was a stroke of genius. "[Goldstein] spent about ten minutes explaining it to me, and I instantly realized … that this was a very smart idea. And it turned out to be much better than even he had imagined, because as much as anything they were responsible for maintaining the tone of this event."[19]

The frantic pace of construction and other preparations also forced the festival staff to make a million quick decisions, some of which bothered Yasgur. Lawrence later admitted that

> I was making decisions very fast—decisions like, "Where shall we put this road? The guy [with the gravel for the road] is here. This is it." "There, put it there…. We gotta commit. This is it. The gravel is here. Do it." Then [Yasgur] would come out and say, "What are you doing? You can't put gravel there," like that kind of thing and then hold his heart, because he had a heart condition. Oh, it was a trip. And then I would have to calm him down. "Max, Max, we're going to clean this up, every piece of gravel. If you don't want it here, every piece of gravel is going to come up. If you don't want that, don't worry, Max." That's the way it was. There was a lot of that kind of thing.[20]

According to Roberts, the exhausting race to get ready for Woodstock also led him to forget about making a profit and just make sure that the show took place. He compared the experience to being on a cresting roller coaster that suddenly plunges downward. "As we were going up … we were always calculating this and that number of tickets and how much the acts cost and what the fences will cost and all that." Once they paid Yasgur $75,000 to rent his property for the weekend, though, "things were going too quickly to think in terms of profit or loss. … Once Max entered the picture, it kind of freed up a generosity impulse on our part, and so we just started spending…. The original budget was out the window."[21]

50

Traffic jams stretched for ten miles around the Woodstock festival site, causing thousands of music fans to abandon their cars and walk.

Arrival of the First Wave

The first concertgoers began arriving on Monday, August 11, even though the campground would not open until Wednesday and the concert was not scheduled to start until Friday, August 15. By Wednesday an estimated 60,000 people had already arrived at the farm. That same day, the New York State Police reneged on a deal to provide traffic direction for the festival. This development outraged and worried the Woodstock promoters. They knew that without the state police routing the massive crowds to designated parking areas, the roads leading to Max Yasgur's farm would soon be tied up in knots.

As the traffic jams worsened in and around White Lake and the greater Bethel area, the festival work force continued its feverish work on the still unfinished stage and festival grounds. Lang, Kornfeld, Rosenman, and Roberts looked on anxiously. By this time they sensed that the crowd could grow to 200,000 or even more; each of them harbored deep concerns about their ability to handle such a massive crowd.

Meanwhile, up on the roads, large numbers of concertgoers simply quit fighting the growing traffic jams. They abandoned their cars and vans by the side of the road and walked to the farm, clothes and blankets on their backs. One of these young rock fans, a sixteen-year-old from Westbury, Long Island, admitted to a *New York Times* reporter that he had made the pilgrimage to Woodstock over the objections of his parents. "My parents knew there'd be drugs there, that it'll be a little wild," he said. "They didn't want me to come. I know there will be drugs everywhere and I wonder what it will all be like. I've never been away from home before. I wonder what will happen to all of us."[22]

Notes

[1] Quoted in Littleproud, Brad, and Joanne Hague. *Woodstock: Peace, Music, and Memories.* Iola, WI: Krause, 2009, p. 15.
[2] Quoted in LIttleproud, p. 15.
[3] Lang, Michael, with Holly George-Warren. *The Road to Woodstock: From the Man Behind the Legendary Festival.* New York: Ecco, 2009, p. 48.
[4] Lang, pp. 52, 53.
[5] Lang, p. 58.
[6] Quoted in Evans, Mike, and Paul Kingsbury, eds. *Woodstock: Three Days That Rocked the World.* New York: Sterling, 2009, p. 59.
[7] Quoted in Lang, p. 87.
[8] Lang, p. 57.
[9] Quoted in Lang, p. 73.
[10] Quoted in Makower, Joel. *Woodstock: The Oral History.* New York: Doubleday, 1989, p. 95.
[11] Quoted in Makower, p. 96.
[12] Quoted in Lang, p. 115.
[13] Quoted in Makower, p. 120.
[14] Quoted in Stuart, Jane. "Rock at Woodstock," *Record Call* (Hackensack, NJ), July 27, 1969.
[15] Lang, pp. 151-52.
[16] Quoted in Makower, p. 124.
[17] Quoted in Lang, p. 130.
[18] Quoted in Makower, p. 147.
[19] Quoted in Evans and Kingsbury, p. 104.
[20] Quoted in Makower, p. 148.
[21] Quoted in Makower, p. 125.
[22] Quoted in Evans and Kingsbury, p. 62.

Chapter Four

THE MUSIC
AT WOODSTOCK

⬥

It wasn't that we were scared of playing in front of that many people because frankly you didn't know it was that many people. It was nighttime when we played, so we could only see the first forty or fifty rows of people. But also, your mind just doesn't count that high.... We were scared because everybody we thought was cool in the world that played music was standing around behind us in a row, all in a huge semi-circle behind the [amplifiers]. Everybody. Everybody that we respected in the world was right there—the Dead, Airplane, Hendrix, Sly, Country Joe, and just a ton of people, you know.

—David Crosby in *Woodstock: The Oral History*

All Thursday and Friday, the crowds came pouring into Bethel. As the mass grew to 200,000 people and kept spiraling upward—eventually reaching as many as 450,000 concertgoers, though no one knows for sure—monster traffic jams paralyzed roadways for miles around. A few of the musical acts reached the stage area before the roads into Woodstock became impassable. Many others, though, did not arrive in time. As a result, Woodstock Ventures hurriedly devised a plan to ferry the performers by helicopter from nearby hotels to the concert site.

The transportation problems wreaked havoc with the promoters' carefully planned schedule of performances from the outset. A folk-rock band named Sweetwater had been slated to open the festival on Friday afternoon. As the announced starting time of 4:00 p.m. approached, however, the Woodstock promoters and staff learned that the band members and their equipment truck were stuck somewhere in traffic. Michael Lang knew that they could not wait forever to get the live music going. If the massive audience—some of whom had been sitting in Max Yasgur's fields since Wednesday—was forced to wait too long for the festival to begin, there was no telling how it might react. With this in mind, Lang began looking around backstage for someone else to get the Woodstock party started.

Richie Havens Sets the Tone

Lang had only two artists to choose from. One was singer-songwriter Tim Hardin, but he was a poor candidate. Hardin at the time had taken steps to free himself from a self-destructive addiction to heroin, but he was still abusing alcohol and other drugs, and he was in no condition to kick off the festivities. The other possibility was Richie Havens, a charismatic black folksinger who was slotted as the fifth act of the opening day. Havens tried to fend off Lang. He admitted that he was terrified of playing in front of so many people and pointed out that his bass player had not yet arrived. But Lang would not give up. As he later wrote, "I knew he could handle it, and his powerful but calm demeanor was just what we needed to set the tone for liftoff."[1]

Lang finally convinced Havens to open the festival, and at 5:07 p.m. Havens and his conga player strode out onstage to an immense roar from the assembled throng. Strumming an acoustic guitar, Havens performed all four of his scheduled songs to a very appreciative audience. When he tried to leave the stage, though, Lang, John Morris, and other top Woodstock staffers had other ideas. With other musical acts still in transit, they pleaded with Havens to play some more. "I was supposed to do maybe forty minutes, thirty-five, forty minutes," Havens recalled. "[But] when I walked off the first time they said, 'Richie, you gotta do four more songs.' So I said 'OK.' I went back, and I did four more songs. I walked off again, and they said, 'Richie, three more....' I sang every song I knew."[2]

Havens finally capped his long set with "Freedom," a largely improvised song that he blended with "Motherless Child," an old folk spiritual. His blazing rendition of the song—and his whole set—set a high musical standard for the rest of the Woodstock bands to meet. Many Woodstock workers and attendees also said that Havens established a feeling of peace and brotherhood that resonated for the rest of the weekend. At one point, for example, the singer proclaimed that the festival was "all about you and me and everybody around the

Folksinger Richie Havens (left) opened Woodstock with a powerful performance that set the tone for the entire weekend.

stage and everybody that hasn't gotten here, and the people who are gonna read about you tomorrow. Yes! And how really groovy you were—all over the world, if you can dig where that's at—that's really where it's really at!"[3]

"Havens saved the day," according to rock historian and author Bob Santelli. "It was a powerful performance and it was lucky that it occurred because there wasn't a whole lot else that was as compelling or as intense on Friday as Richie Havens."[4] Rock critic Pete Fornatale offered similar praise. He described Havens's set as an "omen that … everyone at the festival backstage, onstage, and in front of the stage hoped could make you believe that everything was going to be all right. He did his job and he did it magnificently."[5] For his part, Havens was moved by the entire Woodstock experience. He stayed all weekend, and during that time he said that he was hugged "thousands and thousands" of times by appreciative fans.[6]

> *Richie Havens proclaimed that Woodstock was "all about you and me and everybody around the stage and everybody that hasn't gotten here, and the people who are gonna read about you tomorrow. Yes! And how really groovy you were—all over the world, if you can dig where that's at—that's really where it's really at!"*

A Mellow Friday Evening in Bethel

The next few hours of entertainment at Woodstock unfurled at an easygoing pace. The atmosphere was still frantic behind the scenes, where promoters and staff were trying to keep the overwhelmed facilities in working order. Out in front, meanwhile, many concertgoers were getting high—sometimes dangerously so—on pot, LSD, and other mind-altering drugs. Up on stage, though, a parade of voices and songs kept the atmosphere upbeat and relaxed.

Hindu religious guru Sri Swami Satchidananda gave a ten-minute prayer of peace and love over the gathering. He was followed by the band Sweetwater, which had finally managed to get to the concert site by helicopter. "We didn't really get [how many people had come to Woodstock] until we flew over the scene in a helicopter, and we saw all the people," said keyboardist Alex Del Zoppo. "I couldn't even believe they were people. I thought they were flowers down there. You just saw colors from one end of the horizon to the other. I literally asked the pilot what the crop was, and he says, 'Those are people.'"[7]

Another of the Friday night performers was singer-songwriter Bert Sommer, whose set list included a crowd-pleasing cover version of the popular

Sound engineer Bill Hanley designed and operated the sound system that enabled half a million people to enjoy the music at Woodstock. [Photo Credit: Bill Hanley Woodstock 1969 - Photo by David Marks (3rd Ear Music / Hidden Years Music Archive, South Africa)]

Simon and Garfunkel song "America." Later that evening musician Ravi Shankar took the stage with his sitar, a type of stringed instrument popular in India and Pakistan. Shankar had been a hit at the 1967 Monterey Pop Festival, but his Woodstock set was cut short by the first of several rainstorms that pelted Max Yasgur's farm over the weekend of August 15-17.

Once the downpour ended, twenty-two-year-old Melanie Safka took the stage. "Melanie," as she became known, was relatively new to the music scene. She only appeared at Woodstock as a last-minute replacement for the Incredible String Band. The band had been slotted to play on Friday night, but they refused to play an acoustic set when the downpour made it impossible for them to play their electric instruments. Melanie performed for less than twenty minutes, but she made the most of her opportunity. Journalist Billy Altman later described her brief set as "very emotional, peaceful, and positive."[8] Melanie's Woodstock appearance gave a big lift to her career, and one year later she wrote a hit song "Lay Down (Candles in the Rain)" inspired by the crowd's lighting of thousands of candles, lighters, and matches during her set.

The biggest disappointment of Friday night was Hardin, a talented but troubled singer-songwriter whose well-documented substance abuse problems cropped up again at Woodstock. "He was very stoned," recalled *Woodstock* documentary filmmaker Michael Wadleigh. "The problem with his performance was that he was ripped out of his gourd and didn't perform well."[9]

The next-to-last act of the night was singer-songwriter Arlo Guthrie. He was the son of the legendary political activist and folksinger Woody Guthrie, who had written "This Land Is Your Land" and many other classic American songs. The younger Guthrie, who went on just before midnight, had a big following among the hippie community. His friendly, talkative, and slightly goofy stage demeanor and acoustic guitar-driven songs went over well with the Woodstock crowd. Years later, however, Guthrie admitted that he had been too high to give his best. "So, you know, this was one of those moments you wished you could have done it again. But it is still one of the fonder memories of my entire life."[10]

Guthrie was followed by Joan Baez, the undisputed headliner of Friday's folk-themed lineup. Throughout the 1960s Baez had lent her beautiful voice to the civil rights and antiwar movements, so her appearance on stage at almost 1 a.m. sparked rousing applause. The visibly pregnant Baez began by telling the audience about the recent arrest of her husband, an antiwar draft-resister named David Harris. She then performed several folk songs, closing with "We Shall Overcome," the unofficial anthem of the civil rights movement. Baez's set, which ended around 2 a.m., brought the first round of Woodstock music to a harmonious close.

Hits and Misses on Saturday Afternoon

The Woodstock crowd awoke on Saturday in a state of high anticipation. "If Friday's gentle folk lineup had sent the weekend sailing on a soothing, mellow wave, the roster for the second day's performance promised to crank the excitement level up along with the decibels,"[11] wrote journalist Jack Curry. Acts scheduled to perform on August 16 included the Grateful Dead, Sly and the Family Stone, Creedence Clearwater Revival, the Who, Janis Joplin, and Jefferson Airplane, all of whom had big and enthusiastic followings.

Backstage, however, the mood remained tense. Some of the gathered musicians and band managers were happy to be there. They freely socialized

Making Historical Sense
of a Hazy and Chaotic Weekend

One of the enduring jokes about Woodstock is that "if you remember it, you weren't there." The line is based on the fact that the exhausting length of the event and the rampant drug and alcohol use created wildly different and hazy memories of the weekend among performers and concertgoers alike. For example, historians, musicians, and fans have all argued for years about the exact order in which the various acts performed. These debates have been further muddied by the fact that Michael Wadleigh's *Woodstock* documentary film made no effort to present the concert in chronological order.

In some cases, people do not even agree about which *day* a particular musician or band performed. For example, Country Joe McDonald has always maintained that he performed for the first time on Friday, right after Richie Havens. Other Woodstock histories have made the same claim. When Woodstock promoter Michael Lang published his 2009 memoir *The Road to Woodstock,* however, he claimed that McDonald first performed on Saturday—an assertion shared by a number of other Woodstock participants and attendees. After Lang's book came out, McDonald quickly contradicted the promoter's account of the timing of his first appearance onstage. But when McDonald went back and reviewed audiotape of his performance, he heard the stage announcer state that Santana—who everyone agrees played Saturday—would be taking the stage next. Faced with this evidence, McDonald admitted on his Web site that "I am thinking I have been wrong for 40 years and I did go on Saturday."

McDonald then asked fans who had attended Woodstock to write in with their own recollections of when he took the stage. He received a number of responses—but they were evenly divided between people who insisted that McDonald played on Friday and those who were convinced that he played on Saturday.

Source:

McDonald, Joe. "If You Can Remember the 60s ..." *Country Joe's Place: Woodstock's 40th Anniversary,* 2009. Retrieved from http://www.countryjoe.com/woodstock40.htm.

with each other, which in many cases meant sharing food, booze, and drugs. Other acts, though, were openly unhappy with various aspects of the festival. Some expressed concerns about security at the venue, while others complained about technical problems with the sound system and the time it took to set up for each new act. The Grateful Dead and the Who, meanwhile, voiced angry skepticism about whether they would ever get paid for performing.

Despite all of these distractions, though, Day Two of Woodstock began roughly on schedule. A Boston-based band called Quill got the festivities started a little after noon. The band played a strong set, but problems with the filmmakers' equipment made all the Quill footage unusable for the documentary. By the time Wadleigh and his crew got the problem straightened out, Quill's set was over.

As the afternoon wore on, it became increasingly hot and humid, both onstage and in the surrounding fields. Some of the performers were able to beat the heat and make a connection with the vast audience fanned out before them under the hot sun—including two musicians who had not even been scheduled to play. As on Friday, delays in getting some of the bands to the concert site forced the Woodstock staff to cobble together a new lineup. One of the artists they convinced to fill in was John Sebastian, a well-known figure to rock fans because of his band the Lovin' Spoonful, which had several chart-topping hits in the mid-1960s. By 1969 the Lovin' Spoonful had disbanded, so Sebastian went to Woodstock just to enjoy the scene and hang out with musician friends. He reluctantly agreed to take the stage when asked, though. Clad in a colorful tie-dye outfit and armed with an acoustic guitar he borrowed from Hardin, Sebastian played a well-received set of acoustic numbers.

An even bigger impression was made by Country Joe McDonald. He and his band, the Fish, were not scheduled to play until Sunday, but he also agreed to play a few songs to help fill the time until the scheduled bands arrived. McDonald's solo set was highlighted by one of the most famous moments in Woodstock lore—the so-called "Fish Cheer." The Fish Cheer was a call-and-response chant started by McDonald to rouse the audience out of its heat-induced sluggishness, and it worked in a big way. He started by yelling "gimme an F," and when the crowd roared back, McDonald and the audience proceeded to spell out the most infamous swear word in the English language. The cheer was a huge deal in an era when even big rock stars did not dare utter that word in concert. "It was not like today," said Santelli. "To have that happen was pretty, pretty wild. At that time that was the ultimate word you could use to demonstrate your anger, your frustration, your refusal to accept what was going on, because back then that was 'the word,' you might be able to say shit or hell or damn, but you certainly couldn't say that word. That word was absolutely top to bottom taboo.... It became an anthem. Not because of the word ... but it was basically the attitude of the song."[12]

Some bands wilted in the heat. The jazz-blues-rock stylings of the Keef Hartley Band failed to keep the interest of the crowd. The Incredible String Band, which had been rescheduled to perform Saturday after refusing to go on the night before, also struggled to make a connection with festival attendees. Band manager Joe Boyd later admitted that it was a big mistake going on Saturday afternoon "in the baking sun. People were ready for something heavy and loud and they came on and just—died!"[13]

Saturday afternoon at Woodstock, however, also featured stretches of music that mesmerized the crowd. Most notably, Day Two of Woodstock will always be known for unveiling guitarist Carlos Santana and his Latin-tinged brand of rock and roll to the world. The Mexican musician's band, which was known simply as "Santana," had not even released its first album at the time of the festival. However, famed West Coast manager and promoter Bill Graham had told Lang that he would keep the Grateful Dead from playing at Woodstock unless the festival found a spot for Santana, who Graham described as a sizzling talent. Lang agreed to Graham's demand, which ended up being a stroke of enormous good fortune for everyone at Woodstock (see "Rocking Out with Santana at Woodstock," p. 170). Concertgoers were treated to what Santana biographer Marc Shapiro described as a "relentless rush of primal rock and Third World rhythms, racing through what had been dubbed the Woodstock Nation like an out-of-control forest fire."[14] "I was up onstage," remembered Morris, "and I could look [out] at the audience, so I could see that these guys were just knocking them dead. They were hitting it out of the park."[15]

Playing Until Dawn—and Beyond

The electric blues band Canned Heat performed a solid, energetic set of songs as dusk fell over the Yasgur Farm. They were followed by Mountain, another band that drenched its rock in blues. By this time rain showers and bursts of strong winds were pelting the stage and surrounding fields. The Woodstock staff knew, though, that they were already several hours behind schedule. Determined not to lose any more ground, they convinced the Grateful Dead to go on as planned.

Janis Joplin entertained the crowd during the early morning hours of August 17.

The Dead's set never came together. Guitarist and vocalist Jerry Garcia, guitarist Bob Weir, and other members of the band later complained that they endured electric shocks from their instruments at Woodstock. They also admitted, though, that the band just never got into a rhythm that grabbed the crowd. "They were just horrible," remembered Grateful Dead manager Jon McIntire. "I'd never heard them play so badly."[16] In the early 1990s Weir reflected back on their experience at the festival. "Some people made their careers at Woodstock, but we've spent about 20 years making up for it."[17]

Creedence Clearwater Revival was next, and at 1:30 a.m. on Sunday morning the band launched a valiant effort to recapture the energy that had dissipated during the Dead's set. "I think the Dead's experience made Creedence nervous," wrote Lang, "but they didn't show it. They were practically a hit machine by then, and they played with conviction and intensity."[18] The band poured out blistering versions of songs like "Proud Mary," "I Put a Spell on You," "Commotion," and "Suzie Q," all of which were big hits. By this time, though, many people in the crowd were simply too wiped out to respond. "We were ready to rock out and we waited and waited and finally it was our turn," recalled lead singer John Fogerty. "There were a half million people asleep. These people were out. It was sort of like a painting of a Dante scene, just bodies from hell, all intertwined and asleep, covered with mud. And this is the moment I will never forget as long as I live: a quarter mile away in the darkness, on the other edge of this bowl, there was some guy flicking his Bic, and in the night I hear, 'Don't worry about it, John. We're with you.' I played the rest of the show for that guy."[19]

The next act to appear in the early morning hours of August 17 was Janis Joplin and her new backing group, the Kosmic Blues Band. Some people who were at Woodstock said that Joplin put on a good show, but most felt that she turned in a disappointing set. This feeling was particularly strong among music industry veterans who knew how electrifying Joplin could be in concert. Their prevailing view was that by Woodstock, she had fallen too deep into the patterns of drug and alcohol abuse that would take her life one year later. "She was wasted [at Woodstock]," said Morris. "And that is the worst performance I ever saw her do…. She was sloppy. It was sloppy. The audience didn't react badly, but I would say questioningly."[20]

The atmosphere changed when Sly and the Family Stone took the stage. Sylvester "Sly Stone" Stewart was well-known in the rock world for being vain, irresponsible, and tantrum-prone. But he and his race- and gender-mixed band were also great musicians and charismatic performers, and at Woodstock they virtually forced the crowd to cast aside their blankets and sleeping bags and resume partying. "Sly Stone got the biggest audience reaction of any group," declared Wadleigh. "Sly is legendary for being able to do that.... When he says, 'I wanna take you higher,' the audience was so revved up. When Sly says, 'Dance to the music,' you can't not dance to the music.... I tell you, for an ability to get you going, that group was just stunning.... Sly's two songs that we used [in the *Woodstock* film], 'Dance to the Music' and "I Want to Take You Higher,' we had to use them. We couldn't not have used them. It was impossible. He was just so good."[21] Carlos Santana agreed, declaring that "the main peak for me was Sly Stone. Bar none. He took over that night."[22]

By the time Creedence Clearwater Revival took the stage in the wee hours Sunday morning, "There were a half million people asleep," recalled lead singer John Fogerty. "These people were out. It was sort of like a painting of a Dante scene, just bodies from hell, all intertwined and asleep, covered with mud."

Sly was followed by the Who, which took the stage at Woodstock around 5:00 a.m. on Sunday morning. The English rockers played one of the longest sets of the entire weekend. They performed every song off their double album *Tommy*, and most reports indicate that the Who was one of the musical highlights of the festival. Still, the Who's turn onstage is best known in Woodstock lore for political activist Abbie Hoffman's ill-considered decision to deliver a political speech in the middle of the band's set. When guitarist Pete Townshend saw Hoffman at the lead microphone, he promptly slammed his guitar into the back of Hoffman's head. Hoffman stumbled off the stage and vanished into the crowd.

The Who performed their last song, the anthem "See Me Feel Me," just as the sun rose over Yasgur's farm. That left only Jefferson Airplane from the Day Two list of performers. The band dutifully took the stage at about 7:00 a.m., but nobody had gotten much sleep. "We were supposed to go at ten-thirty [the previous] night and we'd been up and down about four or five times on acid that night, getting ready to go on, and then everything was delayed for whatever reasons," recalled guitarist Paul Kantner. "There were a lot of people just sleeping-bagged out who had gone out actually even before us, during the Who. The fires were starting to go out, and people were crashing and burning."[23] Lead vocalist Grace Slick had similar memories. "We'd been up all night and I sang the ... songs with my eyes closed, sort of half asleep and half singing. We probably could have played better if we'd been more awake, but part of the charm of rock and roll is that sometimes you're ragged."[24]

More Music—and More Rain

Sunday's festivities began with a heartfelt address to the crowd from Woodstock's host, farmer Max Yasgur. English rock and blues singer Joe Cocker then got the final day of Woodstock music off to a rollicking start. Cocker and his band took the stage around 2:00 Sunday afternoon. They put together a crowd-pleasing set that included rave-up versions of several well-known songs by Bob Dylan ("Just Like a Woman," "I Shall Be Released") and the Beatles ("With a Little Help from My Friends"). Cocker walked off stage, though, just as the worst rainstorm of the entire weekend came marching in. It drenched the festival and its inhabitants, forced the concert managers to cut off power to the stage, and stopped the music for a couple of hours.

The heavy rains convinced tens of thousands of people to leave the festival and begin the long trek back home. The crowd was still immense, though, and it became increasingly restless waiting for the show to resume. Once the rain stopped, Country Joe and the Fish volunteered to perform an acoustic set. This would give the stagehands time to clear water off the stage, turn the power back on, and make sure the microphones and amplifiers were safe to use. "Finally, at six thirty, the sun actually came back out and we restored power," recalled Lang. "Some people had left, but those who stayed seemed almost reinvigorated by the storm. Plugged in, [Country Joe and] the Fish launched into their regular set."[25]

Country Joe and the Fish did not finish up until around dusk, which meant that once again, Woodstock was way behind schedule. The next bands to perform were Ten Years After and The Band. They were followed by blues guitarist Johnny Winter, who walked onstage at midnight, and the band Blood, Sweat and Tears, which played until about 2:30 Monday morning.

The Woodstock crowd sagged during the Blood, Sweat and Tears set, but a

Joe Cocker played a rollicking set to open the final day of the Woodstock festival, just before a driving rainstorm sent many fans home.

Legendary guitarist Jimi Hendrix closed the Woodstock festival by playing to a dwindling crowd on Monday morning.

fresh surge of energy rippled through the assembled throng when Crosby, Stills, Nash and Young (also known as CSNY) took the stage around 3:00 a.m. This newly assembled band of established folk-rock stars had been one of the most anticipated acts of the entire weekend, and as the musicians took the stage many of their fellow musicians sitting backstage got up and gathered together to listen.

The group's hour-long set did not disappoint. Renowned *Rolling Stone* rock critic Greil Marcus called them "visually one of the most exciting bands I've ever seen" and described their performance as "scary brilliant proof of the magnificence of music."[26] Jefferson Airplane's Grace Slick was impressed as well. "This was their first large-scale performance as a group, and they were determined to get it right," she recalled. "As it turned out, they were *so* good, it was amazing, and I was jealous of their preparation. They'd obviously rehearsed their harmonies to perfection."[27]

The stream of festivalgoers leaving Woodstock turned into a torrent after CSNY wrapped up its one-hour set. The Paul Butterfield Blues Band then played a long and blistering set of electric blues as the sun rose and ushered in Monday morning. After the group Sha Na Na played a brief set of 1950s-style rock, the only act left to perform was Jimi Hendrix.

When Hendrix and his backing band, which he called Gypsy Sun and Rainbows, strode onto the stage at around 9:00 a.m. on Monday morning, the once-massive Woodstock crowd had dwindled to only 30,000 or so hardcore souls. Most of them were glad they stayed, though, as Hendrix blazed his way through a nearly two-hour set that featured such rock classics as "Foxy Lady," "Gypsy Woman," and "Hey Joe." The most famous song played by Hendrix at

Woodstock, though, was a powerful, hard-edged instrumental version of the American national anthem, "The Star-Spangled Banner." Forty years later, writer Martin Johnson called it "a performance of such rock guitar virtuosity that even today, it functions as Woodstock's keynote address."[28]

Hendrix's "Hey Joe" was the last song of Woodstock weekend to echo out over the hills and fields of Bethel. When the guitarist and his band left the stage, the last dazed, frazzled, but happy remnants of the world's largest-ever concert festival had nothing left to do but begin the long trek back to their everyday lives. As it turned out, however, the sounds and sights of Woodstock would reverberate far longer than anyone could have guessed at the time.

Notes

[1] Lang, Michael, with Holly George-Warren. *The Road to Woodstock: From the Man Behind the Legendary Festival.* New York: Ecco, 2009, p. 181.

[2] Quoted in Evans, Mike, and Paul Kingsbury, eds. *Woodstock: Three Days That Rocked the World.* New York: Sterling, 2009, p. 72.

[3] Quoted in *Woodstock (The Director's Cut),* directed by Michael Wadleigh (DVD release). Warner Home Video, 1997.

[4] Quoted in Fornatale, Pete. *Back to the Garden: The Story of Woodstock.* New York: Touchstone, 2009, pp. 15-16.

[5] Fornatale, p. 14.

[6] "Singer-Songwriter Richie Havens Remembers His Woodstock," *Voice of America,* August 15, 2009. Retrieved from http://www.voanews.com/content/a-13-2009-08-15-voa7-68705132/409291.html.

[7] Quoted in Evans, p. 79.

[8] Quoted in Fornatale, p. 77.

[9] Quoted in Fornatale, p. 67.

[10] Quoted in Lane, Steven. "A Conversation with an American Music Icon…. Arlo Guthrie." *BrooWaha.com,* March 31, 2008. Retrieved from http://www.broowaha.com/articles/3344/a-conversation-with-an-american-music-icon-arlo-guthrie.

[11] Curry, Jack. *Woodstock: The Summer of Our Lives.* New York: Weidenfeld and Nicolson, 1989, p. 189.

[12] Quoted in Fornatale, pp. 38-39.

[13] Quoted in "A Little Upstate Folk Festival: Woodstock and the Incredible String Band." *Be Glad*, Winter 1994. Retrieved from http://www.makingtime.co.uk/beglad/woodstock.htm.

[14] Shapiro, Marc. *Carlos Santana: Back on Top.* New York: St. Martins/Griffin, 2002.

[15] Quoted in Fornatale, p. 122.

[16] Quoted in Greenfield, Robert. *Dark Star: An Oral Biography of Jerry Garcia.* 1996. Reprint. New York: HarperCollins, 2009, pp. 116-17.

[17] Quoted in Evans, p. 145.

[18] Lang, p. 216.

[19] Quoted in Bordowitz, Hank. *Bad Moon Rising: The Unauthorized History of Creedence Clearwater Revival.* Chicago, Illinois: Chicago Review Press, 2007, p. 390.

[20] Quoted in Fornatale, pp. 146-47.

[21] Quoted in Fornatale, pp. 171-72.

[22] Quoted in "Woodstock Nation." *Rock and Roll Is Here to Stay: An Anthology.* Edited by William McKeen. New York: W.W. Norton, 2000, p. 411.

[23] Quoted in Makower, Joel. *Woodstock: The Oral History.* New York: Doubleday, 1989, pp. 239-40.

[24] Quoted in Lang, p. 222.

[25] Lang, p. 231.

[26] Quoted in Downing, David. *A Dreamer of Pictures: Neil Young, the Man and His Music.* New York: Perseus, 1995, p. 59.

[27] Slick, Grace, and Andrea Cagan. *Somebody to Love?: A Rock-and-Roll Memoir.* New York: Warner, 1998.

[28] Johnson, Martin. "Jimi Hendrix's Woodstock." *The Root,* August 14, 2009. Retrieved from http://www.theroot.com/views/jimi-hendrix-s-woodstock.

Chapter Five

THE SCENE
AT WOODSTOCK

By the third day, it had become a survival camp…. This was their country. Their space. But it wasn't all that pleasant all the time. Sometimes, there were great highs. But by the third day with the mud and the food running out and the discomfort, it became like a camp of people who were in retreat from something.

—Concert promoter Bill Graham in "Woodstock Nation,"
Rock and Roll Is Here To Stay: An Anthology

The musicians and bands who played at Woodstock provided the soundtrack for a weekend that concertgoers and festival crew members described in a million different ways. Some people said that Woodstock was fun, exciting, and liberating. Others described the three-day festival as chaotic, miserable, and frightening. Most, however, seemed to view their time at Woodstock as a strange blend of both positive and negative experiences. The concert was both fun *and* chaotic, exciting *and* miserable, liberating *and* frightening.

Traffic Madness

For the hundreds of thousands of rock fans who traveled to Bethel for Woodstock, the festival's horrible traffic snarls would provide many of their most vivid—and frustrating—memories. They came by car, motorcycle, truck, and commercial bus in such great numbers that roadways were paralyzed for miles around. "It's hard to know why everyone knew to come," said writer Susan Silas, who attended as a sixteen-year-old. "All over the country young people packed their cars, got on airplanes, hitchhiked. Before I set out I had no idea

The crowd at Woodstock was so much larger than expected that it overwhelmed local roadways, businesses, and residents.

that the urgency I felt about going—I had to go—was being felt by tens of thousands of other kids in big cities and small towns all across the United States."[1]

By the time the festival officially opened on the afternoon of Friday, August 15, thousands of people had abandoned their cars on the shoulders of local roadways and walked in to the event with little else but the clothes on their backs. "Lines of cars were stretching up to 20 miles from the fair at midnight," reported the *New York Times*. "Traffic on the five key roads that lead and feed into Bethel—Routes 17, 17B, 42, 55, and 97—was bumper to bumper up to four and one-half hours today. An auto club spokesman called the situation 'an absolute madhouse.'"[2]

The Woodstock organizers convinced local radio stations to broadcast announcements warning listeners that the festival crowd was already far too large. The announcements urged people who were not already at Woodstock to avoid the area. These messages, which were echoed by newspaper reports, have been credited with reducing the flow of concertgoers. By the time they were delivered, however, White Lake and other villages in the Bethel area were already overwhelmed. "The residents of the hamlets around Yasgur's land felt trapped," wrote journalist Jack Curry. "Resentment caught on early. Opportunists were already preying upon the unprepared kids, charging a dollar for a slurp of hose water, more than that for a raw tomato from a garden."[3]

Fortunately for concertgoers, these predatory practices were the exception rather than the rule. Many local farmers, storekeepers, and homeowners provided food and other forms of aid to attendees over the course of the weekend, despite suffering property damage from careless youth.

Woodstock Becomes a Free Concert

The Woodstock Art and Music Festival had always been conceived as a moneymaking venture, and in the weeks leading up to the concert more than 100,000 tickets had been sold. The huge and early arriving crowd and last-minute change in location, however, made it impossible for Woodstock organizers and crew to complete its ticket-for-entry system. Fences were never completed, and by Thursday afternoon about 60,000 people had planted themselves in the bowl in front of the stage without handing over a ticket. By early Friday afternoon, hordes of young people had trampled the half-finished fencing system and flooded into every nook and cranny of Max Yasgur's farm. After consulting with top staffers like John Morris, Mel Lawrence, and Wes Pomeroy, event organizers Michael Lang, Artie Kornfeld, John Roberts, and Joel Rosenman were forced to concede that they had no realistic way of securing tickets or money from anyone. Woodstock was going to be a free concert.

Given this swift turn of events, the question came up as to whether the promoters should just cancel the show. The idea was quickly shot down, however. As Bill Belmont, road manager for Country Joe McDonald said, "Crowds turn ugly, especially when things don't go the way they're supposed to. I saw crowds get pissed off [at other festivals] because bands wouldn't do encores. The whole concept of peace and love was a state of mind. It was not a reality. Crowds are always crowds."[4]

"The one major thing that you have to remember tonight, when you go back up to the woods to go to sleep or if you stay here, is that the man next to you is your brother," Woodstock promoter John Morris told the giant crowd. "And you damn well better treat each other that way because if you don't, then we blow the whole thing."

Morris subsequently took the stage on Friday afternoon to inform the crowd that "it's a free concert from now on." When the crowd roared its approval, though, Morris added, "That doesn't mean that anything goes! What that means is we're going to put the music up here for free.... The one major thing that you have to remember tonight, when you go back up to the woods to go to sleep or if you stay here, is that the man next to you is your brother. And you damn well better treat each other that way because if you don't, then we blow the whole thing."[5]

Rain, Mud, Sex, and Drugs

Over the next three days the conditions on Max Yasgur's farm steadily declined as heavy rains, broiling heat, inadequate food and sanitation facilities, and rampant drug use all took their toll on the crowd. Three people died during the course of the weekend—one from a burst appendix, one from a heroin overdose, and one who was run over by a tractor while sleeping next to a road. Wide swaths of the festival grounds reeked of human sweat and bodily waste well before the final evening of performances, and the main bowl area was transformed into an amphitheatre of mud.

Some people who came to the show found it all too crowded, chaotic, and uncomfortable to enjoy. "If you like colossal traffic jams, torrential rain, reeking portable johns, barely edible food, and sprawling, disorganized crowds, then you would have found Woodstock a treat," wrote journalist Mark Hosenball, who attended Woodstock as a seventeen-year-old (see "Bad Memories of Woodstock," p. 176). "For those of us who saw those things as a hassle, good music did not necessarily offset the discomfort."[6]

The extent to which heavy drugs were consumed at Woodstock also shocked some people. "Among the youngsters in the crowd, the generation that had grown up with drugs, the amount and type of drug use were perceived as worrisome by many," according to Curry. "Hardly anyone in the crowd objected to pot and its mild high, but harsher drugs were common too. Kids who had been longstanding potheads were suddenly shocked by the prevalence of amphetamines, psychedelics and downers."[7] One young attendee said that "the drugs that were being done at Woodstock just made zombies out of everyone.... People were burning out left and right, big holes in the brain. I wasn't shocked, just disillusioned."[8]

Peter Beren, who worked at the food concessions at Woodstock, had similar memories. "There were little groups of people with some playing guitars,

When heavy rains turned the festival site into a muddy mess, concertgoers made the best of it by sliding down a hill.

and there were some really sweet aspects to this landscape," he acknowledged. At many campfires, though, it looked "not like a pastoral scene of hippies, but more like what you would imagine in a circle of hell: fires, people fighting with one another, shouting, people freaking out on drugs."[9] This onslaught of drug use produced a lot of people who required medical attention over the course of the weekend. The festival's medical care facility, which was manned by volunteer doctors and nurses, was filled to capacity with young men and women on "bad trips" for the entire weekend.

Nudity was common at Woodstock, and some concertgoers openly engaged in sexual activities without regard for the sensibilities of passersby. These uninhibited displays of sexuality delighted some attendees and elicited disapproval from others. For the most part, however, criticisms of sexual behavior—or any other kind of behavior aside from selfishness—were muted. The countercultural emphasis on "doing your own thing" and rejecting the "uptight" morality of older generations was in full swing at Woodstock. "The environment in general was just wild," recalled Rona Elliot, who helped with public relations for the festival. "Every ten feet, you could see anything.… Anything you could imagine was happening and in a very supportive environment. It wasn't threatening, people were getting stoned and they were doing whatever they were doing."[10]

Keeping the National Guard Away

Once the concert actually began on Friday, Woodstock organizers and crew breathed a huge sigh of relief. They then spent the rest of Friday and all day Saturday working feverishly to keep the festival going and avoid any major disasters. On Sunday morning, though, a potential catastrophe emanating from the state capital of Albany was only narrowly averted.

On Sunday morning, August 17, New York governor Nelson Rockefeller became so disturbed by reports about the deteriorating conditions at Woodstock that he threatened to declare the festival grounds a disaster area. Rockefeller could then send in National Guard troops to clear the entire crowd from Yasgur's farm and all surrounding villages. On the one hand, the men and women running the festival could understand the governor's anxiety. "Here was this ten square miles where no traffic moved, all the arteries were clogged, the kids were essentially in control, and it was lawless," said Roberts. "No one can get there to stop people from doing whatever mischief they wanted to do. If a band of

The crowd's energy level rose and fell throughout the weekend-long concert, with periods of wild excitement followed by periods of mellow recovery.

kids wanted to go and ransack a house, the police couldn't get through to stop them or find them. They would all disappear into the crowd. From the outside, that must have looked very dangerous."[11]

Roberts even admitted that the organizers wondered among themselves about the likelihood that the "anything goes" atmosphere at Woodstock might inspire someone to put LSD in the water supply or engage in other dangerous acts. By Sunday, however, the promoters and crew had received two days' worth of upbeat and generally positive reports from the festival grounds—and even from local residents who found that the Woodstock "kids" were peaceful and well-mannered. They knew that the peaceful vibe circulating through the generally antiwar crowd would be extinguished in a hurry if the festival was invaded by rifle-wielding Guardsmen. "They panicked in Albany," said Morris.

They thought it was a bunch of dope-soaked hippies who were going to tear the place apart. In those towns, there were a number of people who were afraid that there was this horde that was going to come up over the hill and rape their daughters and eat their cows. Or rape their cows and eat their daughters.… Rockefeller's people said we are going to close down the area. We are going to surround it with National Guard and clear it out. And I went, no, you're not. What you're going to have is a gigantic massacre, which doesn't make sense.[12]

Morris, Roberts, and other staff members ultimately convinced Rockefeller and his aides to keep the National Guard away from Woodstock. Then, in what journalist Stephen Dalton described as a "deft bit of diplomacy,"[13] they actually managed to persuade the governor and his staff to fly in food and medical aid.

Most of these supplies were gathered by local groups who launched major donation drives in response to reports of food and medical supply shortages at Woodstock. "The food came from everybody's pantry, everybody's stores," said Gordon Winarick, a local hospital executive who helped coordinate the relief effort. "It was the church, the Boy Scouts, the Girl Scouts, the synagogues, firehouses—any organization.… [The attitude was] they have a problem, we have an obligation, there was care, concern, let's help. And of course, they were all stunned because when the hordes of people came back in the town, they were all so polite and they would all say thank you, and all be so grateful."[14]

Some Woodstock people insist, though, that all the talk about food shortages was exaggerated. "If people wanted to eat, we had the food, if they wanted to walk over to the Hog Farm," said Lisa Law, a commune member who helped prepare and distribute food at the Hog Farm tent. "There was this talk about hunger and I always said, 'What hunger?' If they didn't want to get up and walk over then that was their problem. But there was no lack of food at Woodstock."[15]

A General Spirit of Peace and Harmony

Virtually everyone involved with Woodstock—performers, organizers, crew, and audience members—agrees that the festival was dogged by numerous problems and inconveniences throughout its three-day run. Yet for all the people who soured on the festival because of these difficulties, there were at least as many young men and women who found the entire experience to be an ulti-

Free kitchens set up by the Hog Farm commune provided sustenance to concertgoers who were unprepared for the three-day event.

mately rewarding and affirming one. "We were … in the middle of a crowded mass of humanity that was truly unbelievable," remembered one member of the Woodstock audience. "No one complained about the rain, the heat, the rain, the lack of food, the mud, the rain. In spite of the unpleasant conditions, we were all a bunch of happy clams having the greatest time of our lives, drugs or no drugs, food or no food."[16]

Woodstock veterans speak warmly about numerous aspects of the festival scene (see "Breakfast in Bed for 400,000," p. 167). There was the "hum of hippie commerce"[17] in the woods, where colonies of artisans sold crafts and other wares to young people. There were the ponds, where legions of pale hippies ditched their clothes and frolicked to get relief from the heat. There were the makeshift campgrounds, where people compared their impressions of the musical acts and shared their life stories. There was the pavilion area, where the Hog Farm distributed huge amounts of food to hungry young people. And there

"We Could Have the Largest Mass Electrocution in History"

One of the most famous events of the entire Woodstock festival was the Sunday afternoon storm that buffeted the concert site just after Joe Cocker finished his set. The fierce storm brought such high winds and heavy rainfall that Woodstock organizers feared a massive loss of life. One problem was the concert site's sixty-foot-tall light towers, which began to sway back and forth during the storm. With dozens of young people huddled up in the tower's scaffolding and hundreds more all around its base, a tower collapse would claim many lives. This crisis was averted when John Morris grabbed the stage microphone and convinced the kids hanging on the tower to climb down. When the added weight from the concertgoers disappeared, the towers stabilized.

The other big fear on Sunday afternoon was that as concertgoers churned the rain-soaked bowl into mud, they were exposing buried power cables that ran to the stage area. According to Morris, the concern was that if the "cables wear through and fray and all those people are wet and packed together—we could have the largest mass electrocution in the history of the world." This nightmare scenario was firmly put to rest, though, by lighting director Chip Monck and other engineers. They assured the Woodstock promoters that the cable coverings could withstand far more than the tread of thousands of muddy feet.

Source:

Fornatale, Pete. *Back to the Garden: The Story of Woodstock.* New York: Touchstone, 2009.

was the stage itself, where Santana, Sly and the Family Stone, Crosby, Stills, Nash and Young, the Who, Richie Havens, Jimi Hendrix, and others delivered song after song of great music.

According to many people at Woodstock, these qualities were more than enough to make up for the rain and mud and bad smells (see "A Military Veteran Remembers the Festival," p. 180). "The hippies shared whatever they had—food, carrot salad with raisins, tents, a joint—how they shared everything," remembered Carlos Santana. "Four hundred fifty thousand, or however many people were there, it was a living organism of people. A lot of people saw the mud, a lot of people saw the ugly things, but this is what I saw. I can only give you my vision of what I saw, and what I saw was a true harmonious convergence."[18] According to one concertgoer who was nineteen years old at the time, this spirit of generosity and patience extended even to the most over-crowded sections of the festival. "The closer you got to the stage, the less room there was," recalled Harriet Schwartz. "It was like a mosh pit—*worse* than a mosh pit. So I was literally like an accordion. I would sit, my back would be on somebody else's knees, and somebody else's back would probably be on my knees. If you don't love people that are around you, you're in a lot of trouble. But everybody there generally was sweet, loving, caring. We were all in the same boat together."[19]

It was that spirit of kindness and brotherhood that Max Yasgur focused on when the organizers convinced him to address the crowd from the stage on Sunday morning. "I'm a farmer," he began nervously, to encouraging roars from the crowd.

> I don't know how to speak to twenty people at a time, let alone a crowd like this. But I think you people have proven something to the world. Not only to the town of Bethel or Sullivan County, or New York State. You've proven something to the world. This is the largest group of people ever assembled in one place. We have had no idea that there would be this size group, and because of that, you had quite a few inconveniences as far as water and food and so forth. Your producers have done a mammoth job to see that you're taken care of. They'd enjoy a vote of thanks.

> But above that, the important thing that you've proven to the world is that a half a million kids—and I call you kids because I have children that are older than you are—a half a million young people can get together and have three days of fun and music and have nothing *but* fun and music. And God bless you for it![20]

When the festival finally drew to a close on Monday morning, only a small remnant of the mighty crowd remained. Most attendees had departed during the course of Sunday afternoon and evening (see "Leaving Woodstock," p. 188). Whether they headed home on Saturday, Sunday, or Monday, though, the people who experienced Woodstock shared a common bond. "What outsiders failed

On the final day of the Woodstock festival, landowner Max Yasgur praised attendees for their good behavior.

to understand was that, like the mud clinging to the sneakers of each of the kids trudging homeward, something stuck to the souls of these 500,000," wrote Curry. "[Woodstock] Nation disbanded even more abruptly than it had begun, fairly bursting apart like an incubating pod grown heavy with seeds. But the members of that Nation would carry forever an indelible stamp in the passport of their souls that they would cherish as a special brand of honor giving them the privilege to say, 'We were there.'"[21]

Notes

[1] Silas, Susan. "I Paid for Woodstock." *Exquisite Corpse: A Journal of Letters and Life,* October 2009. Retrieved from http://www.corpse.org/index.php?option=com_content&task=view&id=423&Itemid=1.

[2] Collier, Barnard L. "200,000 Thronging to Rock Festival Jams Roads Upstate." *New York Times,* August 15, 1969.

[3] Curry, Jack. *Woodstock: The Summer of Our Lives.* New York: Weidenfeld and Nicolson, 1989, p. 143.

[4] Quoted in Makower, Joel. *Woodstock: The Oral History.* New York: Doubleday, 1989, pp. 179-80.

[5] *Woodstock (The Director's Cut),* directed by Michael Wadleigh (DVD release). Warner Home Video, 1997.

[6] Hosenball, Mark. "I Was at Woodstock. And I Hated It." *Newsweek,* August 11, 2009. Retrieved from http://www.thedailybeast.com/newsweek/2009/08/11/i-was-at-woodstock-and-i-hated-it.html.

[7] Curry, p. 166.

[8] Quoted in Curry, p. 167.

[9] Quoted in Makower, p. 209.

[10] Quoted in Makower, pp. 195-96.

[11] Quoted in Makower, p. 247.

[12] Quoted in Fornatale, Pete. *Back to the Garden: The Story of Woodstock.* New York: Touchstone, 2009, p. 108.

[13] Dalton, Stephen. "War and Peace." *The National,* July 2, 2009. Retrieved from http://www.thenational.ae/arts-culture/film/war-and-peace.

[14] Quoted in Makower, pp. 211-12.

[15] Quoted in Makower, p. 214.

[16] Northlake, John. "I *Had* to Go." *Woodstock Revisited.* Edited by Susan Reynolds. Avon, MA: Adams, 2009, p. 81.

[17] Curry, p. 198.

[18] Quoted in Fornatale, p. 126.

[19] Quoted in Fornatale, p. 110.

[20] Quoted in Landy, Eliot. *Woodstock Vision: The Spirit of a Generation.* Rev. ed. Milwaukee, WI: Backbeat Books, 2009, p. 171.

[21] Curry, pp. 229-30.

Chapter Six
AFTER WOODSTOCK

No retrospective of the sixties would be complete without footage from the festival. Our film [*Woodstock*] is the dominant popular image of the festival, and give it its place in history.

—Assistant editor Elen Orson
in Dale Bell's 1999 book *Woodstock*

By the time the last notes from the stage of the Woodstock Art and Music Festival echoed over the rolling woodlands and fields of Bethel on Monday morning, the crowd had greatly diminished from its massive weekend levels. Of the estimated 400,000 concertgoers who had squeezed onto Max Yasgur's farm and roamed the surrounding town during the weekend, fewer than 150,000 remained by Sunday night. The majority of them had straggled away over the course of Sunday afternoon, called back home by classes, work, and other obligations. The crowd had dwindled even more, to an estimated 20,000-30,000 hardcore concertgoers, when Jimi Hendrix brought the festival to a close.

As the last diehard festivalgoers packed up and began their homeward journeys, the concert organizers and the townspeople of Bethel faced the task of cleaning up after the three-day party. This was no ordinary job. The gargantuan crowd had generated huge amounts of garbage that overwhelmed the trash cans, trash compactors, portable toilets, and other facilities at the festival site. The promoters had initially planned for a much smaller festival. By the time the true dimensions of the gathering crowd became apparent, it was too late to bring in more equipment to handle the mess.

Meanwhile, the horrible traffic jams in and around Bethel made it impossible for garbage haulers to transport each day's garbage to local landfills. "We contracted for the largest trash compactors available and placed them strategically around the site," said head concert organizer Michael Lang. "We would collect the garbage, take it to the compactors, then load it into trucks to haul to a local dump. A pretty good plan, and it worked beautifully the first day—until we got to the 'haul it away' part—traffic was just too heavy to make it through."[1]

Cleaning Up the Mess

As a result of these factors, the fast-emptying festival grounds "looked like those old photos you see of old Civil War battlefields, where you see a dead horse and these mounds of things that have been left," said concert photographer Henry Diltz.

> The whole field where all these people had been … what was left behind was this incredible sea of mud and all this flotsam and jetsam that was left by this crowd—soggy wet sleeping bags and cardboard boxes and newspapers and picnic wrappers and just a sea of junk all sunk in the mud. There were broken chairs sitting there. There were tents that were all knocked down and trampled on.… There was even an incredible stench. I guess from all this humanity just occupying the field for three days. I don't know what they did there, but it really smelled very, very foul.[2]

On Tuesday, August 19, the massive clean-up effort finally got moving. "In a day … [everyone] was gone, and we had to try to figure out how to clear it up and clear it out and decide what we were going to pack up and save and what we were going to put away and what we had to do to return Max's property to something like it was,"[3] recalled Chris Langhart, one of the festival's technical directors. Over the next several weeks Langhart supervised a crew of more than a hundred workers that dismantled the stage, hauled out the trailers, and covered over land that had been gouged with pipes, trenches, tents, and portable toilets. The clean-up crew used bulldozers to push the trash into vast mounds that could be carted away. Work crews and local community groups also sorted through the refuse to find blankets, sleeping bags, clothing, and other materials that could be used by the Salvation Army and Goodwill.

Max and Miriam Yasgur were shocked by the damage that the festival did to their property. The number of concertgoers that had come to Woodstock far exceeded the number that they had agreed to accommodate in the contract they had signed with John Roberts and the other festival promoters. But the Yasgurs

Tired and dirty music fans jammed area roads as they made their way home from the Woodstock festival.

had enjoyed their experiences with the young concertgoers, they liked Roberts, and they could see that he and the other promoters were making a genuine effort to compensate the Bethel community for the problems their festival had created. With these factors in mind, Max Yasgur rejected the idea of filing a lawsuit against the promoters. As his wife recalled, his attitude was "'Let's work something out here. Leave my place nice and compensate me for the damage and let's remain friends.' And ... that's what happened. And John called us every once in a while and when Max died in 1973, he contacted me. He was a real gentleman about the whole thing. I can't speak highly enough of him."[4]

The clean-up crews also spent a lot of time fixing up the damage that festival attendees had done to the properties of the Yasgurs' neighbors. "People would call up and say, 'My fence was broken down by those festival-goers,' and

85

we'd have to go and fix the fence," remembered Mel Lawrence, the festival operations chief. "We got a phone call one time from a church that said that people had really dirtied up the inside of this old barn of a church. And we went in there and it was all these newspapers from like the 1930s, you know, I mean, it had nothing to do with the festival. We were cleaning up the whole county as it turned out and we'd still be cleaning if we didn't decide to just stop it."[5]

Taking Stock of Woodstock

While the Woodstock organizers tried to fix the damage or otherwise compensate property owners in the Bethel area, the community itself was left to clean up the mountains of litter that had been left along area roadsides. This angered a significant segment of the community, which had always been deeply divided about hosting the festival. Once the event was over, few opponents had changed their minds. They continued to describe Woodstock as a big mistake and the weekend itself as a nightmare. Yasgur's neighbor Clarence W. Townsend, a dairy farmer, complained afterwards that "there were kids all over [our] place. They made a human cesspool of our property and drove through the cornfields. There's not a fence left on the place. They just tore them up and used them for firewood."[6] Lang later estimated that about eighty lawsuits were filed against Woodstock ventures in the days and weeks following the concert. Most were either dropped or settled out of court.

> *"There were kids all over [our] place," one local farmer complained after Woodstock. "They made a human cesspool of our property and drove through the cornfields. There's not a fence left on the place. They just tore them up and used them for firewood."*

Festival coordinator Stan Goldstein acknowledged that Bethel included "a group of very vocal, unhappy people in whose fields and lawns people had settled, who claimed all kinds of damage from the marauding hordes." He emphasized, however, that other townspeople said, "'Wow, what a miraculous thing you guys have done … the kids were great … how did you manage to do it?' Of course, most of the merchants and businesspeople in the area were very happy. They'd never done so much business in such a short length of time."[7]

As the cleanup got underway in Bethel, the rest of America tried to make sense of exactly what had transpired on the Yasgur farm. Some conservative media outlets and commentators condemned the entire festival as a hopelessly disor-

It took clean-up crews several weeks to dispose of mountains of garbage and restore the Woodstock festival site to its original state.

ganized event that exposed the moral bankruptcy of the attendees. According to this perspective, Woodstock just gave hippies an excuse to retreat to a fantasy land of irresponsibility where they could smoke a lot of pot, run around naked, and trash other people's property and belongings without any consequences.

Many of the people who had actually attended the festival or performed on stage, though, seemed to reject that version of events. In conversations with friends, letters and stories to local newspapers, and interviews with journalists, many of these young men and women acknowledged the nudity and pot smoking. They described Woodstock, though, as an almost magical gathering. They emphasized not only the high quality of the music and the freedom they felt, but the way in which the huge gathering had remained harmonious and high-spirited despite the rain and mud and hunger and overcrowding. To them, Woodstock really had been "three days of peace and music," just as the promoters had promised.

The *New York Times* Changes Its Tune

As the days and weeks passed, this positive characterization of the Woodstock experience became the dominant one in America's collective consciousness. Even some outlets that initially criticized the festival began describing it in warm terms. The *New York Times* was by far the most famous example of this shift in attitude.

On August 18—the same day that Woodstock finally drew to a close—the prestigious newspaper ran an editorial called "Nightmare in the Catskills." The paper's editors admitted that "the great bulk of the freakish-looking intruders" who descended on Bethel for the festival "behaved astonishingly well, considering the disappointments and discomforts they encountered." But most of the *Times* editorial painted a grim picture of the proceedings. They described the organizers as incompetent and the concertgoers as "maddened youths": "The dreams of marijuana and rock music that drew 300,000 fans and hippies to the Catskills had little more sanity than the impulses that drive the lemmings to march to their deaths in the sea. They ended in a nightmare of mud and stagnation that paralyzed Sullivan County for a whole weekend. What kind of culture is it that can produce so colossal a mess?"[8]

"[Woodstock] will surely go down in history as a mass event of great and positive significance in the life of the country," wrote the editors of the New York Times. "In a nation beset with a crescendo of violence, this is a vibrantly hopeful sign. If violence is infectious, so, happily, is nonviolence."

One day later, the paper published another editorial about Woodstock, called "Morning After at Bethel." This one described the concert—and the people who showed up for it—in much more upbeat and generous terms. The editors of the paper changed their position on Woodstock after *New York Times* reporters like Barnard Law Collier registered angry objections to the paper's initial accounts. "It was difficult to persuade [the editors] that the relative lack of serious mischief and the fascinating cooperation, caring, and politeness among so many people was the significant point,"[9] said Collier.

Once they heard out their own reporters, the editors were forced to let go of their preconceptions about the festival and its attendees. They sheepishly published a second editorial that emphasized the positive aspects of the experience. The editors even predicted that Woodstock "will surely go down in history as a mass event of great and positive significance in the life of the country.... In a nation beset with a crescendo of violence, this is a vibrantly hopeful sign. If violence is infectious, so, happily, is nonviolence. The benign character of the young people gathered at Bethel communicated itself to many of their elders, including policemen, and the generation gap was successfully bridged in countless cases. Any event which can do this is touched with greatness."[10]

The Horror of Altamont

The good vibes from Woodstock endured through the summer of 1969, but when autumn arrived the mood surrounding America's counterculture darkened. Two events were responsible for this change. The first was the October 1969 arrest of Charles Manson and several of his long-haired followers (known in the press as the Manson Family) for the brutal August 1969 killings of seven people—including pregnant actress Sharon Tate—in an affluent Los Angeles neighborhood. As details about the frightening Manson family and their gruesome crimes emerged, many Americans who had come to see hippies as peaceful (whether they liked them or not) wondered whether they might actually be dangerous. "Before the murders, no one associated hippies with violence and murder, just drugs, peace, free love, etc." explained attorney Vincent Bugliosi, who played a lead role in securing death sentence convictions for Manson and his followers for their awful crimes (California later struck down the death penalty, so the sentences were commuted to life in prison). "Then the Manson Family comes along, looking like hippies, but what they were all about was murder. That was their religion, their credo. That shocked a lot of people and definitely hurt the counterculture movement."[11]

The second event was a one-day rock-and-roll festival that was held at Altamont Speedway in Livermore, California, on December 6, 1969. The free event was envisioned as a triumphant finale to a U.S. concert tour by the Rolling Stones—and a way for the band to blunt criticism about the sky-high ticket prices that marked the rest of the tour. The bill included popular bands like Jefferson Airplane, Santana, and Crosby, Stills, and Nash, with the Stones providing the night's closing set. Rock fans flocked to the show, which organizers touted as a kind of West Coast version of Woodstock. Instead, they witnessed what *Rolling Stone* writer John Burks described as "perhaps rock and roll's all-time worst day."[12]

The Altamont concert was troubled from the start. The speedway itself did not have any of the charm of the Yasgur farm—or of most other outdoor con-

The Hell's Angels motorcycle gang killed a member of the audience while the Rolling Stones were on stage at the Altamont Speedway in California.

cert venues. As tour photographer Ethan A. Russell said, "it was a dull, lifeless landscape. There was no hint of green, not a tree, not a blade of grass. When we arrived there was no palpable feeling of joy or even happiness. It slowly dawned on me that this concert might not turn out to be what I expected."[13] Once the concert started, attendees complained that the sound quality was terrible, that the promoters had not arranged for enough portable toilets or medical tents, and that the crowd was rougher than they expected. Woodstock promoter Michael Lang, who also helped put on the Altamont show, called the concert "one of the worst experiences of my life. I truly got to see the dark side of the drug culture. People high on all kinds of exotic concoctions were just wandering through the crowd."[14]

The biggest problem with the Altamont show, though, was the decision by the Rolling Stones, their management, and the promoters to hire the Hell's

Angels motorcycle gang to provide security for the concert. The Angels had been suggested by the Grateful Dead, who said that the gang had patrolled other concerts in the San Francisco Bay area over the previous few years without any serious problems. The Angels were cheap, too; they agreed to show up in exchange for $500 worth of beer and prime seats on and around the stage. The only other security personnel on hand were personal bodyguards to the musicians and a small number of guards responsible for protecting the speedway grounds. Virtually no police were ever seen at the concert site.

By December 1969, though, the Hell's Angels had become a violent bunch, and they were heavy abusers of alcohol and dangerous drugs like LSD and heroin. This menacing combination was on vivid display as the concert wore on. Members of the gang prowled the stage area armed with pool cues that they used indiscriminately against anyone who irritated them. Drunken Angels also used full beer cans as projectile weapons, hurling them at the heads of unsuspecting concertgoers. Even performers came under attack. When a group of Angels began beating up a young black man near the front of the crowd during Jefferson Airplane's set, lead singer Marty Balin jumped offstage to come to the man's aid. One of the Angels promptly turned on Balin and knocked him unconscious.

The night took an even more frightening turn when the Rolling Stones took the stage. The band was halfway through a song when it stopped and looked toward the area directly in front of the stage. A concert film crew focused its cameras on the same scene. What the Stones and the crew both witnessed was the killing of a young black man named Meredith Hunter by members of the motorcycle gang. The victim was stabbed in the back by an Angel, then savagely stomped by several gang members as he lay helpless on the ground. Stunned by the outbreak of violence, lead singer Mick Jagger pleaded for the Angels and the audience alike to stop fighting. Jagger also used the sound system to call for a doctor and an ambulance for Hunter, who was taken backstage. A doctor who had volunteered to help at the medical tents said, though, that "there's nothing they could have done to save him."[15]

The Stones completed their set, although band members later admitted that the Angels' swarming attack on Hunter

Some said Altamont would have been different without the Hell's Angels. But one concertgoer insisted that "it wasn't just the Angels. It was everybody. There was no love, no joy. In twenty-four hours we created all the problems of our society in one place: congestion, violence, dehumanization. Is this what we want?"

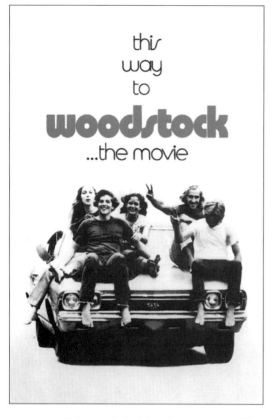

this
way
to
woodstock
...the movie

Director Michael Wadleigh's documentary film allowed millions more people to experience the sights and sounds of the Woodstock festival.

greatly disturbed them. An Angel named Alan Pasarro was later identified as the stabber, but he was acquitted of murder charges when film footage showed that Hunter was holding a gun when Pasarro stabbed him. Hunter's family always maintained, though, that he took out the gun only because he felt threatened by gang members.

News of the grim and bloody Altamont experience spread across the country over the next few days (three other concertgoers died in addition to Hunter; one drowned in a ditch and two others were run over by a car as they sat next to a campfire). People who had been to Woodstock or heard about its peaceful vibe expressed shock that the San Francisco Bay area—birthplace of the Summer of Love—could have been the setting for such a nightmarish concert. Many hippies said that it all would have gone much differently if the Hell's Angels had not been at Altamont. But one woman concertgoer insisted that "it wasn't just the Angels. It was everybody. There was no love, no joy. In twenty-four hours we created all the problems of our society in one place: congestion, violence, dehumanization. Is this what we want?"[16]

Woodstock Immortalized on Film

Altamont is frequently described as the point at which all the violence that had been swirling around the nation during the 1960s—the assassinations of Martin Luther King and Robert F. Kennedy, the attacks on civil rights marchers, the Vietnam War, the riots in Chicago and America's urban slums—finally penetrated the world of rock and roll. Afterwards, some young music fans wondered if the country would ever be able to recapture the feeling of innocence and harmony that had been nurtured at Woodstock.

Fortunately for them, March 1970 brought the release of a film that reminded America of the sounds, sights, and experiences of the Woodstock festival. *Woodstock: 3 Days of Peace and Music* was the creation of director Michael Wadleigh, who in turn relied heavily on the talents of sound designer Larry Johnson, editor Thelma Schoonmaker, producer Bob Maurice, sound engineer Dan Wallin, assistant editor Martin Scorsese (who would later become one of the world's most famous film directors), and an army of cinematographers, camera crew, and production assistants. Their final product distilled 172 hours of concert footage down into a three-hour film. It interspersed musical highlights with scenes that sought to capture what the concert had been like for the young men and women who had sat in the audience, camped in the fields, and swam in the ponds at Woodstock (see "The Saga of the Woodstock Port-O-San Man," p. 183).

The film, which was released by Warner Brothers, was a huge popular and critical hit. Young moviegoers flocked to theaters in such great numbers that the documentary became the sixth-highest-grossing movie of 1970. Meanwhile, lukewarm reviews of the movie in some conservative magazines and newspapers were overwhelmed by rave reviews from most mainstream media outlets. "In terms of evoking the style and feel of a mass historical event, *Woodstock* may be the best documentary ever made in America," wrote reviewer Roger Ebert. "*Woodstock* is a beautiful, complete, moving, ultimately great film, and years from now when our generation is attacked for being just as uptight as all the rest of the generations, it will be good to have this movie around to show that, just for a weekend anyway, that wasn't altogether the case."[17] The film critic for *Time*, meanwhile, called it a "joyous, volcanic new film that will make those who missed the festival feel as if they were there."[18]

According to Lang, though, *Woodstock* was worthwhile not only as a historical document, but as an educational tool to show people the true size, strength, and diversity of the "Woodstock Generation." Lang said that the film revealed "that there was this community that existed in America, that was tied together, and that was so large and so strong and so positive.... I think it brought home to people that it was not just these sort of radical groups that were spread

> *The* Woodstock *movie revealed "that there was this community that existed in America, that was tied together, and that was so large and so strong and so positive,"* Michael Lang *commented. "You look at that crowd, you don't see half a million long-haired freaks, you see kids with crew-cuts, you see kids from every walk of life."*

Pete Townshend's Shifting Assessments of the Woodstock Experience

Most of the musical acts who played at Woodstock have extremely fond memories of the entire experience. They freely admit that the weekend was chaotic and muddy and disorganized, but they say that it also was exhilarating to be part of such a massive and celebratory event. One exception to that viewpoint, though, was lead guitarist Pete Townshend of the Who. Townshend had not wanted to perform at Woodstock in the first place. The band was just finishing an exhausting tour of its own, and he wanted to go back to England to spend time with his family. He agreed to play at the festival only after relentless badgering from the Who's manager.

Townshend was unimpressed by the whole festival, and at one point he even hit hippie radical Abbie Hoffman in the back of the head with his guitar for interrupting the Who's set to give a political speech. Afterward, Townshend expressed contempt for the Woodstock audience. "All those hippies wandering about thinking the world was going to be different from that day on," he said. "I walked through it all and felt like spitting on the lot of them." When Country Joe McDonald, who also performed at Woodstock, heard about Townshend's remarks, he offered a cutting recollection of the guitarist: "I saw Townshend pull up in his limo, then do his set, and leave. That's the sum total of his experience of Woodstock. He played at it but he wasn't really part of it."

Thirty years later, Townshend issued an apology of sorts. Performing as a solo act at the thirtieth anniversary celebration of Woodstock, he declared that America became a better country because of Woodstock. He also said that while he disagreed with Hoffman and other radical hippies of the 1960s about many things, he thought "their hearts were in the right place."

Sources:

Fornatale, Pete. *Back to the Garden: The Story of Woodstock.* New York: Touchstone, 2009.

O'Hagan, Sean. "The Year of Living Dangerously," *Telegraph (UK),* May 16, 2009.

around here and there in the East Village [of New York City] and Haight-Ashbury, but this was everybody's son and daughter who was involved here. You look at that crowd, you don't see half a million long-haired freaks, you see kids with crew-cuts, you see kids from every walk of life."[19]

Playing at Woodstock was a career highlight for many performers, like Arlo Guthrie.

Some Stars Burn Brighter, Others Burn Out

The *Woodstock* film (and a hugely popular soundtrack album that was released around the same time) also provided a snapshot of many of the most popular bands and most talented musicians of the 1960s rock world. It was true that neither the Beatles nor Bob Dylan appeared at Woodstock, but by 1969 both artists had virtually stopped performing live. The Beatles broke up one year later. Dylan resumed playing live in the 1970s and later became known for his never-ending touring.

Many other top acts were featured, though, including several who remained top concert draws for years after Woodstock. Such performers included the Grateful Dead, Joe Cocker, Crosby, Stills, Nash, and Young (CSNY), and the Who (see "Pete Townsend's Shifting Assessments of the Woodstock Experience," p. 94). Other musical acts exploded in popularity as a direct result of their Woodstock appearances. "There was the Woodstock gig followed by the Woodstock film followed by the Woodstock album, which was a monster," pointed out legendary rock promoter Bill Graham. "Woodstock *made* Joe Cocker, Ten Years After, Mountain, Sly Stone, and Santana."[20]

For other acts who performed at the festival or were featured on the film, Woodstock represented the peak of their careers. A number of the artists faded out of the spotlight within months of the festival, while big names like Sly and the Family Stone, The Band, Jefferson Airplane, Creedence Clearwater Revival, Ten Years After, and Blood, Sweat and Tears dissolved by the mid-1970s. Other performers, like Joan Baez, Richie Havens, and Arlo Guthrie, went on to have long and impressive careers in rock and folk music. They never again achieved the level of adulation that they received for their turn on the stage at Max Yasgur's farm, but Guthrie did not mind. "I think anyone who played at Woodstock … attained a status within the American culture, actually in the sort of global culture, that was beyond anything we ever dreamed of being," he said. "I still don't need reservations in restaurants in Italy, or *India*, or wherever, simply because I was at Woodstock. Which is, you know … I'll take it."[21]

Finally, the Woodstock lineup included two iconic performers who became casualties of the hardening "rock-and-roll lifestyle," which glorified hard drugs and alcohol consumption. Jimi Hendrix had used his 1967 performance at Monterey and his 1969 Woodstock appearance to cement his reputation as one of rock and roll's greatest guitarists. Thirteen months after he closed out the Woodstock festival, on September 18, 1970, Hendrix died after a long night of partying. According to the coroner, Hendrix choked to death on his own vomit. Two weeks later, on October 4, the body of singer Janis Joplin was found in a Hollywood hotel room. Medical examiners later determined that Joplin—another artist who had vaulted to stardom at Monterey during the 1967 Summer of Love—died of a heroin overdose.

Authorities believed that both deaths were accidental, but they still triggered a great surge of sorrow and disillusionment within America's so-called Woodstock Nation. For many people, wrote historians Ron Eyerman and Andrew Jamison, the deaths of Hendrix and Joplin "symbolized the death of a generation, a lifestyle, the counterculture itself."[22] They were not the only Woodstock artists whose lives were shortened by drugs, either. As rock critic Pete Fornatale wrote, "the list of deaths by drug of performers who appeared at the festival reads like a who's who of progressive rock: Hendrix, Joplin, [Who drummer Keith] Moon, [songwriter Tim] Hardin, [Grateful Dead guitarist Jerry] Garcia, et cetera.… I'm tempted to say that there is a huge chasm between moderate, recreational drug use versus severe addiction.… But how can anyone ignore the body bags piled up in the years since the festival?"[23]

Notes

[1] Lang, Michael, with Holly George-Warren. *The Road to Woodstock.* New York: Ecco, 2009, p. 196.
[2] Quoted in Makower, Joel. *Woodstock: The Oral History.* New York: Tilden Press, 1989, pp. 288-89.
[3] Quoted in Makower, p. 292.
[4] Quoted in Makower, p. 292.

[5] Quoted in Makower, p. 295.

[6] Quoted in Rand, Ayn. *The New Left: The Anti-Industrial Revolution.* New York: New American Library, 1971, p. 71.

[7] Quoted in Lang, p. 243.

[8] "Nightmare in the Catskills." *New York Times,* August 18, 1969. Retrieved from www.graphics8.nytimes.com/packages/pdf/topics/Woodstock/1969WoodstockEditorial.pdf.

[9] Quoted in Fornatale, Pete. *Back to the Garden: The Story of Woodstock.* New York: Touchstone, 2009, p. xxii.

[10] "Morning After at Bethel." *New York Times,* August 19, 1969. Retrieved from www.woodstockpreservation.org/Gallery/NYT-PDF/19_MorningAfterAtBethel.pdf.

[11] Sachs, Andrea. "Q&A: Manson Prosecutor Vincent Bugliosi." *Time,* August 7, 2009. Retrieved from www.time.com/time/nation/article/0,8599,1915134,00.html.

[12] Burks, John. "In the Aftermath of Altamont." *Rolling Stone,* February 7, 1970, p. 7.

[13] Russell, Ethan A. "The Rolling Stones at Altamont: The Day the Music Died." *The Telegraph (UK),* December 2, 2009. Retrieved from www.telegraph.co.uk/culture/music/rockandpopfeatures/6690506/The-Rolling-Stones-at-Altamont-the-day-the-music-died.html.

[14] Lang, p. 259.

[15] Quoted in Gleason, Ralph J. "Aquarius Wept." *Esquire,* August 1970, pp. 84-92. Retrieved from www.esquire.com/features/altamont-1969-aquarius-wept-0870.

[16] Quoted in Gleason, "Aquarius Wept."

[17] Ebert, Roger. "Woodstock: May 1970." *Awake in the Dark: The Best of Roger Ebert: Forty Years of Reviews, Essays, and Interviews.* Chicago: University of Chicago Press, 2006, pp. 267-71.

[18] "Hold Onto Your Neighbor." *Time,* April 13, 1970, p. 100.

[19] Quoted in Bell, Dale, ed. *Woodstock: An Inside Look at the Movie That Shook Up the World and Defined a Generation.* Studio City, CA: Michael Wiese, 1999, p. 251.

[20] Graham, Bill, and Robert Greenfield. *Bill Graham Presents: My Life Inside Rock and Out.* 1990. Cambridge, MA: De Capo Press, 2004, p. 289.

[21] Quoted in Bell, p. 91.

[22] Eyerman, Ron, and Andrew Jamison. *Music and Social Movements; Mobilizing Traditions in the Twentieth Century.* New York: Cambridge University Press, 1998, p. 131.

[23] Fornatale, Pete. *Back to the Garden: The Story of Woodstock.* New York: Touchstone, 2009, p. 67.

Chapter Seven

THE LEGACY
OF WOODSTOCK

―⟪⟫―

If someone thinks that love and peace is a cliché that must have been left behind in the Sixties, that's his problem. Love and peace are eternal.

—John Lennon

With each passing year, the Woodstock Art and Music Festival fades a little deeper into the mists of American memory. At the same time, though, the concert has emerged as perhaps the single most recognized symbol of the 1960s—or at least an idealized version of the era, when young people came together to celebrate the power of peace, love, and music over war, materialism, and racism.

Woodstock also changed many other aspects of American society. The event sent shock waves through the nation's music industry, transforming it in numerous important ways. It also was a wake-up call to "Madison Avenue"—U.S. advertising agencies—which suddenly realized that the youth market had great untapped potential. Even as various aspects of the festival and the decade it came to represent became commercialized, though, supporters continued to defend passionately the *idea* of Woodstock and the 1960s. Some of the foremost supporters of the idea of Woodstock Nation, in fact, are men and women who were not even alive when the famous concert took place.

Music Becomes Big Business

The most obvious and immediate ripple effects from Woodstock were seen in the music industry. Prior to Woodstock, rock and roll musicians supported

> *"Woodstock changed the music industry," said festival organizer Stan Goldstein. "For the first time you could see the power of artists to attract not just crowds, but crowds of people with money."*

themselves primarily through record sales. Concerts were not big money makers. Instead, they were seen by bands and managers alike as promotional events designed to raise public interest in a new record or album. The 400,000-strong audience at Woodstock, though, provided clear evidence of something that earlier concert events like the 1967 Monterey Pop Festival had suggested: concerts could generate a lot of money by themselves. "Woodstock changed the music industry," confirmed Stan Goldstein, one of the festival's main organizers. "For the first time you could see the power of artists to attract not just crowds, but crowds of people with money."[1]

According to observers like Woodstock promoter Michael Lang, the impact of this lesson could be seen immediately. "The amount of money that bands demanded from their performance [laughs] skyrocketed! Instantly!" he said. "I paid [Jimi] Hendrix $15,000, which was the top [fee we paid to Woodstock performers] ... and three weeks later I think he was getting $150,000 at the Isle of Wight"[2] music festival in England.

Within a matter of a few years, popular rock bands had learned to negotiate contracts that gave them a far higher share of the concert "gate"—the money collected from concert ticket sales—than ever before. Long national tours became more and more popular as a result, and by the late 1970s musical acts such as the Rolling Stones, Led Zeppelin, Elton John, and the Eagles were becoming stupendously rich. This phenomenon continues today as popular performers like U2, Bruce Springsteen, Lady Gaga, Taylor Swift, and Madonna regularly sell out huge basketball and football stadiums for their concerts.

Woodstock also became a blueprint of sorts for future multi-day music festivals. Promoters learned from Woodstock that events that brought together a wide assortment of popular acts were irresistible to many music fans. These fans were attracted not only by the prospect of listening to their favorite bands live, but by the idea of experiencing that music in a community setting with thousands of other like-minded people. Promoters came to understand that for many fans, the feeling of being part of a special *event* was just as important as the opportunity to enjoy music. "[Woodstock] stands out in everybody's mind as the originator,"[3] said Michele Scoleri of the Bumbershoot Music Festival, which takes place in Seattle every Labor Day weekend.

The success of Woodstock led to a surge in large-scale outdoor music festivals in later years.

Of course, concert promoters learned from the problems that cropped up at Woodstock as well. Today's music festivals are better organized and more professionally executed than the show that took place in Bethel, New York, in August 1969. At Bonaroo, Lollapalooza, Pitchfork, Coachella, and other prominent music festivals around America, "lineups are well-curated, portable toilet lines are short, security is mostly handled professionally, the sound is generally good and amenities are easily purchased," observed journalist Robert Lang. "Promoters are more responsible than Woodstock's were, too, taking green measures to blunt the environmental impact and clean up after themselves."[4]

Finally, Woodstock showed that the music industry had a lot of room to grow. After the festival, radio executives and record companies worked feverishly to claim their share of a pie that was much bigger than they had previously believed. They were convinced that rock critic Greil Marcus was right when he said after Woodstock that "all over the nation, kids are moving to rock and roll. It's the most important thing in their lives."[5] Media companies began snapping

101

up radio stations and organizing them into big music-playing networks. Meanwhile, record labels devoted to rock and other popular music like country, rhythm and blues, disco, and soul all exploded in size and influence. As rock historian Robert Santelli wrote, "Woodstock sent the music industry in a frenzy to sign new bands and take advantage of the vast new commercial potential of rock."[6]

The Buying Power of Youth

At the same time that the music industry was becoming big business, executives in other industries that heard the stories about Woodstock or saw footage from the *Woodstock* documentary realized that they had not been paying enough attention to the cultural changes that had been taking place during the 1960s. "Madison Avenue suddenly came out of the fifties ... and into the sixties and seventies, realizing that this was their future," said Michael Lang. "And things had to start appealing to this culture and these kids, or they weren't going to survive through the seventies."[7]

Advertising campaigns in America became increasingly focused on making sure that the products they were promoting came off as "hip" and "cool." Corporations began using popular rock songs and counterculture imagery to sell clothing, automobiles, movies, beer, and numerous other types of consumer products. This embrace of Woodstock's music and image for the purposes of commerce outraged some musicians and activists from the 1960s. "Woodstock ... was a beautiful experience for hundreds of thousands of our people which we produced ourselves," wrote John Sinclair, the politically radical manager of the MC5 rock band, in 1972. "But the ... record companies and movie companies and vampires of all kinds swooped down on it and grabbed it and took it into their factories and cooked the reality of Woodstock down into records and movies and shit which they now sell back to us."[8]

Despite such condemnations, however, the effectiveness of these advertising campaigns was undeniable. Some observers also point out that despite all the warm remembrances of Woodstock as a weekend of sharing and brotherhood, the festival *was* originally envisioned as a for-profit event. In any case, rock-and-roll music became deeply interwoven into the world of business marketing. Today's consumers, whether they are teenagers, young parents, or "baby boomers" (people in their mid-forties through mid-sixties), have become thoroughly accustomed to commercials that use classic rock songs or more modern hits to sell everything from music-playing cell phones and computers to cologne and vacation destinations.

Rock band Coldplay has refused to allow its songs to be used in advertising, thus bucking the trend toward increasing commercialization of music.

Trying to Recapture the Magic

Since the 1969 Woodstock festival, several anniversary concerts designed to commemorate—and in some cases profit from—the original event have also been organized. In 1989 a twentieth-anniversary concert was proposed by Louis Nicky, who had become the owner of the Yasgur Farm where the original festival had been held. He was unable to get the necessary permits from Bethel authorities, but several thousand Woodstock alumni and fans nonetheless congregated at the site on the third weekend in August that year. The weekend featured no big-name acts, but many people who made the journey said that the atmosphere was warm, friendly, and non-commercial.

In 1994 two concert events to mark the twenty-fifth anniversary of Woodstock were organized in New York State. The smaller one, which drew more than 10,000 people, was a free concert held at the original site. It featured live performances from several beloved acts from the original festival, including Richie

Woodstock promoter Michael Lang has been involved with several later efforts to celebrate the legacy of the famous music festival.

Havens (who helped organize the show) and Arlo Guthrie. The event was called A Day in the Garden Festival because the organizers of the larger, competing festival had secured all legal rights to the Woodstock name. According to many participants, though, the modestly sized Bethel event did a great job of capturing the friendly, easygoing vibe of the original.

By contrast, the official Woodstock '94 twenty-fifth anniversary festival was crafted as a big moneymaking venture. Held on an 800-acre farm in Saugerties, New York, the extravaganza's organizers included original Woodstock promoters John Roberts, Michael Lang, and Joel Rosenman, as well as record executive John Scher. Their event, sometimes known as Woodstock II, attracted a crowd of 350,000. From August 12-14, 1994, concertgoers were treated to a diverse selection of acts, ranging from legendary artists like Bob Dylan, Aerosmith, Crosby, Stills, and Nash, and Peter Gabriel to newer sensations such as Sheryl Crow, the Red Hot Chili Peppers, Nine Inch Nails, and Metallica. Some of the performers and concertgoers complained about the high ticket prices and obvious commercialism of the event, including highly visible sponsorship from Pepsi-Cola. Others, though, praised the quality of the music and the energy of the performances. Some attendees also expressed happiness about a mid-festival rainstorm that turned the field into a mud pit that was reminiscent of the original Woodstock.

Woodstock '99

In 1999 Lang and Scher joined with U2 manager Ossie Kilkenny to put on a thirtieth anniversary Woodstock concert from July 23-25. The event was held at a former air force base in upstate New York's Mohawk Valley, more than 100 miles from the much-loved grounds of the original Woodstock site (see "The Bethel Woods Center for the Arts," p. 107). Despite $150 tickets and an agreement for portions of the concert to be broadcast nationally by the MTV network, Woodstock '99 attracted a crowd of about 250,000 to see a line-up that featured a heavy dose of aggressive rap, metal, and punk bands.

Many of the groups featured at Woodstock '99 were quite popular, but they hardly reflected the peaceful spirit of the original Woodstock festival. For example, sets by metal and rap groups like Korn and Limp Bizkit attracted hordes of young, drunken males who turned the mosh pit in front of the main stage into a war zone. Journalist Jeff Stark wrote afterward that the pit during Limp Bizkit's appearance was "a sweaty, dirty, roiling mass of vicious guys knocking the [crap] out of one another. It's not a fun scene. It's nasty, and people are getting hurt—bad. Bodies on cardboard stretchers emerge from the audience a couple of times per song."[9]

The atmosphere at the festival continued to sour throughout the weekend, as oppressive heat, overpriced concessions (including $4 bottles of water), and heavy drug and alcohol abuse all took their toll on fan morale. The great majority of concertgoers still enjoyed themselves and conducted themselves peacefully, but several hundred attendees spiraled out of control during the closing Sunday night set by the Red Hot Chili Peppers. The festival grounds became a cauldron of arson, vandalism, and violence, with rowdy mobs of concertgoers overturning cars, looting vendor booths, and setting bonfires. At one point they even toppled a speaker tower near the main stage. "The whole scene was scary," said MTV news correspondent Kurt Loder. "There were just waves of hatred bouncing around the place."[10]

A monument marks the site of the historic Woodstock music festival in Bethel, New York.

The reputation of Woodstock '99 took further blows in subsequent weeks, as media outlets reported that the festival had been marred by multiple rapes and other sexual assaults against female attendees. "It's a bad mark on our generation," said one young man who attended the festival. "We're going to be known as the ones who killed Woodstock."[11]

An Example for Future Generations?

Despite the many problems that dogged Woodstock '99, some people insist that the problems at the 1999 festival do not diminish or tarnish the vibrant legacy of the original 1969 concert. This is especially true of the men and women who performed at Woodstock '69 or experienced that festival's peaceful and happy spirit as members of the vast crowd.

Veterans of the first Woodstock, though, emphasize that many different factors contributed to its overall success and still-legendary status. According

The Bethel Woods Center for the Arts

The site of the original 1969 Woodstock Art and Music Festival is now home to the Bethel Woods Center for the Arts. The 1,700-acre grounds of the center include all 600 acres of Max Yazgur's famous dairy farm, which was the central staging area for the Woodstock concert. One of the prime attractions of the facility is an outdoor music pavilion that can accommodate up to 15,000 concertgoers. Since opening in 2006, the pavilion has featured top performers from the worlds of rock, country, classical, and jazz music, including Bob Dylan, the Dave Matthews Band, Carlos Santana, Willie Nelson, Lady Antebellum, and the New York Philharmonic Orchestra. Another focal point of the center is a museum full of exhibitions about the original Woodstock festival and the big political and cultural events of the 1960s. In addition, the center hosts an annual Harvest Festival at Bethel Woods, which fuses a traditional farmers' market with an arts and crafts show, educational programs, and special performances by musical artists from around the region.

The center owes its existence to Alan Gerry, who grew up in New York State before making a fortune in the cable television business. In 1996 Gerry established a foundation to start buying up land around the original Woodstock site. A decade later the center formally opened its doors.

The Bethel Woods Center for the Arts has been criticized in some quarters as nothing more than a "hippie museum," but staff, volunteers, and other supporters say that it provides valuable educational resources on a pivotal period in American history. They also emphasize the center's ability to attract famous artists who might otherwise never perform in upstate New York. For their part, politically conservative officials and business owners in Bethel, White Lake, and other towns in Sullivan County have expressed strong support for the center, which they hope will bring badly needed tourist dollars to the region.

Sources:

Bethel Woods Center for the Arts. *Celebrating the Human Spirit: Report to the Community, 2010-2011.* Liberty, NY: Bethel Woods, 2011.

Bethel Woods Center for the Arts web site. Retrieved from www.bethelwoodscenter.org/home.aspx.

to singer Arlo Guthrie, "Woodstock showed that, in times of disaster or difficulty, people can take care of each other, and for that reason alone it reaffirmed my faith in people."[12] David Crosby of the group Crosby, Stills, Nash, and Young pointed to the sense of community that emerged from the gathering at Max Yasgur's farm. "The important thing about it wasn't how many people were there or that … a lot of truly wonderful music got played," he said. "The important thing was it's the moment when all of that generation of hippies looked at each other and said, 'Wait a minute, we're not a fringe element. There's millions of us! We're what's happening here!' It was that self-awareness, you know, that, up to that point, it really hadn't happened."[13] Crosby and other defenders of Woodstock's legacy believe that as members of Woodstock Nation realized just how large their tribe was, they became more convinced than ever that they could change the world for the better (see "A Moment of Muddy Grace," p. 199).

Not all Americans share this positive interpretation of Woodstock—or the turbulent decade that it is often used to symbolize. The United States, in fact, contains plenty of people who believe that Woodstock is an accurate symbol of the 1960s *not* because it was so innocent and harmonious and peaceful, but rather because it showcased spectacularly self-indulgent, childish, and irresponsible behavior (see "Ayn Rand Denounces the 'Phony' Values of Woodstock," p. 192). They think that Woodstock Nation badly weakened America's social and cultural foundations—and many believe that the country has yet to recover from the moral degradation of the 1960s.

Defenders of Woodstock and the liberal political activism of the 1960s strongly object to this dark portrait. To the contrary, they continue to describe the decade as one in which idealistic young Americans stood strong against an immoral war, fought for racial equality, and rejected social conformity and materialism. "If the Sixties were overrated," declared rock legend Neil Young in *Rolling Stone*, "then I don't know what you would say about some of the … other generations. Compared to what?"[14]

Champions of the social activism that flowered during the 1960s also frequently claim that the decade's cultural impact could be felt across the United States for years afterward. They assert that the counterculture lent important strength and support to a wide range of major social and political causes of the 1970s and 1980s, including environmentalism, feminism, and racial diversity. As historian Philip Kopper wrote, "citizens of the 'Woodstock nation' claimed to have proved that love could conquer a lot, if not all."[15] All across the United States, meanwhile, the cultural symbols of Woodstock—peace signs, tie-dye

Young people today, like these visitors to the Bethel Woods Center for the Arts, continue to be fascinated by the Woodstock experience and 1960s hippie culture.

clothing, and other "hippie" fashions—have continued to endure. Nearly half a century after the concert took place, these symbols remain popular with kids, college students, and middle-aged parents alike.

Even some people who treasure the continued symbolic meaning of Woodstock, though, have said that efforts to "re-create" the concert are doomed to fail. After all, the decade that brought the festival into being has long since passed into the history books. The Vietnam War, for example, ended long ago. In early 1973 American combat troops left South Vietnam. Two years later the country was conquered by North Vietnam, which promptly merged the two nations into a single Communist-ruled country called the Socialist Republic of Vietnam. "If there wasn't a war called Vietnam going on, recollections of Woodstock would be truly different," asserted novelist and Vietnam War veteran Tim O'Brien. "It would [just] be one more jamboree. Because there was a war that the music was bouncing off, it made it an important social event in the history of this country."[16]

> *"If the Sixties were overrated," declared rock legend Neil Young in* Rolling Stone, *"then I don't know what you would say about some of the ... other generations. Compared to what?"*

"There can never be another Woodstock," agreed folksinger and political activist Joan Baez, who closed the first night's music at Bethel. "Woodstock, in all its mud and glory, belonged to the sixties, that outrageous, longed for, romanticized, lusted after, tragic, insane, bearded and bejeweled epoch. It is over and will never return."[17]

The problems that afflicted the Woodstock '99 event might also have had the side-effect of killing off any interest in future Woodstock anniversary festivals. "There's always been a problem with trying to reenact Woodstock, because you'll never get back there," explained historian Maurice Isserman. "There will never be an event again—under that name—that has such a dramatic impact or creates such a durable myth. And it would be better, I think, if other future events were organized that may be were like Woodstock, but had had a different name, and a different logo, and a different set of expectations, and you don't bring in a few of the old acts to make it feel as if it's just a continuation of the original. Every generation should create its own mythology and have its own transcendent experience."[18]

Notes

[1] "Woodstock: Fresh Dawn or Last Gasp?" *Sydney Morning Herald,* August 10, 2009. Retrieved from www.smh.com.au/news/entertainment/music/woodstock-fresh-dawn-or-last-gasp/2009/08/10/1249756 244995.html.

[2] Quoted in Bell, Dale, ed. *Woodstock: An Inside Look at the Movie That Shook Up the World and Defined a Generation.* Studio City, CA: Michael Wiese, 1999, p. 252.

[3] Quoted in Lang, Robert. "A Heroes' Welcome at Woodstock 40th Festival Legacy," *Daily Mail (UK),* August 16, 2009. Retrieved from www.dailymail.co.uk/tvshowbiz/reviews/article-1206905/Woodstock-40th.html.

[4] Lang, "Heroes' Welcome."

[5] Quoted in Wiener, Jon. *Come Together: John Lennon in His Time.* New York: Random House, 1985, p. 103.

[6] Santelli, Robert. "The Rock and Roll Hall of Fame and Museum: Myth, Memory and History." In Evelyn McDonnell, ed. *Stars Don't Stand Still in the Sky: Music and Myth.* New York: New York University Press, 1999, p. 241.

[7] Quoted in Bell, p. 253.

[8] Sinclair, John. *Guitar Army: Street Writings/Prison Writings.* New York: Douglas, 1972, p. 210.

[9] Stark, Jeff. "Taking Woodstock: What a Riot," *Slate.com,* July 27, 1999. http://www.salon.com/1999/07/27/woodstock/

[10] Quoted in Oldenburg, Ann. "MTV's Loder Flees Out-of-Control Fest," *USA Today,* July 27, 1999, p. D2.

[11] "A Look Back at Woodstock '99," *The Post-Standard/Syracuse.com,* July 26, 2009. Retrieved from www.blog.syracuse.com/entertainment/2009/07/a_look_back_at_woodstock_99.html.

[12] Nikkhah, Roya. "Woodstock 40 Years On: The Legend, the Legacy." *Telegraph (UK),* August 8, 2009. Retrieved from www.telegraph.co.uk/culture/music/5995703/Woodstock-40-years-on-The-legend-the-legacy.html.

[13] Quoted in "The Way the Music Died," *PBS Frontline,* May 27, 2004. Retrieved from www.pbs.org/wgbh/pages/frontline/shows/music/interviews/crosby.html.

[14] Quoted in Brokaw, Tom. *Boom! Voices of the Sixties, Personal Reflections on the '60s and Today.* New York: Random House, 2007, p. 663.

[15] Kopper, Philip. "Flashback to Woodstock," *American Heritage,* Summer 2009. Retrieved from www.americanheritage.com/content/flashback-woodstock.

[16] Quoted in "Woodstock Helped Us Get Through 'Nam," *PRWeb Newswire,* August 4, 2009.

[17] Baez, Joan. *And a Voice to Sing With: A Memoir.* New York: Summit Books, 1987, p. 165.

[18] Quoted in Storm, Geoff. "Historical Memory and the Woodstock Legacy," *WRPI "Talking History"* [transcript], 2009. Retrieved from www.archives.nysed.gov/apt/magazine/archivesmag_fall10_woodstock.pdf.

BIOGRAPHIES

Joan Baez (1941-)
Folksinger, Political Activist, and Woodstock Performer

Joan Chandos Baez was born on January 9, 1941, in Staten Island, New York. She was the middle daughter of Albert Vinicio Baez, a prominent Mexican-American physicist who focused his talents on the worlds of education and medicine, and Joan Bridge Baez. In 1951 the Baez family moved to Baghdad, Iraq, where Albert spent a year establishing a new physics department at Baghdad University. In 1952 the family returned to California, settling in Palo Alto. Raised by her parents in the pacifist Quaker faith, Joan became politically aware at an early age. By the time Joan graduated from Palo Alto High School in 1958, she had already established herself as a young woman who was unafraid to speak out on perceived injustices and problems in American society.

A New Folk Sensation

Baez also enjoyed music, and by her late teens she could often be found strumming a guitar and singing folk songs. In 1958 her father took a teaching post at the prestigious Massachusetts Institute of Technology (MIT). Baez suddenly found herself living in Cambridge, Massachusetts, one of America's hottest incubators of folk music. She quickly became a fixture on stage at coffeehouses and folk clubs around Cambridge and Boston. Baez also enrolled at Boston University, but she dropped out after several weeks to focus on her musical dreams.

Baez's beautiful voice and charismatic stage presence impressed folk fans and musicians alike. Nationally known folk artist Bob Gibson was so impressed with Baez that he invited her to perform with him at a folk festival that was being held in Newport, Rhode Island, in July 1959. The inaugural Newport Folk Festival—which quickly became the leading concert event in the folk music world—introduced Baez to a much larger audience. Baez's unbilled performance at Newport established her as a new star; when she appeared at Newport again one year later, she was one of the event's headliners.

Baez's star continued to rise throughout the early 1960s. In 1960 she released the first of fourteen records on the Vanguard label, where she stayed until 1971. These early recordings further burnished her reputation as a talented and sensitive interpreter of traditional folk ballads and songs written by other up-and-coming artists. The most prominent of these new folksingers was Bob Dylan—or "Bobby," as Baez affectionately called him. Baez and Dylan became romantically involved in late 1962, around the same time that Dylan's own career began to take off. They performed together on several occasions, and their songs and statements in support of the civil rights movement made them the unofficial "first couple" of early 1960s protest music. Baez sang "We Shall Overcome" at the famous 1963 March on Washington led by Martin Luther King Jr., with whom the singer established a friendship.

Baez's romantic relationship with Dylan continued on and off until 1965, by which time Dylan had become one of the biggest stars in the rock-and-roll universe. Around this same time, Baez became increasingly involved in protest actions against the Vietnam War. Her passion for civil rights remained strong as well, and in March 1965 she participated in the famous Selma-to-Montgomery voting rights march. Over the next several years Baez also performed benefit concerts to raise money for causes ranging from migrant farmworker rights to campaigns to outlaw the death penalty.

On a few occasions, Baez's political activism landed her in legal trouble. In October 1967 she and more than 100 other demonstrators were arrested for unlawfully blocking a military induction center in Oakland, California. She served ten days in jail for that offense. After her release, she went right back to the same induction facility for another demonstration. This time her arrest resulted in a month-long jail stay.

Baez at Woodstock

On March 26, 1968, Baez married David Harris, a prominent antiwar activist and military draft resister. In July 1969 Harris was sent to prison after being convicted of draft evasion, a felony offense. He served twenty months before authorities released him. During Harris's incarceration, Baez agreed to perform at the famous Woodstock Music and Art Fair, which was held August 15-17, 1969, in Bethel, a small farming community in upstate New York.

Baez was the headliner on the first night of the festival. When she strode on stage with guitar in hand at one o'clock in the morning, she received a warm welcome from the huge throng of concertgoers. Baez opened by briefly telling the story of her husband's recent legal troubles. The six-months-pregnant singer then launched into a set of well-known folk and gospel standards, including "Joe Hill" and "Swing Low Sweet Chariot," as well as a cover of Dylan's "I Shall Be Released." Baez closed the first night's music with a beautiful version of "We Shall Overcome," which had become the anthem of the civil rights movement. "She was the queen," said festival coordinator John Morris. "Everybody loved her. I mean, I was totally in love with her.... She was the perfect person to end it on because everybody was wearing down that first night.... She was the lullaby so that they could make it through that night."[1]

Like many other people who performed at Woodstock, Baez was stunned by the size of the crowd and how concertgoers persevered through a weekend of storms, heat, bad drugs, and overwhelmed toilet facilities. "It was three extraordinary days of rain and music," she wrote in a 1987 memoir. "I sang in the middle of the night. I just stood up there in front of the residents of the golden city who were sleeping in the mud and each other's arms, and I gave them what I could at the time. And they accepted my songs. It was a humbling moment, in spite of everything. I'd never sung to a city before."[2]

A Lifetime of Music and Advocacy

Baez gave birth to Gabriel Earl Harris in December 1969. Gabriel would grow up to become a musician himself. He has even been the drummer in his mother's touring band. David Harris was released from prison in March 1971. He and Baez were reunited, but the marriage lasted for only two more years before ending in divorce.

Baez's stature as a folk music icon gradually faded after Woodstock, although she continued to release highly acclaimed albums such as *Diamonds and Rust* (1975) and *Ring Them Bells* (1995). Over the course of her career, in fact, Baez has released over thirty albums containing her interpretations of songs by such diverse artists as the Beatles, Woody Guthrie, Paul Simon, Stevie Wonder, Josh Ritter, Natalie Merchant, and Steve Earle. Baez also continues to perform in concert—often in support of efforts to raise funds for social and political causes that are close to her heart. In 2007 she received a Grammy Lifetime Achievement Award for her rich body of musical work.

Since the 1960s, though, Baez has arguably become best known for her political activism. Over the years she has lent her voice to a wide range of caus-

117

es around the world, including women's rights, civil rights, antipoverty, gay rights, and antinuclear campaigns. In 2011 the human rights organization Amnesty International paid tribute to her decades of activism by establishing the Amnesty International Joan Baez Award for Outstanding Inspirational Service in the Global Fight for Human Rights. The award is intended to recognize musicians, filmmakers, painters, and other artists who devote their talents to the cause of human rights.

Sources:

Baez, Joan. *And a Voice to Sing With: A Memoir.* New York: Summit Books, 1987.

Baez, Joan. *Daybreak—An Intimate Journal.* New York: Dial Press, 1968.

"Biography," JoanBaez.com, n.d. Retrieved from http://www.joanbaez.com/officialbio08.html. http://www.joanbaez.com/officialbio08.html.

Hajdu, David. Positively *4th Street: The Lives and Times of Joan Baez, Bob Dylan, Mimi Baez Fariña, and Richard Fariña.* New York: Farrar, Straus and Giroux, 2001.

Notes

[1] Quoted in Fornatale, Pete. *Back to the Garden: The Story of Woodstock.* New York: Touchstone, 2009, pp. 91-92, 98.

[2] Baez, Joan. *And a Voice to Sing With: A Memoir.* New York: Summit Books, 1987, p. 165.

Bob Dylan (1941-)
Influential Rock and Folk Music Singer-Songwriter

Robert Allen Zimmerman, who later changed his name to Bob Dylan, was born on May 24, 1941, in Duluth, Minnesota. He was raised in Hibbing, Minnesota, a working-class town in northern Minnesota's so-called Iron Range, a region known for its iron mining industry. By the time he was in his teens, Dylan had learned to play the guitar, harmonica, and piano. He enjoyed the early rock-and-roll songs that came through his radio from Elvis Presley, Little Richard, and other stars of the 1950s, but his greatest enthusiasm was for the music of folk, blues, and country legends like Woody Guthrie and Hank Williams.

Dylan briefly attended the University of Minnesota, but he spent most of his time performing traditional folk songs at campus-area coffeehouses. In late 1960 Dylan dropped out of college and moved to New York City's Greenwich Village, which was the center of America's folk music movement at the time. He spent the next several months scrambling for gigs in the Village's various folk clubs, bars, and coffeehouses. Dylan gradually built a reputation as a new talent, and in 1961 he was signed to the Columbia Records label by legendary music producer John Hammond.

Taking the Folk Music World by Storm

Dylan's self-titled first album, which was released in 1962, consisted mostly of covers of traditional folk and blues classics. It did not get a lot of attention. In May 1963, however, Columbia released his second album, titled *The Freewheelin' Bob Dylan*. This work was stuffed with songs written by Dylan himself, and they set the folk music world ablaze. Offerings on the album ranged from protest songs that became instant classics ("Blowin' in the Wind") to wrenching songs of love and romantic regret ("Girl from the North Country").

In 1964 Dylan released two more classic albums, *The Times They Are A-Changin'* and *Another Side of Bob Dylan*. These works cemented Dylan's reputation as one of America's most gifted songwriters. The albums featured stunning songs about everything from racism and civil rights ("The Times They Are A-Changin'," "Only a Pawn in Their Game") to messy and doomed personal relationships ("It Ain't Me, Babe"). By the close of 1964, Dylan was being widely hailed as the spokesman of his generation and the country's most powerful voice of social and political protest.

At the same time, however, these albums hinted at Dylan's growing desire to break out of the boundaries imposed by traditional folk music—and at his mounting discomfort with his role as the "Prince of Protest." In 1965 he decisively and gleefully blew up his "protest singer" image, and in the process he changed the world of rock and roll forever. Over the course of that year he released two albums, *Bringing It All Back Home* and *Highway 61 Revisited*, that featured heavy doses of raw, electric rock and surrealistic, cryptic imagery. They also included such enduring rock classics as "Subterranean Homesick Blues" and "Like a Rolling Stone."

In between the release of these two albums, Dylan blasted the tradition-minded Newport Folk Festival in July with a set of blistering electric rock that shocked and outraged folk music purists. His performance prompted people like Irwin Silber, editor of the folk magazine *Sing Out!*, to call Dylan a traitor to the folk movement. Dylan was unapologetic. "What I did to break away was to take simple folk changes and put new imagery and attitude to them ... [to create] something different that had not been heard before," he wrote many years later. "Silber scolded me ... for doing this, as if he alone and a few others had the keys to the real world. I knew what I was doing, though, and wasn't going to take a step back or retreat for anybody."[1]

Rebellion and Resentment

In 1966 Dylan completed his transition from traditional folk music to electric rock and roll with *Blonde on Blonde,* a two-record set of amazing creativity that interspersed hit singles like "Rainy Day Women #12 & 35" and "I Want You" with blues stompers ("Stuck Inside of Mobile with the Memphis Blues Again") and haunting, surreal love songs ("Visions of Johanna"). By this time, the songwriter had also radically altered his public image. Gone was the earnest, friendly young fellow who had burst onto the folk scene a few years earlier. In his place was a scowling, shades-wearing rock star whose songs and public statements reflected cynicism and disillusionment about everything from modern society to personal relationships.

Ironically, this musical and personal transformation made Dylan an even more popular public figure. Many young people who opposed the Vietnam War and fought their parents' conservative views on sex, drugs, and rock and roll saw Dylan as a great (though sometimes inscrutable) truth teller, and they waited breathlessly for his next song or interview. When Dylan suffered a serious motorcycle accident in the summer of 1966, his extended absence from the recording studio and concert stage further heightened the air of mystery that surrounded him.

This hero worship made Dylan increasingly uneasy. During the mid-1960s Dylan had purposely cultivated the image of a young man who understood things that others did not. In the years following the release of *Blonde on Blonde*, however, Dylan rebelled against escalating demands that he continue serving as "the conscience of a generation,"[2] as he put it. His resentment steadily grew as he and his wife Sara Lowndes (whom he married in November 1965) started raising a family in Woodstock, New York. "Having children changed my life and segregated me from just about everybody and everything that was going on," Dylan wrote in a 2004 autobiography.

> Outside of my family, nothing held any real interest for me and I was seeing everything through different glasses. Even the horrifying news items of the day, the gunning down of the Kennedys, King, Malcolm X ... I didn't see them as leaders being shot down, but rather as fathers whose families had been left wounded.... Someone else would have to step up and volunteer. I really was never any more than what I was—a folk musician who gazed into the gray mist with tear-blinded eyes and made up songs that floated in a luminous haze. Now it had blown up in my face and was hanging over me. I wasn't a preacher performing miracles. It would have driven anybody mad.[3]

Dylan's last two albums of the 1960s, *John Wesley Harding* and *Nashville Skyline*, were introspective, acoustic-oriented works that avoided political statements. In 1969 concert promoter Michael Lang approached Dylan to see if he might consider making a surprise appearance at the upcoming Woodstock Music and Art Fair, which was being held in Bethel, New York, less than 100 miles from the songwriter's Woodstock home. Dylan did not flatly reject the offer, but he made no promises, either. In the end, he decided to stay home and remain out of the public spotlight that he had come to dislike so much.

Triumphs and Tribulations

Dylan gradually emerged from hiding in the 1970s. One of his albums from that decade, 1975's *Blood on the Tracks,* was greeted as a masterpiece on a par with *Blonde on Blonde* and *Highway 61 Revisited.* Others, such as *Street-Legal* (1978), were critical and commercial flops. Dylan also resumed touring in the 1970s, most notably with a 1975-1976 tour that he dubbed the Rolling Thunder Revue. In June 1977 Dylan and his wife underwent a painful divorce. Two years later he released *Slow Train Coming,* the first of three successive albums that displayed the artist's unexpected (and temporary) turn to fundamentalist Christianity.

Dylan remained a legendary figure in the rock-and-roll universe during the 1980s and 1990s. In 1988 he was inducted into the Rock and Roll Hall of Fame in only the hall's third year of existence. Singer Bruce Springsteen spoke at the ceremony about Dylan's explosive impact on popular music, remarking that "Bob freed the mind the way Elvis freed the body.... To this day, wherever great rock music is being made, there is the shadow of Bob Dylan."[4]

These decades, though, also left Dylan's fans frustrated and perplexed. Some of his work from this period, such as *Infidels* (1983), *Oh Mercy* (1989), and *Time Out of Mind* (1997) were seen as strong reminders of his gifts as a songwriter and performer, but other albums were criticized as sloppy or uninspired. The same criticisms were leveled at his concert performances from this period. Dylan himself later admitted that he had lost the energy and creativity that had made him a star. "It had become monotonous," he wrote. "My performances were an act, and the rituals were boring me.... In reality, I was just above a club act. Could hardly fill small theaters."[5]

Dylan's struggles were further underscored by the release during this period of two retrospective box sets that retraced his amazing career. *Biograph* (1985) and *The Bootleg Series, Vols. 1-3* (1991) lovingly chronicled the amazing tapestry of work that the songwriter had crafted since his emergence in the early 1960s. But they also reminded people of the dwindling relevance and popularity of his more recent work.

A Revitalized Career

In the late 1990s and the first decade of the new century, though, Dylan resurrected his fading career and reputation with a series of stellar albums. Dylan followed 1997's *Time Out of Mind* with *Love and Theft* (2001), *Modern*

Times (2006), and *Together Through Life* (2009). All three albums were bursting with well-crafted, thoughtful, and emotionally rich songs that effectively mixed country, folk, blues, gospel, and rock influences. They brought Dylan some of the most favorable reviews he had seen in years. Dylan rediscovered his enthusiasm for live performing around this same period, and he has maintained a busy touring schedule for years.

Dylan's career renaissance was also aided by the 2004 publication of *Chronicles: Volume One*, the first in a three-book series of memoirs that he agreed to write for the Simon and Schuster publishing company. *Chronicles* was widely hailed as a candid and eloquent account of Dylan's early career. Meanwhile, new installments in *The Bootleg Series* treated music fans to a cascade of previously unreleased Dylan music from the 1960s to the present.

Today, Bob Dylan's reputation as the poet laureate of rock and roll remains unchallenged. Recent honors and awards bestowed upon him have reflected his unique and enduring influence on American music and culture. In 2009 he was awarded the National Medal of Arts, the highest award given to artists by the U.S. government. Three years later Dylan received the Presidential Medal of Freedom, the country's most prestigious civilian honor. "There is not a bigger giant in the history of American music," said President Barack Obama during the award ceremony. "[Bob Dylan] helped redefine not just what music sounded like, but the message it carried and how it made people feel."[6]

Sources:

Dylan, Bob. *Chronicles: Volume One*. New York: Simon and Schuster, 2004.
Marcus, Greil. *Like a Rolling Stone: Bob Dylan at the Crossroads*. New York: Public Affairs, 2005.
Wilentz, Sean. *Bob Dylan in America*. New York: Doubleday, 2010.

Notes

[1] Dylan, Bob. *Chronicles: Volume One*. New York: Simon and Schuster, 2004, p. 67.
[2] Dylan, p. 118.
[3] Dylan, pp. 117-18.
[4] Quoted in "Bob Dylan Biography." American Rock and Roll Hall of Fame Web site, n.d. Retrieved from http://rockhall.com/inductees/bob-dylan/bio/.
[5] Dylan, pp. 152,155.
[6] "Bob Dylan Awarded Presidential Medal of Freedom." *Rolling Stone,* May 29, 2012. Retrieved from http://www.rollingstone.com/music/news/bob-dylan-awarded-presidential-medal-of-freedom-20120529.

Jimi Hendrix (1942-1970)
Rock-and-Roll Guitarist and Performer at Woodstock

James Marshall "Jimi" Hendrix (born Johnny Allen Hendrix) was born on November
27, 1942, in Seattle, Washington. He was
the oldest of five children born to James Allen
"Al" Hendrix and Lucille Jeter, whose marriage was wracked by fighting and alcohol
abuse. The family was impoverished as well,
and Jimi and his siblings spent much of their
young lives in a succession of cheap apart-
ments and hotels around Seattle. When the
turmoil at home became particularly bad, the
children were sometimes sent off to live with
Seattle-area relatives until things calmed down.
His parents finally divorced in 1951, and from that time on Hendrix rarely saw
his mother.

Hendrix's troubled home life did not give him a good foundation to suc-
ceed in school, and he left high school without graduating. He later claimed that
he was kicked out of school for holding hands with a white girlfriend, but admin-
istrators at the school said that he simply flunked out because of bad grades and
poor attendance. Hendrix spent the next few years working odd jobs, pursuing
a growing interest in guitar playing, and experiencing occasional brushes with
the law. In May 1961 he enlisted in the U.S. Army. After completing basic training he was stationed at Fort Campbell in Kentucky. By all accounts he was not
a model soldier, and his indifferent attitude rubbed his commanding officers the
wrong way. He was discharged from military service after one year.

Paying His Dues

Hendrix received his first guitar—a used one—when he was fifteen years
old, and from that point forward he displayed a single-minded determination
to make his mark on the world as a guitarist. Unable to read music or afford
an instructor, he taught himself to play through hours of experimentation and
repetition. His inspirations were early rock and blues legends like Elvis Presley, B. B. King, Muddy Waters, and Robert Johnson. In early 1959 his father gave

him his first electric guitar, and he began playing with local blues bands, usually for free.

After leaving the army, Hendrix moved to Tennessee. Living first in Clarksville and then in Nashville, he and an army buddy named Billy Cox, who played bass guitar, put together a band called the King Kasuals. They also supported themselves by playing backup for better-known African-American musicians who toured the South in the early 1960s. Despite being relegated to black-only concert halls, these artists—including Ike and Tina Turner, Little Richard, and Sam Cooke—were enormously talented, and they continued Hendrix's education in the ways of soul and blues.

In early 1965 Hendrix left the South for New York City, where he put together his own band, called Jimmy James and the Blue Flames, and further burnished his growing reputation as a wildly talented guitarist. In 1966 he agreed to take Chas Chandler as his manager. Chandler thought that Hendrix had the potential to be a big star, but he also thought that the guitarist would benefit from exposure to the evolving psychedelic and blues rock scene in England. Hendrix subsequently relocated to London, where his journey to stardom suddenly accelerated.

Once in London, Hendrix changed the spelling of his first name to Jimi and went about the process of forming a new band. Within a few weeks Hendrix, bassist Noel Redding, and drummer Mitch Mitchell were performing as the Jimi Hendrix Experience. Their live shows—and Hendrix's fiery guitar work in particular—became a sensation in England among fans and fellow rock musicians alike. They raved about his technique and creativity (such as his pioneering use of amplifier feedback as part of his sound) and marveled at the left-handed Hendrix's practice of playing right-handed guitars upside-down. By early 1967 famous British rock and rollers such as Pete Townshend, John Lennon, Paul McCartney, and Eric Clapton had all made a point to see Hendrix perform in concert.

A Star in the States

In the summer of 1967 the Jimi Hendrix Experience released its first album, called *Are You Experienced?* It featured four enduring hits in "Hey Joe," "Purple Haze," "Foxy Lady," and "The Wind Cries Mary." The album was enormously popular not only in England, but back in Hendrix's native United States. Hendrix returned to the United States to tour in support of the album, and his appearance at the June 1967 Monterey Pop Festival—in which he ended his performance by setting his guitar on fire—further enhanced his reputation as the newest "guitar god" in the rock-and-roll universe.

In 1968 Hendrix and his band mates released two more albums, *Axis: Bold as Love* (featuring the hit "Little Wing") and *Electric Ladyland.* The latter album, which Hendrix put together in his own new recording studio in New York City, was highlighted by a scorching cover version of Bob Dylan's "All Along the Watchtower." In 1969 the band dissolved, but Hendrix maintained his frantic schedule of touring and recording.

In the spring of 1969 Hendrix was approached about playing at the Woodstock Music and Art Fair, a massive three-day concert event to be held in upstate New York in mid-August. Hendrix agreed, and he showed up with a new band called Gypsy Sun and Rainbows that included his old army friend Billy Cox. Hendrix and his band were slated as the grand finale for Sunday, August 17, the last day of the festival. The festival schedule suffered so many delays due to bad weather and technical malfunctions, though, that Hendrix and his band did not take the stage until Monday morning, August 18.

By that time only a fraction of Woodstock's legendarily massive audience remained. The rock fans who stuck around, though, were treated to one of the best performances of the entire weekend. Hendrix's stunning, feedback-fueled rendition of the "Star-Spangled Banner," in particular, is frequently cited as a Woodstock highlight.

A Life Cut Short

After Woodstock Hendrix reduced his band to a trio called Band of Gypsys, with Cox on bass guitar and Buddy Miles on drums. The new band performed at the famous Fillmore East in New York City on New Year's Eve, 1969, and New Year's Day, 1970. Highlights from these shows were released in 1999 as *Hendrix: Live at the Fillmore East.* Hendrix continued to record and tour, but on September 18, 1970, his star was suddenly extinguished. After a night of heavy alcohol and drug use, Hendrix suffocated to death on his own vomit in a hotel in London.

Hendrix's legions of fans were saddened by the guitarist's tragic end, which was followed two weeks later by the overdose death of singer Janis Joplin. The loss of Hendrix and Joplin in quick succession was interpreted by many people as a grim warning for rock and rollers and countercultural figures who had glorified drug use during the 1960s.

Despite the circumstances surrounding Hendrix's death, he is remembered as one of the true legends of rock and roll. In 1992 he was posthumously inducted into the American Rock and Roll Hall of Fame. "Hendrix was arguably the greatest instrumentalist in the history of rock music," according to the Hall of Fame. "He expanded the range and vocabulary of the electric guitar into areas no musician had ever ventured before … and the impact of his brief but meteoric career on popular music continues to be felt."[1]

Sources:

Cross, Charles R. *Room Full of Mirrors: A Biography of Jimi Hendrix.* New York: Hyperion, 2005.

"The Jimi Hendrix Experience Biography." American Rock and Roll Hall of Fame Web site, n.d. Retrieved from http://www.rockhall.com/inductees/the-jimi-hendrix-experience/bio/.

Roby, Steven, and Brad Schreiber. *Becoming Jimi Hendrix: From Southern Crossroads to Psychedelic London, the Untold Story of a Musical Genius.* Cambridge, MA: Da Capo Press, 2010.

Notes

[1] "The Jimi Hendrix Experience Biography." American Rock and Roll Hall of Fame Web site, n.d. Retrieved from http://www.rockhall.com/inductees/the-jimi-hendrix-experience/bio/.

Artie Kornfeld (1942-)
Woodstock Promoter and Recording Industry Executive

Arthur "Artie" Lawrence Kornfeld was born in Brooklyn, one of the five boroughs of New York City, on September 9, 1942. His parents were Shirley and Irving Kornfeld, who worked as a policeman in the city. When Artie was thirteen years old, his family moved to Charlotte, North Carolina, which was embroiled in racial tensions over segregation and African-American civil rights.

As a Jewish family from the North, the Kornfelds experienced occasional hostility from southern white Protestants in their community as well. The family refused to shrink away or hide from the ugliness that sometimes flared up around them, though. Kornfeld's mother, in fact, became a leading activist in the state's civil rights movement. She was a founding member of the Congress of Racial Equality (CORE), one of the most important civil rights groups of the late 1950s and early 1960s, and she regularly spoke out in defense of racial justice and expressed pride in her own Jewish heritage. She and her husband also enrolled their son in the only integrated private high school in the entire state. After graduating from high school Kornfeld attended Adelphi College (now Adelphi University) in Long Island, New York, and American University in Washington, D.C.

Early Musical Career

Kornfeld spent much of his youth immersing himself in the world of early rock and roll. This passion was fed by a teenage job as an usher at the Charlotte Coliseum, where top musical acts played when they came to town. The job, he later recalled, "allowed me to see Fats Domino, Buddy Holly, Little Richard, Elvis Presley, and all my generation's rock 'n' roll idols. It was like being paid to visit rock 'n' roll heaven."[1]

Kornfeld obtained his first guitar in 1956. He practiced for hours and sought out every opportunity to play and sing. Over the next few years he managed to secure a couple of small record deals and made occasional concert appearances as a backup singer for well-known acts like Dion and the Belmonts. During the early and mid-1960s, however, Kornfeld became best known as a writer of songs for other artists. He penned big hits like "Dead Man's Curve" for Jan and Dean, and by 1966 he had written an estimated seventy-five songs that had appeared on the *Billboard* charts, which ranks the most popular songs in the country by a combination of sales and radio play.

Kornfeld's contacts with musicians, band managers, and promoters in the music industry became so extensive that Capitol Records approached him in 1964 with a job offer that was unique at the time. The company wanted him to become the first-ever vice president for its rock-and-roll division. Kornfeld accepted the offer, and over the next few years he became a highly visible figure at the promotional end of the music industry.

Making Woodstock Happen

In May 1968 Kornfeld was visited at Capitol by Michael Lang, a concert promoter, band manager, and head shop owner. Lang failed in his efforts to get Kornfeld interested in a band he was managing, but the two young men nonetheless struck up a friendship. As the months passed by, they began fantasizing about opening their own recording studio upstate in Woodstock, New York, which was a well-known enclave of musicians and other artists.

Kornfeld and Lang kicked around the idea of raising funds for the studio by arranging a rock concert. Both men later admitted, though, that the concert idea might never have progressed beyond idle chatter if they had not met John Roberts and Joel Rosenman. Roberts was heir to a family fortune and Rosenman had a background in law. Most importantly, both of the men—though "square" in comparison to the "hippies" Lang and Kornfeld—were willing to invest their time, money, and talents in a music festival. "We were from different worlds and backgrounds," Kornfeld later wrote, "but the four of us made a perfect partnership for what was to follow. In my estimation, without each of our unique talents coming together, Woodstock would never have happened."[2]

The four young men joined together to form Woodstock Ventures in early 1969. The partnership and festival got their "Woodstock" names from the town where Kornfeld and Lang had always dreamed of holding the concert. When Woodstock and their second choice, a small upstate New York town called Wallkill, rejected the concert, however, they ended up having the festival in Bethel, which was about forty-five miles west of Wallkill.

The months leading up to the festival, which was scheduled to run from August 15 to August 17, were chaotic for Kornfeld and the other partners. Each of the men had huge and time-consuming responsibilities, and Kornfeld was no exception. As the head promoter of the festival, Kornfeld had the responsibility for publicizing the event through traditional newspapers, radio stations, record shops, and the underground press. The time demands quickly became so great that he left Capitol Records.

The Woodstock Music and Art Fair was a famously muddy, overcrowded, and drug-fueled affair, but it also featured memorable music and a remarkably peaceful and laid-back atmosphere. Kornfeld was immensely proud of the event and his role in making it happen. Afterwards, however, the four-man partnership dissolved, in part because of tensions over the cost of the festival, which advance ticket sales had failed to cover. "[Rosenman and I] were the financial partners," explained Roberts. "We were the ones who were charged with cleaning [the concert site] up and paying all the bills.... Since Michael and Artie didn't really have that much of a financial stake in it ... we felt, you know, that they were less than helpful and responsible about the aftermath."[3] Kornfeld went on to collaborate with Lang for several more years, but their friendship frayed and they eventually parted ways.

Kornfeld continued to work as a concert and band promoter after Woodstock. His career was hampered during the 1970s by a worsening addiction to cocaine, but in 1982 he managed to kick the habit before it completely derailed his life. He frequently speaks publicly on Woodstock and its legacy, and in 2010 he became chairman of Relax Music Group, a New York-based music marketing, management, and promotion firm. In addition, Kornfeld in recent years has hosted an Internet music program titled "The Spirit Show" that highlights up-and-coming bands and musicians.

Sources:

Kornfeld, Artie. *The Pied Piper of Woodstock*. Delray Beach, FL: Spirit of the Woodstock Nation, 2009.
Makower, Joel. *Woodstock: The Oral History*. New York: Doubleday, 1989.
Official Web Site of Artie Kornfeld. Retrieved from http://www.artiekornfeld-woodstock.com/.

Notes

[1] Kornfeld, Artie. *The Pied Piper of Woodstock*. Delray Beach, FL: Spirit of the Woodstock Nation, 2009, p. 18.
[2] Kornfeld, p. 66.
[3] Quoted in Fornatale, Pete. *Back to the Garden: The Story of Woodstock*. New York: Touchstone, 2009, p. 105.

Michael Lang (1944-)
Concert Promoter and Co-founder of the
Woodstock Music and Art Fair

Michael Lang was born on December 11, 1944, in Brooklyn, New York. He was raised in a middle-class neighborhood by his parents, Harry and Sylvia Lang, who owned and operated a heating system installation business and had financial interests in several other Brooklyn-area businesses. As young Michael grew older, his parents would occasionally take him to listen to live music at local nightclubs in which they had part-ownership. These experiences gave Lang a taste of the glamour and energy of live music—as well as a realization that entrepreneurial business opportunities could take all kinds of shapes and forms.

Ups and Downs in Florida

Lang's high school years included experimentation with marijuana and the hallucinogenic drug LSD. Around this same time he became fascinated by the counterculture movement emerging in some American cities and college campuses. After securing a deferment from the military draft and thus avoiding a potential posting in Vietnam, Lang began taking classes at New York University (NYU) in 1962. In 1964 he transferred to the University of Tampa, only to return to NYU after a few months.

In 1966 Lang's boredom with college studies and his increasingly countercultural lifestyle led him to once again leave New York for Florida. This time he moved to Coconut Grove, a community at the southern end of Miami. Lang quickly opened a head shop where he sold a wide assortment of "hippie" goods, including posters, strobe lights, beads, bong pipes, and other smoking paraphernalia. Lang's shop became a popular gathering place for Miami's hippie crowd, and before long the ambitious Lang was also trying his hand as a rock concert promoter. He started with a few small events, but in 1968 he played a pivotal role in organizing the Miami Pop Festival, which featured national acts like Jimi Hendrix, the Mothers of Invention, and Steppenwolf. The two-day concert drew a big crowd of 100,000 people, but the high expense of putting on the show made it a financial failure for Lang.

After the festival, Lang became increasingly unhappy with his life in Coconut Grove. "Police continued to hassle hippies, rents and condos were going up, the old wooden houses were being torn down, and head shops were proliferating," he wrote in his autobiography, *The Road to Woodstock*. "Broke and a bit burned out on South Florida, I thought it was time to head back to New York."[1]

Turning the Woodstock Dream into Reality

Upon returning to New York State, Lang bought a small house in Woodstock, a small arts-oriented town located about ninety miles north of New York City. Although he had left his head shop behind in Florida, Lang was still working as a band manager and concert promoter. Shortly after settling in Woodstock, he went to the New York offices of Capitol Records to see if he could interest the company in signing a band he was managing. On his visit to Capitol he met Artie Kornfeld, a young record executive who had also grown up in Brooklyn. The two young men bonded over their mutual love of rock music, and before long they became good friends.

In the fall of 1968 Lang and Kornfeld began talking about arranging a rock concert in order to raise funds to build a recording studio in Woodstock. In early 1969 they met two young entrepreneurs, John Roberts and Joel Rosenman. Roberts and Rosenman were not enthused about the recording studio, but they agreed to provide funding and legal assistance for the concert. The four men subsequently created Woodstock Ventures, a partnership built for the purpose of organizing a big multi-day rock festival in upstate New York.

The next several months were chaotic for Lang and his partners. They had to move the concert site twice—the final time only a month before the August 15-17 concert was scheduled to open—publicize the festival to rock fans across the country, and put together a lineup of musical acts capable of stirring up excitement. Another top priority for Woodstock Ventures was hiring concert people with the expertise to make the show a success. Lang took the lead on this score, and by all accounts he put together a top-notch staff of production people and technical engineers.

By late July, Lang and his partners were in a state of perpetual motion at the concert site in Bethel, New York. "We were trying to finish a four-month job in a month," Lang recalled. "We were in the midst of dealing with endless building permits, which were actually the only permits we were required to have. Stage construction was the main priority. The scaffolding had been delivered and we were starting to build the kids' park, clear the woods and put roads in. I remember desperately trying to get the phone lines eight miles down the track to the site.... There were 300 of us on 24/7 duty.... At Woodstock, we were building a city from scratch."[2]

During these final frantic days of preparation, some members of the construction crew and Lang's business partners expressed frustration with Lang, who in many ways had become the public face of the upcoming festival. They criticized him for displaying a smug attitude and being careless with other people's money and time. Other staff members, though, said that Lang's optimistic disposition and confidence were essential in making Woodstock happen. "He had this cosmic aura to him," recalled one Woodstock staffer. "I don't mean to overdo this, but he always had this little smile on his face like he knew something that none of us knew. Which, as it turns out, was not necessarily true.... But he managed to glow a lot of things into existence that I don't think any other one of [the partners], given the personalities—none of them could have done that."[3]

A Free Concert for the Ages

When the Woodstock Festival finally arrived, it was a disaster in some respects. The crowd was so huge that it paralyzed roadways for miles around, overwhelmed the concert site's facilities, and made it impossible for Woodstock Ventures to collect or sell tickets for the event. Lang and his partners had no choice but to make Woodstock a free concert—a development that took a big financial toll on Roberts and Rosenman, who had paid for a good portion of the festival's costs out of their own pockets.

Despite the immense crowd (as many as 500,000, though no one knows for sure), downpours that drenched the festival, and several disappointing musical performances, however, the concert as a whole was widely hailed as a stunning success. The festival goers remained peaceful and enthusiastic through every setback, and performers such as Jimi Hendrix, Sly Stone, the Who, and Crosby, Stills, Nash, and Young delivered legendary sets.

Years later, Lang still marveled at how Woodstock succeeded against all odds. "For me," he wrote,

> Woodstock was a test of whether people of our generation really believed in one another and the world we were struggling to

133

create. How would we do when we were in charge? Could we live as the peaceful community we envisioned? I'd hoped we could…. Over that August weekend, during a very tumultuous time in our country, we showed the best of ourselves, and in the process created the kind of society we all aspired to, even if only for a brief moment. The time was right, the place was right, the spirit was right, and we were right. What resulted was a celebration and confirmation of our humanity.[4]

After Woodstock was over, hard feelings between Lang and Kornfeld on one side and Roberts and Rosenman on the other made it impossible to keep Woodstock Ventures together. Roberts and Rosenman ultimately bought out Lang and Kornfeld after long and acrimonious negotiations. After leaving Woodstock ventures, though, Lang remained an active presence in the American music industry.

In the four decades since Woodstock, Lang has managed nationally known recording artists, owned and operated his own record companies, and produced numerous music festivals. He even reconciled with Roberts and Rosenman to help produce the controversial Woodstock '94 and Woodstock '99 concert events and rejoined the Woodstock Ventures group. In 2009, in honor of the fortieth anniversary of the famous concert, Woodstock Ventures unveiled Woodstock.com, a Web site that celebrates the history and music of the original Woodstock event. That same year Lang published *The Road to Woodstock*, an autobiographical account of the festival that was warmly received by critics and music fans alike.

Sources:

Lang, Michael, with Holly George-Warren. *The Road to Woodstock: From the Man Behind the Legendary Festival*. New York: Ecco, 2009.

Makower, Joel. *Woodstock: The Oral History*. New York: Doubleday, 1989.

Notes

[1] Lang, Michael, with Holly George-Warren. *The Road to Woodstock: From the Man Behind the Legendary Festival*. New York: Ecco, 2009, p. 34.

[2] "Inside Woodstock: Michael Lang Q&A." *Mojo* [online], July 28, 2009. Retrieved from http://www.mojo4music.com/blog/2009/07/inside_woodstock_michael_lang.html.

[3] Makower, Joel. *Woodstock: The Oral History*. New York: Doubleday, 1989, p. 132-33.

[4] Lang, p. 4.

John Roberts (1945-2001)
Woodstock Promoter and Business Entrepreneur

John P. Roberts was born in 1945 into a wealthy East Coast family that had made its fortune as a manufacturer of dental and pharmaceutical products. His parents subsequently established a trust fund (a program of regular, scheduled financial benefits) for Roberts and arranged for him to receive inheritance money when he turned twenty-one years old.

Roberts enrolled at the University of Pennsylvania in 1961 and graduated with a business degree in 1966. A short time later, he established a strong friendship with Joel Rosenman, a recent graduate of Yale University's law school. Roberts and Rosenman became roommates and began kicking around the idea of going into business together. Over a period of months they decided to try their hand at producing a television sitcom (situation comedy) about two rich pals who become involved in various wacky business schemes. As part of their research for the proposed show, Roberts and Rosenman took out advertisements in the *Wall Street Journal* and *New York Times,* stating, "Young men with unlimited capital looking for interesting, legitimate investment opportunities and business propositions."

News of the advertisement eventually reached concert promoter Michael Lang and record executive Artie Kornfeld, who were seeking investors for a proposed music recording studio and music festival in Woodstock, a small town in upstate New York. The four men got together, and over a period of weeks Roberts and Rosenman discarded their television show idea. Instead, they agreed to form a genuine partnership called Woodstock Ventures with Lang and Kornfeld for the purpose of organizing a big weekend music festival in August 1969. The concert would bring together many of the world's top rock-and-roll acts, and all four men believed that it could be a big moneymaker.

Roberts used $500,000 of his inheritance money to provide the initial financing for the festival, which the partners decided to call the Woodstock Music and Art Fair. He received little support or encouragement from his family, however. Roberts later recalled that when his father learned about Woodstock, he bitterly responded, "I just knew it. I just knew the minute you got your hands on your inheritance, you would do something like this."[1]

Planning—and Paying—for Woodstock

Roberts was deeply involved in the planning for Woodstock during the spring and early summer of 1969. Advance ticket sales for the event brought some money into the venture, but Roberts remained the primary source of funding. He later estimated that he spent a total of $1.8 million on the festival, and that he did not fully pay off all debts associated with Woodstock until 1980. Roberts and Rosenman knew that they were not as "hip" as Lang, who was deeply familiar with the counterculture vibe of the late 1960s. In recognition of Roberts's role as the main money man for the show, though, Lang, Kornfeld, and the senior festival staff regularly consulted with him on all major financial decisions, from the selection of bands to the location of the festival itself.

As the festival weekend of August 15-17 drew nearer, preparations for the concert became famously frantic and chaotic. Roberts poured hundreds of thousands of dollars into a concert site in Wallkill, New York, only to have the town's leadership withdraw its offer to host the event a month before the show. Woodstock Ventures quickly found a new festival site on a farm outside of Bethel, New York, but the last few weeks before the festival turned into a mad scramble to obtain the necessary licenses, publicize the switch in locale, and prepare the grounds for as many as 100,000 music fans.

The Woodstock concert was scheduled to begin on Friday, August 15, but by Wednesday the fields surrounding the stage were already swollen with tens of thousands of people. Concertgoers continued to pour into the festival site over the next two days, and by Friday Roberts and the other promoters recognized that they had no way to take or sell tickets. The concert was going to be free, whether they liked it or not. Roberts took this turn of events in stride. "I … started to see that [failing to turn a profit] was somehow very unimportant," he recalled. "I don't know why, but a sort of curious calm overcame us and it seemed like the gates [earnings from purchased tickets] just weren't really what was important here anymore. It spelled instant doom, financially. And that didn't seem that terribly important at that particular moment, either.… I think all of us found ourselves in a situation that we had never been in before and would never be in again, with pressures and considerations that don't usually happen to you."[2]

After Woodstock

After the Woodstock festival drew to a close and entered the annals of legendary American cultural events, Roberts and Rosenman bought out Lang and Kornfeld to become the sole owners of Woodstock Ventures. They thus retained legal rights to the Woodstock name and the famous Woodstock symbol of a dove perched on the neck of a guitar. Roberts and Rosenman also received a financial windfall from royalties generated by an immensely popular Woodstock documentary film and record album.

Roberts's involvement in the music business waned after Woodstock, though he and Rosenman were important early investors in New York's Mediasound Recording Studios. This studio, which Roberts and Rosenman first invested in back in 1968, became well-known in the 1970s and 1980s as a favorite recording destination for many of the era's top musical acts. Roberts and Rosenman also reconciled with Lang in 1994 and 1999 to stage twenty-fifth-anniversary and thirtieth-anniversary Woodstock concerts.

Most of Roberts's career energies, however, went into JR Capital, an investment company he co-founded with Rosenman in the 1970s. He also became a nationally known bridge player. Roberts lived for many years in Manhattan, where he and his wife, Rona Roberts, raised two children. He died of cancer on October 27, 2001, at the age of fifty-six.

Sources:

Makower, Joel. *Woodstock: The Oral History.* New York: Doubleday, 1989.

Sisario, Ben. "John P. Roberts, 56, a Producer of Woodstock and Its Revivals." *New York Times,* November 2, 2001. Retrieved from http://www.nytimes.com/2001/11/02/arts/john-p-roberts-56-a-producer-of-woodstock-and-its-revivals.html.

Notes

[1] Quoted in Evans, Mike, and Paul Kingsbury, eds. *Woodstock: Three Days that Rocked the World.* New York: Sterling, 2009, p. 36.

[2] Quoted in Makower, Joel. *Woodstock: The Oral History.* New York: Doubleday, 1989, p. 181.

Hugh "Wavy Gravy" Romney (1936-)
Leader of the Hog Farm Commune and Social Activist

Hugh Nanton Romney, who eventually became known as the countercultural figure "Wavy Gravy," was born on May 15, 1936, in East Greenbush, New York. He grew up in East Princeton, New Jersey, where his father worked as an architect, and in 1954 he voluntarily enlisted in the U.S. Army. Romney received an honorable discharge after two years of service. He then used the GI Bill—a government financial assistance program for military veterans seeking a college education—to enter Boston University in 1957. Over the next several months Romney developed a keen interest in theater, poetry, and music, as well as a fascination with the emerging "beatnik" lifestyle. By 1959 he had moved to New York City to pursue his growing passion for art, literature, and the counterculture.

From New York to California

During the early 1960s Romney served as the poetry director at New York City's Gaslight Cafe, a hip coffeehouse that was one of the top venues of that era's exploding folk music scene. He also jumped on stage himself from time to time, and his humorous stream-of-consciousness storytelling style was a hit with audiences. Romney also became familiar with well-known cultural figures like comedian Lenny Bruce, poet Allen Ginsberg, jazz musician Thelonious Monk, and folksinger Tom Paxton during this time.

Another of Romney's friends in New York was a promising young songwriter named Bob Dylan. According to Romney, in fact, Dylan wrote the first draft of "A Hard Rain's A-Gonna Fall," one of his most famous songs, on a typewriter in Romney's apartment. Romney also ended up marrying one of Dylan's former girlfriends. After a brief marriage in the early 1960s that ended in divorce, Romney met Bonnie Beecher, who had previously dated Dylan. Romney married Beecher, who eventually changed her name to Jahanara Romney, in 1965.

In 1962 Romney moved to California, where he dove headlong into San Francisco's evolving hippie culture. He became friends with members of the

Grateful Dead and floated into and out of the orbit of novelist Ken Kesey's Merry Pranksters, a hippie commune that promoted the use of LSD and other psychedelic drugs as a way to reach higher levels of consciousness. Romney spent the next few years teaching acting classes (one of his students was Harrison Ford), selling marijuana, and caring for hogs on a farm in the hills outside of Sunland, California. Bonnie, meanwhile, found steady work as a television actress.

The Sunland Farm, where Romney and his wife lived rent-free in exchange for serving as caretakers, became the foundation for his famous Hog Farm commune. Growing numbers of personal friends, countercultural artists and musicians, and assorted West Coast hippies began paying extended visits to the farm in 1965. After a while, recalled Romney, "the people began to outnumber the pigs"[1] and the place became an actual hippie commune known to its residents as the Hog Farm.

In 1966 Romney and other members of the Hog Farm began making extended trips around California and the wider western United States. Traveling in brightly colored converted school buses, Romney and his gang produced several concert light shows for rock bands like the Grateful Dead, Jimi Hendrix, and Cream. In 1968 Romney and other Hog Farm residents acquired a small plot of land in rural New Mexico and began making plans to relocate their commune there. These hazy plans were interrupted, though, when the organizers of the 1969 Woodstock Music and Art Fair asked Romney if the Hog Farm would be willing to build fire pits and trails at the concert site and manage a free kitchen for the festival.

Breakfast in Bed for 400,000

Romney happily accepted the offer, and shortly thereafter he, his wife, and the rest of the Hog Farm members were being whisked to New York City by jet. When they arrived, just a few days before the scheduled August 15 opening of the three-day festival, Romney learned that the Hog Farm had also been appointed to provide most of the security for the event. Romney and his colleagues took on that task as well, but they put their own comical spin on it. They announced that they would be forming a "Please Force" rather than a police force at Woodstock, and that cream pies and seltzer water would be their main law enforcement tools.

Romney and the Hog Farm worked furiously to prepare for the coming crowds. Like everyone else at Woodstock, they were overwhelmed by the sheer size of the audience that came to the festival. Nonetheless, they kept their sense of humor and good cheer throughout the weekend. In fact, many of the festival's promoters and executive staff later credited Romney and his fellow commune members with helping to establish the peaceful and generous tone of the event. "Having the Hog Farm at Woodstock was a great move," said commune member Tom Law, who at one point led the audience in yoga exercises from the concert stage. "What would Woodstock have been like without the Hog Farm? I don't know, man."[2]

For Romney personally, his big festival moment came on Sunday morning. Before the day's music began, he strode confidently on stage and declared to the wet and tired—but enthusiastic—audience that "What we have in mind is breakfast in bed for 400,000!" Romney's remark was forever immortalized in the *Woodstock* documentary film. According to Romney, he and other Hog Farm members then waded into the crowd and "introduced hippies to granola. We had ... Dixie cups full of granola and [gave] it to hippies in their sleeping bags. And they looked at it and said, 'What is this [stuff], gravel?' But obviously, they liked it because granola is the staple of conscious people on the planet now."[3]

Wavy Gravy Is Born

Two weeks after Woodstock, on Labor Day weekend, Romney and the Hog Farm agreed to provide security services at the Texas International Pop Festival in Dallas. During the course of the weekend the famed blues guitarist B. B. King reportedly gave Romney the nickname "Wavy Gravy." Romney liked the name so much that he adopted it for everyday use, and he has been known as Wavy Gravy ever since.

During the 1970s Wavy Gravy became increasingly involved in political activism and efforts to help children and families in need. In 1974 he and his wife established Camp Winnarainbow, a summer performing arts camp for underprivileged children, in Mendocino, California. Four years later, he helped found the Seva Foundation, a nonprofit organization that works to improve health and living standards in poor communities all around the world. He also became known for his appearances at hospitals, where he would dress up as a clown to cheer up sick children and other patients.

In the early 1980s Romney and about fifty Hog Farm commune members purchased a big tract of land in Laytonville, California. The land, which is located in the northern part of the state and is known as Black Oak Ranch, became the primary home of the commune (and the new locale for Camp Winnarainbow) in the early 1990s. In 1992 the Ben and Jerry's ice cream company

140

unveiled a new ice cream flavor that it dubbed "Wavy Gravy" in honor of Romney. For the next ten years or so, royalties from the sale of the ice cream—which blended caramel, cashew, and Brazil-nut ice cream with almonds and a chocolate-hazelnut swirl—were used to help underprivileged and homeless kids from the San Francisco Bay area and a South Dakota Indian reservation attend Camp Winnarainbow. The ice cream flavor was discontinued in 2003.

In recent years, Wavy Gravy has divided his time between the Black Oak Ranch and a communal house in Berkeley, California. During the summer months he remains heavily involved in the operation of Camp Winnarainbow, but the rest of the year he is devoted primarily to Seva Foundation projects to reduce blindness in India, Nepal, Cambodia, and other Asian countries. In 2010 Romney was the subject of a critically acclaimed documentary film called *Saint Misbehavin': The Wavy Gravy Story*. The movie, which was written and directed by Michelle Esrick, focuses on Romney's life as a countercultural icon, political activist, and humanitarian.

Sources:

"A Clown for Our Time." *Wavygravy.net,* n.d. Retrieved from http://www.wavygravy.net/bio/biography.html.

Gravy, Wavy. *Something Good for a Change: Random Notes on Peace Thru Living.* New York: St. Martin's Press, 1992.

Issitt, Micah L. *Hippies: A Guide to an American Subculture.* Westport, CT: Greenwood, 2009, pp. 104-106.

Notes

[1] Gravy, Wavy. *Something Good for a Change: Random Notes on Peace Thru Living.* New York: St. Martin's Press, 1992, p. 229.

[2] Quoted in Fornatale, Pete. *Back to the Garden: The Story of Woodstock.* New York: Touchstone, 2009, p. 197.

[3] Quoted in Fornatale, p. 197.

Joel Rosenman (1942-)
Woodstock Promoter and Business Entrepreneur

Joel Rosenman was born in 1942 and grew up on Long Island, New York, in the town of Cold Spring Harbor. The son of a prominent orthodontist, Rosenman graduated from high school at age sixteen. He earned a bachelor's degree in English from Princeton University in 1963 and a law degree from Yale University in 1966. In addition to his studies, Rosenman enjoyed singing and playing guitar. He was a member of a highly regarded a cappella singing group at Princeton, and he played with a number of East Coast bands during the mid-1960s.

In the fall of 1966 Rosenman met John Roberts, a young man whose family owned a large business that sold pharmaceutical products and dental equipment and products. They became good friends, and by the winter of 1967 they were rooming together and trying to figure out what career paths they wanted to chart for themselves. Around this time they decided to develop a television sitcom (situation comedy) about "two pals with more money than brains and a thirst for adventure," in Rosenman's words. "Every week they would get into a different business venture in some nutty scheme. And every week they would be rescued in the nick of time from their fate."[1]

Rosenman and Roberts subsequently placed a classified advertisement in the *Wall Street Journal* and the *New York Times* in hopes of stirring up some script ideas. They described themselves as "young men with unlimited capital" actively seeking business opportunities. The two young men received numerous responses, most of which they disregarded. One respondent, though, convinced them to actually invest in a new recording studio in Manhattan, New York. Mediasound Recording Studios opened in 1969, and over the next decade it became a popular studio for musical acts ranging from Frank Sinatra to several top disco bands of the 1970s.

Helping Bring Woodstock to Life

News of the advertisement also reached Michael Lang and Artie Kornfeld, two other ambitious young men who were seeking a way to make their mark on the world. Lang and Kornfeld had been idly discussing the idea of holding a rock-and-roll music festival to raise funds for a new recording studio to be built in Woodstock, New York. When they heard about the ads, they approached Rosenman and Roberts in the hope that they might be interested in forming a business partnership.

The four men met several times in early 1969, and before long they agreed to form a partnership called Woodstock Ventures with the goal of building a studio and organizing a music festival. Roberts provided the seed money for the enterprise, while Rosenman lent his knowledge of contracts and other legal matters to the effort. In fairly short order, though, the studio idea fell by the wayside and the concert became the main area of focus. According to Rosenman, he and Roberts were responsible for this shift. "Ultimately, we had the money," he said, "so what we said went."[2]

The next several months of Rosenman's life were consumed by the challenge of organizing a major three-day rock concert in upstate New York. Rosenman joined with his partners, top festival staff members, and an ever-expanding crew of technicians, carpenters, and other laborers to make the Woodstock dream of "three days of peace and music" a reality. The obstacles were enormous throughout the process. They ranged from a change in concert location a mere month before the show to a monster crowd that obliterated all previous music festival attendance records. As many as 500,000 concertgoers showed up at the festival, which ran from Friday, August 15, through Monday morning, August 18. The audience overwhelmed the concert facilities and created shortages of shelter, toilets, food, and drinking water.

Yet peace reigned over the festival, people enjoyed the live music, and the event became a legendary cultural milestone of the 1960s. "[The festival] seemed like the dawn of a new age," Rosenman later said. "Kids who had previously been convinced by the establishment that they were aberrations stood up, looked around, and saw half a million of themselves as far as the eye could see, and suddenly realized that they were not weirdos, that they were the new generation."[3]

A Lifetime Association with Woodstock

After Woodstock concluded, the four Woodstock Ventures partners were left to sort out the financial and legal problems left behind. By this time relations were strained between the Lang-Kornfeld camp and the Roberts-Rosenman duo. Kornfeld and Lang ultimately left Woodstock Ventures in exchange for a financial payment. (Rosenman and Roberts later reconciled with Lang, though, to team up for the production of twenty-fifth and thirtieth anniversary concert celebrations of the original Woodstock show.)

After the departure of Lang and Kornfeld, Rosenman and Roberts controlled the famous Woodstock name and logo, which became very profitable over the years thanks to licensing deals for Woodstock-related merchandise ranging from albums and videos to t-shirts and key chains. Roberts died in 2001, but his family retained part-ownership in Woodstock Ventures.

Rosenman has emphasized that he does not approve every Woodstock merchandising offer that comes down the line. He places a high value on products that are environmentally friendly, and he relies on gut instinct in assessing whether a proposed deal is consistent with Woodstock's values. "That may sound a little fuzzy, but in fact there's no more definitive way of telling whether it's the right product for us or not," he said. "We trust ourselves on that because we've been doing it for so long."[4] All Woodstock merchandise is available on Woodstock.com, a Web site owned and maintained by Woodstock Ventures.

In addition to his Woodstock-related business activity, Rosenman has worked for many years as an investor and investment advisor with JR Capital, which he co-founded in the 1970s with Roberts. In 2007, news reports indicated that Rosenman and his business associates lost as much as $40 million to Norman Hsu, a businessman who has since been convicted of numerous counts of fraud. Hsu is in federal prison in Michigan and is not scheduled to be released until 2030.

Sources:

Lang, Michael, with Holly George-Warren. *The Road to Woodstock: From the Man Behind the Legendary Festival.* New York: Ecco, 2009.

Rosenman, Joel, John Roberts, and Robert Pilpel. *Young Men with Unlimited Capital: The Story of Woodstock.* Houston, TX: Scrivenery Press, 1989.

Notes

[1] *Times Herald-Record.* "How Woodstock Happened...." Woodstock Commemorative Edition, 1994. Retrieved from http://www.edjusticeonline.com/woodstock/history/index.htm.

[2] *Times Herald-Record,* "How Woodstock Happened...."

[3] Quoted in Rubin, Mike. "Summer of 69." *Spin,* September 1994, p. 64.

[4] Waddell, Ray. "Peace and Prosperity: How a Three-Day Concert Became a Four-Decade Business." *Billboard,* August 8, 2009, pp. 23-24.

Michael Wadleigh (1942-)
Documentary Filmmaker Who Directed
Woodstock

Michael Wadleigh was born September 24, 1942, in Akron, Ohio. He credits his parents, both of whom were educators, with instilling in him a deep curiosity about the world around him. Wadleigh also developed an interest in film at an early age, and after a brief flirtation with Columbia University's medical school, he decided to make a career out of moviemaking.

During the mid-1960s Wadleigh and his business partner, producer Bob Maurice, made several cutting-edge documentaries on black civil rights and the Vietnam War, as well as exciting concert films featuring African-American artists Aretha Franklin and James Brown. He also worked as a cinematographer on a handful of low-budget independent films.

Going to Woodstock

In the late spring of 1969, Wadleigh was approached by Artie Kornfeld and Michael Lang, two young, ambitious music industry people who were planning a major rock concert event in upstate New York. The concert, which they called the Woodstock Music and Art Fair, was scheduled for August 15-17. The two entrepreneurs wanted someone to make a documentary film of Woodstock's musical performances. When they reviewed Wadleigh's exciting and innovative concert footage of Aretha Franklin, they decided that the twenty-six-year-old filmmaker was an ideal choice.

Financial negotiations between Lang and Kornfeld's Woodstock Ventures group and Wadleigh were sometimes tense. Neither camp was able to convince a major Hollywood studio to join the deal, which would have offset some or all of the film production costs. Wadleigh forged ahead with plans to film the festival, though, and the Warner Brothers film studio ultimately agreed to invest in the project.

When Wadleigh and Maurice arrived at Bethel a few days before the festival's opening, they came with a crew of more than two dozen people, including assistant editor Martin Scorsese (who would later direct such Hollywood film classics as *Taxi Driver, Raging Bull, Goodfellas,* and *The Departed*), film editor Thelma Schoonmaker, associate producer Dale Bell, sound engineer Dan Wallin, and sound designer Larry Johnson. The crew's equipment included fifteen cameras (only two of which were working by the end of the festival) and more than a thousand reels of film.

Capturing the Look and Feel of Woodstock

Over the course of that long August weekend in Bethel, which featured a record-setting audience of perhaps 500,000 people, stormy and unpredictable weather, terrible sanitary conditions, and musical sets from many of the world's top rock-and-roll acts, Wadleigh was determined to get footage of every single act. "We of course had limited footage and so what we would do was first get a list of the songs that the performers were going to perform and from our own knowledge of their music, we decided on certain songs that we wanted to cover," he recalled.

> The problem with that strategy was that the … musicians would just throw away the set list and start performing everything. What we had to do was start [recording] every song and then after about 30 seconds, because I didn't want to waste the footage, I would make a decision about whether to cut it off or keep going. That was really the only sensible strategy.… After all, remember that for most of the performances, we were shooting with four or five cameras, which was necessary because we wanted to do the multiple images.[1]

Wadleigh and the rest of his crew were not satisfied to document only the music of Woodstock, however. They also wandered the festival grounds all weekend, interviewing concertgoers and filming how they ate, slept, partied, and interacted with one another through periods of blazing heat, torrential rain, and middle-of-the-night electric guitar solos.

After Woodstock was over, Wadleigh and his crew retreated to Los Angeles, where they spent the next several months editing hundreds of hours of footage down into a three-and-a-half hour film that Warner Brothers could release nationwide. "We relived it in the editing room," remembered Larry Johnson. "We spent a whole year making the movie, and it was so exciting. Because we really did, every time we would see something, we would just go nuts. We'd say, 'Come here! Look at this,' and people would run over ... and we would all stand around and say, 'Play that again!'"[2] It was during this editing process that the filmmakers also introduced a wide range of visual effects, including split screens and overlapping images, to give the documentary an added jolt of visual and narrative interest.

Woodstock: 3 Days of Peace and Music was released on March 26, 1970. To the great surprise of nervous Warner Brothers executives, the film was a spectacular success with audiences and critics alike. Many historians also believe that the sounds and imagery in Wadleigh's movie became locked in America's collective memory as the definitive record of "the Woodstock experience." Twenty-six years after its release, *Woodstock* was selected for preservation in the United States National Film Registry by the Library of Congress in recognition of its enduring cultural, historical, and aesthetic significance. In 1994 an expanded "director's cut" edition of the documentary was released, and in 2009 a 40th-anniversary version was unveiled. The 2009 release included remastered footage of the entire director's cut of the film, as well as two hours of footage of previously unseen performances from the festival.

A Nomadic Life

Woodstock was a big moneymaker for Warner Brothers. Wadleigh, on the other hand, received only a small percentage of the profits. But the director expressed satisfaction when the film received the Academy Award for Best Documentary Feature of 1970 (the movie also received two Oscar nominations for best film editing and best sound).

During the 1970s Wadleigh wrote a number of film screenplays for Hollywood. He was paid handsomely for several of them, but most of these works never ended up being made into films. Wadleigh's lone directorial credit after *Woodstock* was a 1981 horror movie called *Wolfen*, which film critics have praised as an underrated gem in that genre. In 1985 Wadleigh decided to leave filmmaking altogether. "I was always a serious guy and got into filmmaking with a political agenda," he later explained. "I blamed myself because I had an agenda and I didn't have the personal ability to get the films that I wanted made. Therefore, unlike other directors like Scorsese, I was never in love with filmmaking. I was in love with certain messages and if I couldn't make them ... I was wasting my time."[3]

After leaving the world of filmmaking, Wadleigh traveled widely through Africa, Asia, and Latin America. During these years he became particularly interested in research and education projects on "sustainable development," which seeks ways for humankind to extract and consume natural resources at a slower pace so that the environment is not ruined for future generations. Many of Wadleigh's efforts in this area have been undertaken with his longtime partner Birgit Von Munster and have been supported with funding from organizations such as UNESCO (United Nations Educational, Scientific and Cultural Organization).

Sources:

Bell, Dale, ed. *Woodstock: An Inside Look at the Movie That Shook Up the World and Defined a Generation.* Studio City, CA: Michael Wiese, 1999.

Elwakil, Mai. "The Homo Sapiens Report: Michael Wadleigh on the Future of Egypt." *Egypt Independent,* March 15, 2011. Retrieved from http://www.egyptindependent.com/news/homo-sapiens-report-michael-wadleigh-future-egypt.

Makower, Joel. *Woodstock: The Oral History.* New York: Doubleday, 1989.

Sobcynski, Peter. "Interview: Michael Wadleigh on *Woodstock.*" *efilmcritic.com,* June 10, 2009. Retrieved from http://www.efilmcritic.com/feature.php?feature=2774.

Notes

[1] Sobcynski, Peter. "Interview: Michael Wadleigh on *Woodstock.*" *efilmcritic.com,* June 10, 2009. Retrieved from http://www.efilmcritic.com/feature.php?feature=2774.

[2] Quoted in Fornatale, Pete. *Back to the Garden: The Story of Woodstock.* New York: Touchstone, 2009, p. 277.

[3] Sobcynski.

Max Yasgur (1919-1973)
*Owner of Yasgur Farms and Host of the
Woodstock Festival*

Max B. Yasgur was born on December 15, 1919, in New York City. His parents, Samuel and Bella Yasgur, were Russian Jewish immigrants who built a successful dairy farm operation in upstate New York. After graduating from high school Max went on to New York University, where he studied real estate law. He then returned home, where he gradually assumed responsibility for running his family's farming operations. By the late 1960s Yasgur had developed the farm, which was located in the small community of Bethel, into the largest milk producer in the county.

In 1969 Yasgur and his wife Miriam were leading a comfortable, quiet life. Their two children had reached adulthood, and the Yasgur Farms dairy enterprise remained solid and prosperous. On the afternoon of July 16, however, their quiet country existence was turned upside down when a rock concert promoter named Michael Lang came calling.

Hosting Woodstock

Lang came to Bethel in desperate need of a new site for Woodstock, a massive three-day rock music festival that he and his three business partners—John Roberts, Joel Rosenman, and Artie Kornfeld—had been planning for months. Only one day earlier, the organizers had lost their long-planned site for the concert in Wallkill, New York, a town about forty-five miles east of Bethel. Wallkill's city fathers rejected the show out of concerns that it would result in a hippie invasion of their community, and this decision sparked a panicked search for an alternative site. Fortunately for Lang and the others, Yasgur Farms was an ideal location—provided they could convince the farmer to host the event. As one of Woodstock's production staff later recalled, "Max's land was manicured. He was a farmer who cared about his land. His fences were painted. Everything was in good repair.... The land had been tilled and turned and all obstructions removed. The land was just gorgeous. Max had a lovely, lovely farm."[1]

149

Lang had stumbled upon Yasgur's property by chance, but he was determined to make the most of it. He introduced himself to Max and Miriam Yasgur and pitched Woodstock as a great business opportunity for the couple. Max Yasgur knew all about the troubles in Wallkill, and he recognized that he could charge a king's ransom for leasing some of his farmland. But Yasgur believed that the promoters had received a raw deal in Wallkill. As a result, he negotiated a property rental deal that he believed would be profitable for him and his wife—without ruining Lang and his partners.

Once the lease agreement was signed and workers began pouring onto his property, Yasgur behaved with admirable fairness and patience. "I'll say this about Max," recalled Rosenman. "He never hit us up for another dime after we paid him. I remember that every time we went over there [to his home], Max would hand you one of those little cartons of chocolate milk. Every time. We ended up with all these cartons of milk around the office."[2]

Standing Up for Young People

Yasgur's decision to lease his property for the Woodstock Music and Art Fair was not well-received by some of his neighbors. They angrily denounced him in town board meetings and in downtown stores, but these complaints further strengthened the farmer's resolve to host the concert. "He believed that [the youth coming to Woodstock] had a right to express themselves," recalled his son, Sam Yasgur. "He certainly didn't have anything in common with them. He was a forty-nine-year-old hardworking man. Lived all his life on a farm, which meant very long days.... He had no comprehension at the time this thing started about their culture, certainly not about their music, but those things didn't make any difference to him."[3]

Yasgur became particularly upset after neighboring farmers posted big signs on area roadways urging people not to buy milk from Yasgur Farms. From that point forward, Yasgur was determined to make sure that the concert happened, despite his growing anxiety about the size and scale of the festival. "When those signs went up, the signs themselves made him the kids' ally, a very forceful and dynamic ally," wrote his son. "The plain fact was that Max Yasgur hated haters."[4]

During the course of the festival itself, Max and Miriam Yasgur openly worried about the well-being of the hundreds of thousands of concertgoers who descended on their property. As the days passed and the festival's atmosphere remained peaceful, however, they began to relax. Max Yasgur even made an appearance on stage before the third day's music began. His simple, heartfelt address of appreciation and respect for the crowd further heightened his reputation as an unlikely but enduring counterculture hero.

After Woodstock, life on Yasgur Farms mostly returned to normal. Tensions remained high with some neighbors who never forgave the Yasgurs for hosting the event. Many others, though, expressed appreciation for his decision, which brought huge amounts of money into their community. According to Miriam Yasgur, her husband even became a mentor and counselor to several troubled youth in the area.

In 1971 the Yasgurs sold their farm and retired to Florida. Max Yasgur died of a heart attack in Marathon, Florida, on February 9, 1973. *Rolling Stone* magazine honored his passing with a full-page obituary—a rarity for any musical artist, let alone a non-musician.

Sources:

Lang, Michael, with Holly George-Warren. *The Road to Woodstock: From the Man Behind the Legendary Festival.* New York: Ecco, 2009.

Makower, Joel. *Woodstock: The Oral History.* New York: Doubleday, 1989.

"Max Yasgur, Woodstock Patron." *Rolling Stone,* March 14, 1973.

Yasgur, Sam. *Max B. Yasgur: The Woodstock Festival's Famous Farmer.* Maxyasgurfarms.com [self-published], 2009.

Notes

[1] Quoted in Makower, Joel. *Woodstock: The Oral History.* New York: Doubleday, 1989, p. 116.

[2] *Times Herald-Record.* "How Woodstock Happened...." Woodstock Commemorative Edition, 1994. Retrieved from http://www.edjusticeonline.com/woodstock/history/index.htm.

[3] Quoted in Evans, Mike, and Paul Kingsbury, eds. *Woodstock: Three Days That Rocked the World.* New York: Sterling, 2009, p. 46.

[4] Yasgur, Sam. *Max B. Yasgur: The Woodstock Festival's Famous Farmer.* Maxyasgurfarms.com [self-published], 2009.

PRIMARY SOURCES

Historian Arthur Schlesinger Jr. Predicts the "Mood" of the 1960s

American historian and social critic Arthur Schlesinger Jr. was a prominent observer of national politics and culture in the second half of the twentieth century. He also served as a close advisor to President John F. Kennedy in the early 1960s. Before, during, and after this time in the White House, Schlesinger championed an optimistic and vigorous brand of liberalism to address the nation's problems and challenges.

One of Schlesinger's most prophetic works was an essay titled "The New Mood in Politics," which was first published in 1960 and is excerpted here. In this piece, Schlesinger argued that the United States and its people were on the verge of making major changes in the way they looked at and interacted with the world around them. He thought that Americans were growing weary of the materialism and caution of the 1950s, and he believed that they were ready to seek out a new sense of individual and national purpose. Schlesinger predicted, in fact, that in the 1960s and beyond, new attitudes and social reforms would wash over American society like water unleashed from a broken dam.

At periodic moments in our history, our country has paused on the threshold of a new epoch in our national life, unable for a moment to open the door, but aware that it must advance if it is to preserve its national vitality and identity. One feels that we are approaching such a moment now—that the mood which has dominated the nation for a decade is beginning to seem thin and irrelevant; that it no longer interprets our desires and needs as a people; that new forces, new energies, new values are straining for expression and for release. The Eisenhower epoch—the present period of passivity and acquiescence in our national life—is drawing to a natural end.

As yet, the feeling is inchoate [partially completed] and elusive. But it is beginning to manifest itself in a multitude of ways: in freshening attitudes in politics; in a new acerbity in criticism; in stirrings, often tinged with desperation, among the youth; in a spreading contempt everywhere for reigning clichés. There is evident a widening restlessness, dangerous tendencies toward satire and idealism, a mounting dissatisfaction with the official priorities, a deepening concern with our character and objectives as a nation.

Let me list some expressions of the discontent, the desire for reappraisal, the groping for something better:

Credit: SCHLESINGER, JR., ARTHUR M. *THE POLITICS OF HOPE AND THE BITTER HERITAGE.* © 2008 by Princeton University Press. Reprinted by permission of Princeton University Press.

The rise of the Beat Generation is plainly in part the result of the failure of our present society to provide ideals capable of inspiring the youth of the nation.

The revival in the last two or three years of satire (not altogether to be dismissed by the appellation "sick humor") is another expression, as in the '20's, of contempt for the way things currently are going.

The religious boom (Billy Graham, etc.) suggests the wide-spread yearning for spiritual purpose of some sort in life.

The top book on the fiction best-seller list for many months was Pasternak's *Doctor Zhivago*—again a symptom of the felt need for some kind of spiritual affirmation.

A book like J. K. Galbraith's *The Affluent Society* sells fifty thousand copies in hard cover; David Riesman's *The Lonely Crowd* and W. H. Whyte's *The Organization Man* sell hundreds of thousands in paper-back—all this means that our intellectuals are beginning to draw the new portrait of America out of which new political initiatives will in due course come, and that people are responding to their portrayal.

Somehow the wind is beginning to change. People—not everyone by a long way, but enough to disturb the prevailing mood—seem to seek a renewal of conviction, a new sense of national purpose. More and more of us, I think, are looking for a feeling of dedication, for a faith that what we are doing is deeply worthwhile—the kind of inspiration and lift we had for a while in the '30's and again during the Second World War.

The threats of communism and nuclear catastrophe ought perhaps to be enough to give us this sense of purpose, but they don't seem to. Certainly the goal of adding to our material comforts and our leisure time has not filled our lives. Are we not beginning to yearn for something beyond ourselves? We are uncertain but expectant, dismayed but hopeful, troubled but sanguine. It is an odd and baffled moment in our history—a moment of doubt and suspense and anticipation. It is as if increasing numbers of Americans were waiting for a trumpet to sound.

At bottom, perhaps, we are seeking a new articulation of our national values in the belief that this will bring about a new effectiveness in our national action. For national purpose is not something that is enshrined in monuments or preserved in historic documents. It acquires meaning as part of an ongoing process; its certification lies not in rhetoric but in performance. The values of the '50's have been, to a great degree, self-indulgent values. People have been largely absorbed in themselves—in their own careers, their own lives, their own interests. We tend to cover up our self-absorption by saying that what is good for our own interests is good for the country; but this is a gesture of piety. In fact, we start from our own concerns and work outward, rather than start from the national needs and work inward.…

Our situation would be troubling enough if there were no world civil war. But the existence of the world civil war trebles every bet. We are coming to realize that we need a new conviction of national purpose not only as a matter of taste but as a matter of desperate necessity. And so the time is drawing near for a revision of our national priorities, a revaluation of our national values, a renewal of our national purpose. This process of reorientation will be the mainspring of the politics of the '60's. As we commit ourselves to this vast challenge, we will cross the threshold into what promises to be one of the exciting and creative epochs in our history.

Now there is little to be gained in denouncing the values of the '50's as meager and mean. It is important rather to understand why we have dallied with such values—why our nation, in a time of danger, should have lowered its sights, renounced older concepts of high national purpose, and elevated private consumer satisfaction into a controlling national ethic. There is, I believe, no insoluble mystery here. Nor can we properly shift the blame for our condition from ourselves to our leaders. Certainly our leadership has failed in this decade to develop our potentialities of national power and to meet the onward rush of national needs. But it has just as certainly succeeded in expressing the moods and wishes of the electorate.

What accounted for the torpor of the '50's? The answer, I think, is plain enough. The basic cause was the state of national exhaustion produced by the two preceding decades of continuous crisis. During the '30's, '40's and into the '50's the American people went through the worst depression of their history, the worst war of their history, the worst cold war of their history, the most frustrating limited war of their history. During these decades, two aggressive Presidents kept demanding from us a lively interest in public policy and kept confronting us with tough problems of national decision. But no nation can live in tension indefinitely. By the early '50's, the American people had had it. We were weary and drained. We were tired of subordinating the reality of our daily lives to remote and abstract national objectives. We wanted a vacation from public responsibilities. We wanted to take up the private strands of existence, to bury ourselves in family, home, career.

The politics of the '50's were, in consequence, the politics of fatigue. Twenty years of intense public activity, first at home, then abroad, had left the nation in a state of moral and emotional exhaustion. Lull was the natural and predictable result. President Eisenhower was the perfect man for the new mood. Where his predecessors had roused the people, he soothed them; where they had defined issues sharply, he blurred them over; where they had called for effort and action, he counseled patience and hoped things would work themselves out. Perhaps his particular contribution to the art of politics was to make politics boring at a time when the people wanted any excuse to forget public affairs. The nation needed an interval of repose in order to restore its physiological balance, and repose was what President Eisenhower gave them.

In so doing, he was playing his part in the larger rhythm of our politics. For the national life has always alternated between epochs of advance and epochs of consolidation, between times of action and times of passivity. We began the 20th century with two decades of active and insistent leadership under the dominating Presidents—Theodore Roosevelt and Woodrow Wilson. These Presidents raised the national sights. They stood for a crusading fervor in politics, directed first to reform at home and then to carrying the gospel of democracy to the world. After two decades of this, the people could stand it no longer: 1920 was like 1952. They wanted "normalcy," and that is what they got from Warren G. Harding and his successors.

And so the '20's were the decade of "normalcy." The politics of purpose gave way to the politics of lassitude. The nation swung from affirmative government to negative government. But, after a time, negative government began to seem insufficient. As the national energies began to be replenished, people started to tire of the official mood of aimlessness and complacency. Moreover, new problems, nurtured by the years of indifference, began to emerge—problems which required direction and vigor in their solution. The Wall Street crash and its aftermath provided dramatic evidence that drift was not enough as a national policy. The time had come for the reconquest of purpose.

And so the cyclical rhythm has continued. In the '30's and '40's we had decades of purpose until we were tired again; in the '50's, quiescence and respite until problems heaped up and batteries began to be recharged. If this rhythm continues according to schedule, the '60's and '70's should be decades of affirmation until we fall back into drift in the '80's. The pattern of American politics has been an alternation between periods of furious performance which accomplish a lot of things but finally wear the people out to periods of stag-

158

nation which go on until new issues accumulate, flagging national energies revive, and forward motion can be resumed. There is no reason to suppose now that this pendular motion has suddenly come to a full stop.

The question remains whether the nation could afford that holiday from responsibility in the '50's which its every nerve demanded—whether it was wise to choose this point to rest on its oars. No doubt the condition of national weariness made it hard to exercise vigorous leadership in any case; but this scarcely excuses our leaders from not having tried harder. When America "took five," so to speak, in the 1880's or the 1920's, it didn't much matter. But the 1950's were fatal years for us to relax on the sidelines. The grim and unending contest with communism was the central international fact of the decade, and the Communists took no time out to flop in the hammock. We did, and we have paid a cruel price for it....

This is the challenge of the '60's: the reorganization of American values. If we are going to hold our own against communism in the world, if we are going to build a satisfying life at home for ourselves and our children, the production of consumer goods will have to be made subordinate to some larger national purpose. As more and more people perceive the nature of our dilemma, they will demand the revival of public leadership, until in time the gathering discontent will find a national voice, like Theodore Roosevelt in 1901 and Franklin Roosevelt in 1933, and there will be a breakthrough into a new political epoch.

The hallmark of the '50's has been the belief that what is good for one's own private interest is good for all. Charles E. Wilson gave this idea its classic formulation when he suggested that what was good for General Motors was good for the country. And many critics of Wilson have seemed to object less to the principle of Wilson's law than to his choice of beneficiary. Too many tend to assume that what is good for what we care about is good for the country; if we don't like business, then we suppose, if government would only cater to labor or to the farmers, everything would be all right.

But people can't fool themselves indefinitely into supposing that the national interest is only the extension of whatever serves their own power and pocketbook. I believe that millions already feel that the road to national salvation no longer lies in pushing their own claims to the uttermost. Farmers dislike the excesses of the farm program. Workers begin to wonder whether higher wages are the answer to everything. Businessmen know that everything else in society cannot be sacrificed to their own profits.

If the hallmark of the '50's has been the belief in the sanctity of private interests, the hallmark of the '60's, I suggest, may well be the revival of a sense of the supremacy of the public interest—long with the realization that private interests and the public interest often come into harsh conflict. Theodore Roosevelt once said, "Every man holds his property subject to the general right of the community to regulate its use to whatever degree the public welfare may require." If unlimited private indulgence means that there are not enough resources left for national defense or for education or medical care or decent housing or intelligent community planning, then in a sane society private indulgence can no longer be unlimited.

The new attitude toward the public interest will bring in its wake a host of changes. There will be a change, for example, in the attitude toward government. One of the singular developments of the last decade was the rise of the notion that government was somehow the enemy. This was not George Washington's attitude toward government, nor Alexander Hamilton's, nor Andrew Jackson's, nor Abraham Lincoln's. The great American statesmen have all seen government as one means by which a free people achieves its purposes. But in the '50's we tended to suppose that a man engaged in making money for himself was in nobler work than a man serving the community (and that the more money he made, the greater his wisdom and virtue). That attitude will diminish in the '60's. Young men will go into public service with devotion and hope as they did in the days of T. R., Wilson and F. D. R. Government will gain strength and vitality from these fresh people and new ideas.

Of course, affirmative government per se can no more be a sufficient end for a good society than consumer goods per se. The object of strengthening government is to give force to the idea of public interest and to make possible the allocation of resources to necessary public purposes. There is no other way to meet the competition of communism. There is no other way to bring about a higher quality of life and opportunity for ordinary men and women.

This point—the quality of life—suggests the great difference between the politics of the '60's and the politics of the '30's. The New Deal arose in response to economic breakdown. It had to meet immediate problems of subsistence and survival. Its emphasis was essentially quantitative—an emphasis inevitable in an age of scarcity. But the '60's will confront an economy of abundance. There still are pools of poverty which have to be mopped up; but the central problem will be increasingly that of fighting for individual dignity, identity, and fulfillment in an affluent mass society. The issues of the new period will not be those involved with refueling the economic machine, putting floors under wages, and farm prices, establishing systems of social security. The new issues will be rather those of education, health, equal opportunity, community planning—the issues which make the difference between defeat and opportunity, between frustration and fulfillment, in the everyday lives of average persons. These issues will determine the quality of civilization to which our nation aspires in an age of ever-increasing wealth and leisure. A guiding aim, I believe, will be the insistence that every American boy and girl have access to the career proportionate to his or her talents and characters, regardless of birth, fortune, creed, or color.

The beginning of a new political epoch is like the breaking of a dam. Problems which have collected in the years of indifference, values which have suffered neglect, energies which have been denied full employment—all suddenly tumble as in a hopeless, swirling flood onto an arid plain. The chaos of the breakthrough offends those who like everything neatly ordered and controlled; but it is likely to be a creative confusion, bringing a ferment of ideas and innovations into the national life. Thus the '60's will probably be spirited, articulate, inventive, incoherent, turbulent, with energy shooting off wildly in all directions. Above all, there will be a sense of motion, of leadership, and of hope.

When this happens, America will be herself again. She will deal affirmatively and imaginatively with her problems at home. More than that, she will justify once again her claim to leadership of free peoples—a claim which cannot be founded on wealth and power alone, but only on wealth and power held within a framework of purpose and ideals.

Very little in history is inevitable. The cyclical rhythm we have identified in our national affairs offers no guarantee of national salvation. It will work only as men and women rise to a towering challenge. But nothing is stronger than the aspiration of a free people. If the energy now bottled up in American society can win its release in the decade ahead, we will reverse the downward curve of American power and charge the promise of American life with new meaning. From the vantage point of the '60's, the '50's, instead of marking a stage in the decline and fall of the American republic, will seem simply a listless interlude, quickly forgotten, in which the American people collected itself for greater exertions and higher splendors in the future.

Source

Schlesinger, Jr., Arthur. "The New Mood in Politics." First published in *Esquire,* January 1960. Reprinted in Schlesinger, Jr., Arthur. *The Politics of Hope and the Bitter Heritage.* Princeton, NJ: Princeton University Press, 2008, pp. 105-120.

Michael Lang Recalls the Frantic Search for a New Concert Site

During the spring and early summer of 1969, the principal organizers of the Woodstock Music and Art Fair—Michael Lang, Artie Kornfeld, Joel Rosenman, and John Roberts—prepared to hold the music festival in Wallkill, New York. As time passed, however, opposition to the festival steadily increased among Wallkill residents. In mid-July the township's zoning board decided to withhold the permits necessary for the festival, effectively killing the event. This development stunned the owners of Woodstock Ventures, but within twenty-four hours Lang found another concert site. In the following excerpt from Lang's 2009 memoir The Road to Woodstock, *he recalls the series of events that led him to Max Yasgur, the Sullivan County farmer who ultimately agreed to lease his land for the festival.*

D-day arrived on Tuesday, July 15: With none of us present, the ZBA [Wallkill's Zoning Board of Appeals] released a four-page decision, REJECTING our application for a permit. The ruling stated: "Generally, the plans submitted are indefinite, vague, and uncertain. Furthermore, the estimated number of persons attending has been too indefinite and uncertain, and based upon the amount and type of advertising, the venture would be contrary to the intent of the Zoning Ordinance. Problems of fire, police protection, and health would be contrary to the health and safety of the public."

Disbelief, shock, anger, frustration. From our field office, where he was packing boxes, Stan [Goldstein] told a journalist: "There's a field out there, and come August fifteen, sixteen, and seventeen, there are going to be people out there listening to some boss sounds. If you ask me how we're going to do it, I don't know. But we're going to do it."

I too knew we were going to do it, but *not* in Wallkill, and I was strangely relieved. Wallkill had not felt right to me from the beginning and things had only gotten worse. I spoke to John [Roberts] and could sense he and Joel [Rosenman] were crushed. They also knew that we would not recover in Wallkill. I tried to reassure them we'd find a new site, but they had grown weary of my saying, "It's *covered!*" and felt that this was the final blow.

Calling Artie [Kornfeld] next, I had a similar conversation except that—as always—he was energized by my optimism and I was energized by his belief in me. I had a talk with the rest of the team and told them, "Don't worry, I've got this covered. This is going to happen. Just get ready to move."

We could appeal the ZBA decision, but we knew that would take longer than the month until the festival date. John immediately issued a press release stating that we had been unjustly kicked off the site and that we were going to sue those responsible:

> The statements … that have been made by the Wallkill town zoning board of appeals and other individuals are entirely false. Accordingly, we have instructed legal counsel in New York City and in Wallkill to institute damage proceedings and to provide relief from this offensive harassment and the totally dishonest statements of certain individuals. Never in the history of an outdoor event of this kind have such massive and thorough preparations been made for the security and well-being of everyone in attendance. There will be a Woodstock festival—make no mistake about it!

… We had to find a new location for the festival—and fast. I knew morale would go down the tubes if I didn't refocus everyone into action immediately. I put anyone who was not packing up the site or office [at Wallkill] onto the phones to talk to press, local radio stations, realtors, and others who might help us find a new home.…

All the ensuing radio coverage resulted in several phone calls coming in from people suggesting locations. Some were crackpots, but we checked out everything. The day after the verdict, on July 15, Ticia [Bernuth Agri] got a call in our Village office from a guy [Elliot Tiber] who said he had a place in Sullivan County that would be perfect for the festival.…

As soon as I heard from Ticia, I called Mel [Lawrence] and Stanley [Goldstein] and told them to meet me at the address Ticia had been given for the El Monaco Motel in White Lake. My one perk from Woodstock Ventures—a '69 Porsche 912 I'd rented for the duration of the project—could make it to the location in about ninety minutes. Ticia and I zipped up the New York State Thruway to Route 17, followed it to Route 17B and County Road 52. Our Catskills destination—the Sullivan County township of Bethel—brought back memories of family vacations there when I was a kid.

Following Elliot's directions, we pulled up to one of the sorriest-looking motels I've ever seen. The sagging sign said EL MONACO, so we knew we were at the right place. A chubby guy in his early thirties bounded out to greet us, introducing himself as Elliot Tiber. I discovered that his real name is actually Eliyahu Teichberg and he grew up in Bensonhurst, right around the corner from me. He told us the motel belonged to his parents and that only a couple of its eighty rooms were occupied.

At one point, a seemingly crazed Jewish lady with a thick Russian accent rushed outside, and she and Elliot started screaming at each other. She turned out to be his mother. Despite her bossing him around, Elliot remained cheery and upbeat. It was obvious that this kind of thing went on all the time between them. Elliot seemed overjoyed to see us and determined to somehow involve himself in our festival. He started talking about a theater he'd built in a barn on the property. "I put on a theater festival every summer," Elliot told us, "and I already have a permit for this year's production—so you've got your permit!" An off-off-off-Broadway troupe, the Earthlight Theatre, was there for two months, crashing in a dilapidated rooming house on the property. We decided to wait for Mel and Stan, who were driving the thirty-five miles from Wallkill to meet us, before seeing the site.

Finally they arrived and it's, "Okay, Elliot, let's go see what you've got!"

"Follow me! It's a natural bowl and perfect for the festival!" Elliot promised with a big grin.

On the way around the back of the motel, we passed all kinds of handmade signs on different run-down buildings named for various celebrities like Jerry Lewis and Elvis Presley. Scattered bungalows were caving in, and there was an empty swimming pool filled with debris. As we walked toward a sloping meadow, the ground felt soggy and springy under my boots. This did not bode well.

We started descending a gradual incline—straight down into a large swamp filled with nubby growth and amputated saplings. As we trudged through, I asked, dreading the answer, "So how much farther to the site?"

"You're in it!" Elliot answered, with a grand sweep of his arm. "Of course, we can bulldoze and drain all of this."

"This is the place we've been waiting to see?" Mel exploded at Elliot. "What an idiot! What do you think you're doing? You really think we could use this?"

I agreed, as diplomatically as I could. "This isn't going to work at all." When we got back to the motel office, I asked Elliot, "Maybe there's someone who could show us around?"

"I'll call a friend of mine," Elliot offered, perking up after having looked pretty crestfallen. "He's in real estate." Stan departed, but Mel decided to go with Ticia and me. About a half hour later, a sleazy-looking guy named Morris Abraham arrived in a big Buick. He was happy to take us to check out some properties.

A few miles from Elliot's, we drove along 17B through magnificent farmlands—it's absolutely beautiful farm country with open fields everywhere. We took a right turn off 17B onto Hurd Road. About a quarter mile up, we broached the top of the hill and there it was.

"STOP THE CAR!" I shouted, barely able to believe my eyes. It was the field of my dreams—what I had hoped for from the first. It was not lost on me that we had left *Wallkill* to arrive in *Bethel*—"the House of God." I left the car and walked into this perfect green bowl. There at its base was a rise just waiting for our stage. The others joined me. Mel, Ticia, and I exchanged looks of wonder. "Who does all this land belong to?" I asked Abraham.

"Max Yasgur," he replied. "He's the biggest dairy farmer in the county. He owns ten farms and two thousand acres. I can call him and see if he's interested in renting to you."

"Yes, let's do that," I said. I had to work hard at remaining calm. I didn't want to appear too excited to this guy. We passed a sign that said HAPPY AVENUE, and drove until we got to a pay phone and Abraham reached Max. We drove on to his home—a simple white farmhouse—and met Miriam and Max Yasgur, a handsome couple in their late forties.

"These people are interested in renting some of your land, Max, to put on a music festival," Abraham explained.

Max had a sharply intelligent face and looked me in the eye. "You're the people who lost your site in Wallkill, aren't you?" I was preparing for the worst when he added, "I think that you young folks were done a grave injustice over there. Yes, I'll show you my land—we might be able to strike a deal for your music fair."

Max got in the car with us and Morris told him we'd seen the field off Hurd Road and would like to start there. As we drove, Max pointed out some of the land he owned. My heart was beating so fast I hoped no one would hear it. We arrived back at the field and I told Ticia and Mel to wait in the car and keep Morris occupied while Max and I took a walk into what had become *home* in my mind.

"Max, can we talk about this field?" I asked. "This is the perfect place for us. It's the right size and shape and has great sight lines and great vibes." Something about the way Max carried himself told me to be completely candid with him. "It feels like we're meant to be here." I wanted to seal the deal right there in the field. We walked over the rise above the bowl.

"How much land would you say you'd need?" he asked.

"Well, in addition to this field and whatever you have surrounding it, we need another six hundred acres, including land for camping and parking," I told him.

"I still have a crop of alfalfa growing here and crops in several other fields as well," Max said. "How soon do you think you'd need them?"

"Would *now* be too soon?" I asked, with a smile.

Max laughed and pulled a pencil from the protector in his shirt pocket. He wet the tip of the pencil with his tongue and started to scribble numbers on a pad. A sharp guy, he figured how much he was going to lose on his crop and how much it would cost him to reseed the field. When he came up with a number for the bowl, it seemed a fair price and I said yes immediately. We agreed that he would calculate the other fields in much the same manner, taking into consideration whether or not he could harvest crops before we needed to prepare the ground. It was going to be a hefty sum, but I knew that this land was our Woodstock—and Max was our savior. As we shook hands, I realized for the first time that he had only three fingers on his right hand. But his grip was like iron. I was thinking, He's cleared this land himself.

Source

Lang, Michael, with Holly George-Warren. *The Road to Woodstock: From the Man behind the Legendary Music Festival.* New York: HarperCollins, 2009, pp. 113-119.

Breakfast in Bed for 400,000

One of the most remarkable aspects of the Woodstock Music and Art Fair operations was that the membership of a hippie commune known as the Hog Farm assumed responsibility for much of the festival's food, medical assistance, and security needs. Lisa Law was one of the most prominent Hog Farm members, and she was deeply involved in the preparations for Woodstock. In the following essay, Law fondly recalls her experiences at the weekend festival.

Since the Hog Farm, of which I was a member, was a large communal group, the Woodstock festival organizers thought we would know how to take care of masses of people, especially if they were taking drugs. We were well versed in those departments, so agreed to become caretakers and food preparers for what was expected to be about 50,000 people a day.

Our party of about eighty-five, with fifteen Indians from the Santa Fe Indian School, turned up on the assigned day at the Albuquerque International Airport to take the American Airlines jumbo jet the organizers had sent down from New York to fly us to the festival. My husband, Tom Law, and I decided to take our tipi to stay in while there, and the baggage handlers looked like Keystone Kops loading the poles into the baggage compartment. It had to have been a first.

Many reporters met us at New York's Kennedy Airport. They wanted to know if we were handling security at Woodstock. One reporter asked Wavy Gravy, our "minister of talk," what he was going to use for crowd control. He answered, "Seltzer bottles and cream pies."

From the airport, we were whisked off to White Lake in big, comfortable buses and made camp with members of our crew who had arrived earlier, having driven from New Mexico in buses loaded with supplies. Ken Kesey's bus, along with four others, came from Oregon loaded with forty Pranksters, minus Kesey himself, with his best friend Ken Babbs at the helm.

We had nine days to put together the free stage, medical tents, free food kitchen, serving booths, and information centers, and to set up the trip tents for those who, having partaken of mind-expanding drugs, needed to escape the noise, lights, people, and rain.

The advance crew had built a wooden dome, covered it with plastic, and had set up a kitchen inside. Max Yasgur, our host, provided us with milk, yogurt, and eggs every day. Bonnie Jean Romney, Wavy Gravy's wife, was in charge of the kitchen and had gathered together odds and ends of aluminum pots and pans.

We got a flash that the concert could be much, much larger than what was projected. I traveled to New York City and spent $6,000 on food and supplies, including 1,200 pounds of bulgur wheat and rolled oats, two dozen 25-pound boxes of currants, almonds, and dried apricots, 200 pounds of wheat germ, five wooden kegs of soy sauce, and five big kegs of honey, 130,000 paper plates and spoons and forks, about 50,000 paper Dixie cups, pots, pans, five huge stainless steel bowls, and thirty-five plastic garbage pails to mix large portions of muesli. I also bought 250 enameled cups for our crew and our volunteers. (There was no recycling in those days and we were into conservation.)

As Friday approached, things were looking good. The stage was almost built, but there were too many fences to be built and the turnstiles never got up. More and more people would just walk right up to a fence, lay it down and walk over it. Then they would plop themselves down on tarps, making a cushion of their sleeping bags, take off their tops to enjoy the sun, and wait for the music. There must have been 50,000 of these squatters on the main field Friday morning. The promoters told Tom and Wavy Gravy it was time to clear the fields and to start taking tickets. Wavy said, "Do you want a good movie or a bad movie?" The producers had a palaver [conference] and decided to make the festival free.

People just kept coming, a tidal wave of people. When the amphitheater ran out of space, communities popped up everywhere else. The free stage across the forest and down by the Hog Farm camp had its own music and audience. Some of those groups, and some of the crew, never even saw the main stage. The festival chiefs had hired off-duty police to help with traffic and crowd control. They wore T-shirts that read Please Force. It was supposed to establish peaceful security. It worked.

It rained Friday night and on and off all throughout the festival. What were once beautiful grassy fields became mud bogs and slides. It would start to pour, and people would stand up and just let the water rush over them. Then they would sit down again, not wanting to leave their place lest they lose it. Everyone was sharing their food with their neighbors. All the food concessions started giving their food away and the National Guard dropped supplies from planes. I would go to a neighboring farm with a truck and buy whole rows of vegetables. On Saturday morning, after Tom taught yoga off the main stage, Wavy got up and said, "What we have in mind is breakfast in bed for 400,000."

Realizing that a lot of people on the main field were not eating, late on Saturday we filled twenty-five of the plastic trash cans with muesli mix and served it out of Dixie cups at the side of the stage along with cups of fresh water to wash it down.

I had a Super 8 camera and about forty reels of film and was shooting everything that was happening with that and my trusty Nikon. Once a day I would hail a helicopter, say I was with the Hog Farm, and get a lift into the sky. Yeow, what a view! We had created our own city, a half a million loving, sharing freaks. I could see the traffic for miles. People were still coming. Traffic was backed up all the way to the interstate. The lake behind the stage was filled with naked bathers. Helicopters were everywhere, dropping off and picking up performers who had no other way to get into the festival.

Sleep was the furthest thing from my mind. I think I got one hour a day. I was seven months pregnant with our son, Solar. Tom and I were pretty busy multitasking, so Pilar, our two-year-old daughter, spent most of the time with the rest of the Hog Farm kids. On Sunday I got my first shower when the Hog Farmers rigged up a hose at the top of a ladder to be aimed down on the naked bodies below.

I know the music at Woodstock was phenomenal. They said Crosby, Stills, Nash & Young played their second gig there and that Santana wooed the crowd with master drummer Michael Shrieve backing him up. Jimi Hendrix played the National Anthem and made that guitar sing like no one else had ever done. But for me, Woodstock was the people, the masses getting along with each other, sharing, caring, doctoring, feeding. Woodstock marked the dawning of the Age of Aquarius and revealed the soul of the sixties generation awakening. The vibe that made Woodstock a household word lives on in many parts of the world. It's the force that drives us to save the planet, to bring aid to other countries, and to make things right for native cultures. The spirit of that soul, that Woodstock vibe, will endure. After all, we are all members of the same family on Turtle Island.

Source

Law, Lisa. "Breakfast in Bed for 400,000." In Reynolds, Susan, ed. *Woodstock Revisited*. Avon, MA: Adams Media, 2009, pp. 7-10.

Rocking Out with Santana at Woodstock

One of the musical highlights of the Woodstock music festival was the Saturday afternoon set unleashed by Santana, a largely unknown California band helmed by guitarist Carlos Santana. The youngest member of Santana's band was drummer Michael Shrieve, who had turned nineteen only a month earlier. After Woodstock, Carlos Santana and his band became one of the best-known rock groups in America, and Shrieve emerged as one of the rock world's premier drummers. He continued to tour and record with Santana in subsequent decades, but he has also worked on many other recordings and musical projects over the years. In 1998 Carlos Santana and his namesake band, including Shrieve, were inducted into the Rock and Roll Hall of Fame.

In this interview with Dale Bell from 1999, Shrieve talks about his lasting memories of the Woodstock festival, the sequence of events that brought him into Santana's band, and the tremendous, enduring impact of the concert—and the Woodstock *movie—on him and his fellow band members.*

DALE: You were the youngest performer on that stage at Woodstock. What did you see when you went out there for the first time, and what did it feel like?

MIKE: I had turned 19 a month prior in July, so I was young. But everything felt in place for me. I remember thinking when walking up towards the stage and then on the stage at Woodstock that it was like standing on the beach and looking at the ocean. And there were people as far as you could see until the horizon. It was nothing like anything I'd seen before. It was a fantastic feeling actually.

DALE: How did you get to the site?

MIKE: We soon found out that the way we were gonna have to get to the site was by helicopter. And so it was all very exciting. We did fly in on a helicopter and it was an incredible sight to see. The interstate was closed and there were cars parked out as far as you could see. Also, I think it's important to recognize—I'm sure a lot of people have explained the mindset at this time. People wanted to change the world, and the music and the culture was the vehicle that people wanted to change things with. So to see the interstate closed and then to fly over the site and see all the people was absolutely incredible. And you realize that this hippie thing had gotten to this point. You felt like it was really peaking and that something was seriously going on now. It was all exhilarating. It wasn't something that you felt afraid of. You felt a part of something larger than yourself.

DALE: Mike, what led you to be a drummer? What was the path that you took as a young person to end up in Carlos Santana's band?

MIKE: I was living in the [San Francisco] Bay Area. I was a young drummer, very much into jazz and R&B and not so much into rock and roll as a drummer.

My father listened to a lot of jazz when I was growing up. And the house was filled with music. I just started picking music up that I liked. And I started playing drums in the 8th grade and then got really serious through high school and practiced a lot and got into stuff.

Obviously, the Beatles were happening and this was the beginning of the San Francisco scene. Jefferson Airplane, the Grateful Dead and these kinds of groups were playing around and I was very young, but they would come and play down the peninsula, the Palo Alto area.

Jefferson Airplane played once in Palo Alto and I remember going and thinking—looking at Jack Casady and Jorma [Kaukonen]—how does one get like that? What do you do to become that? There's such a great distance from where I am and where they are. Not particularly that I wanted to be them. But the way they dressed and the way that they appeared to be was such a great distance from where I was. I was curious.

I started going to the Fillmore up in San Francisco and seeing such great music. I mean Cream and Yardbirds. And Yardbirds with Jeff Beck and Eric Clapton and Miles Davis and B. B. King and Ray Charles and Charles Lloyd. A lot of good stuff going on. And Michael Bloomfield was the guitar god at the time. And there was a concert going on there called Super Session. With Michael Bloomfield and Stephen Stills and Al Kooper. And for some reason I started calling my friends. I was still living with my folks, and I said, "Let's go see if we can sit in," which was absolutely absurd. I don't know why, but I thought about it. That it was even possible. But everybody said no. Everybody said that's crazy. And I decided that I would go by myself, just so that I could say that at least I tried.

So I borrowed my father's car and I went up and made my way up to the front of the stage and pulled on Michael Bloomfield's pant legs and said, "Could I sit in?" And I figured that he'd kick me in the face and say, "Get out of here, kid."

DALE: Right. Kicking sand on the skinny kid at the beach?

MIKE: Absolutely. He was the deal. And the shocking thing was he said, "Well, what do you play?" I said, "Drums." He said, "Well, the drummer's a really nice guy, let me go ask him." And at that point, panic set in and I thought, oh my God, I was doing this to say that I tried. And next thing I know he said, "Yeah. It's okay." And I actually sat in at the Fillmore, which was the Mecca. This was the place that every musician wanted to play. So here I was sitting in with these guys—Bloomfield and Stills and Al Kooper—who were great to me.

Stan Markum, the manager of Santana, and David Brown, the bass player, came up to me and said, "We heard you play and you sound really nice and we're thinking about getting another drummer. We have a band called Santana." I was very familiar with the band, and I really wanted to play with these guys. They were already playing the Fillmore. Well, I didn't hear from them. I saw them once play at a high school in our area and I went back stage and said hello. Met the other guys.

A year passed and I was hustling recording-studio time at a local studio in San Mateo, California, for my own band. As I was walking in the door, the drummer in Santana was literally walking out. They had just had a big fight, a big falling out.

But a couple other guys remembered me and recognized me from that night. They said, "You wanna jam?" So it was a year later. We're jamming in the studio until dawn. They took me in a room and said, "Would you like to be in the band?" And it was just like that.

They literally followed me home to my parents' house in my car. I woke my folks up. I said, "See ya later. This is where I get off." I packed some things and I got in the car with all of them and drove up to the Mission District in San Francisco where I slept on the couch.

And I'll say one thing, although it was a time of peace and love and hippies everywhere, I soon found out that this band was not so much about peace and love. It was more like a street gang. And its weapon was music.

I was very young and very white and here I was living with a black militant, a Mexican, a Nicaraguan, a Puerto Rican, one other guy from down the peninsula, Greg Rawley. So things started happening fast from there.

DALE: Go back to when you went on the stage at Woodstock.

MIKE: It was Saturday. On that day it was Canned Heat and Creedence and the Dead, Janis Joplin, Jefferson Airplane, the Who. John Sebastian played as well. I'm not sure of what the scheduling was supposed to be. We were there hanging around back stage and something happened. They said, "You're going on now, instead of two or three hours later down in the afternoon."

We were very aware that there was cameras. There were a lot of photographers and there was—it's not the sort of thing that you go and check your hair for. We must've been nervous, but as a group we played to each other. We didn't see ourselves so much as performers, but as musicians. And I think that's part of the strength of us being in a situation like that.

We were an unknown band. Bill Graham got us on the bill. If it wasn't for Bill, we'd never been on there. I believe we got paid five hundred dollars to do the gig. Just sort of token money to get on the bill. So yes, we were aware that there were cameras and it was being filmed. Of course, nobody realized the outcome of that.

DALE: When was the first time that you saw yourself in the film?

MIKE: I recall that we were in New York. We had a day off and *Woodstock* was showing. So as a group, we went to see the movie. We had heard nothing about it, except that we were in it. We were waiting in line like everybody else and the prior showing was coming out. People were pointing at us and looking at us. We weren't famous yet or anything. We were a working band with a record out and working really hard.

We went in to see the movie and there we were sitting together. It was unbelievable. It was an unbelievable experience for me personally. Seeing myself split on screen into six times or whatever it was. I didn't know whether to shrink down in my chair or stand up and say that's me, that's me! They picked the best piece, "Soul Sacrifice." We had a tough time that day, because it was hard staying in tune. There were a lot of problems with the sound and I believe that might have been the only good piece of music we played that day.

Seeing myself split up on screen during the drum solo was really something. To see yourself in a big movie theater playing a drum solo. Even today, I cringe when I got so soft and when I left space in it. And then I'm thinking, "Come on! There's over half a million people, keep the beat going!" I was more kind of into this jazz thing and all that. But after the performance, even at the movie theater, the theater burst into applause. It was the most unbelievable experience for us to see that. It goes without saying that clip changed our lives.

DALE: Do you recall what Carlos [Santana]'s reaction was?

MIKE: I don't recall specifically, but I know that Carlos was having a difficult time staying in tune that day. It shows on the film a lot of things about Carlos. It shows his intensity and his passion and his urgency. He was doing his best to stay in tune. As he says now, he was saying, "Lord, please just keep me in tune."

I think everybody in the band was completely amazed at seeing themselves on the big screen, for one. And that the performance came off as something really very special. It captured the band—I mean it was great at the concert. Wow. We were a perfect group for that day. We were a perfect group for that festival. We were tribal. Rock and roll is one thing. There was a lot of great acts there. But we were really tribal and it just works for that many people. It still works, but that sound was very effective.

DALE: You say that clip changed—what did it change?

MIKE: First of all, it broke us as a band internationally. My first clue of that was one of our first trips over to Europe and Montreaux Festival. And I took a walk to the local train station to pick up some magazines, 'cause I was always a magazine freak. And I walked in and I see this magazine called *Rock & Pop* and I'm on the cover. And it's a big picture of me from *Woodstock*. I had never, of course, been on the cover of a magazine before, or anything like that. Reviews were coming out and I guess the [*Woodstock*] record was out. Or the film was out, of course. It just broke us everywhere and Santana took off after that film happened.

I remember when I was about 35, I was living in New York and walking down Fifth Avenue and somebody said, "Hey, Mike Shrieve! Man, I just loved your solo in *Woodstock!*" Which is something, of course. I'd be rich if I had a dollar for everyone in my life that I heard that. And the guy looked at me for a while and said, "Look, man, what's happened? You've gotten older!" And I was 35 and it really upset me.

And I just thought, "Is this what I'm gonna be trapped as? Known as the drummer from the *Woodstock* movie all my life?" It really upset me. What I realize now is that the concert meant so much to so many people. To them personally. I meant so much to so many young people who have told me that, "We saw you there with all those guys. All those heavy hitters and you were our age. And you didn't seem to be any older than us and you inspired me to play the drums," and it just goes on and on. And you can't fight it.

Finally, you just have to be gracious enough to say, "I'm grateful I was there." It was a wonderful day. It broke the band. There's nothing that I'm gonna do in my life that is more momentous than *Woodstock*. I may do better work. I may play better drums. I may record better solos. None of it matters. It does matter, but it doesn't matter in the big scheme of things. Remember the reasons that you started doing music initially, because you love the music. So just be grateful. Don't be bitter.

Source

"Michael Shrieve: Our Weapon Was Music." In Bell, Dale, ed. *Woodstock: An Inside Look at the Movie That Shook Up the World and Defined a Generation.* Studio City, CA: Michael Wiese Productions, 1999, pp. 101-105.

Bad Memories of Woodstock

Not all concertgoers who made the pilgrimage to Woodstock enjoyed the festival. Some people, in fact, found the whole affair to be a miserable experience. One such participant was Mark Hosenball, who later became a journalist for Newsweek. *On the occasion of the fortieth anniversary of Woodstock in 2009, Hosenball wrote a short essay in which he detailed his unpleasant memories of the concert and challenged the cultural importance of the event.*

If it's toxic to overdose on saccharine, then over the next few days, you should try to avoid the gathering deluge of reminiscence about Woodstock. It's the 40th anniversary of the upstate New York rock-and-roll extravaganza, and we in the media are already gorging ourselves on hazy recollections of the event—memories borne not so much from what actually happened, but from what hippie folklore says happened and from how popular imagination and wishful thinking transformed a chaotic mudfest into an epic pageant of peace and love. This wallow in artificially sweetened nostalgia is being supplemented by entertainment-industry efforts to exploit the occasion: according to The Associated Press, we'll soon be blessed with a remastered music CD of the festival, a new director's-cut DVD of the original film epic *Woodstock*, and a Woodstock comedy called *Taking Woodstock,* directed by Ang Lee. Several anniversary concerts have also been scheduled at the site of Max Yasgur's farm, which now features a concert stage and a museum dedicated to the 1960s.

As an authentic Woodstock attendee (or should I say victim?), I hate to rain on the procession of warm memories and good vibrations, but I will say this: wake up, folks. For some—maybe quite a few of us—who made the journey, Woodstock was, if not a nightmare, then a massive, teeming, squalid mess. If you like colossal traffic jams, torrential rain, reeking portable johns, barely edible food, and sprawling, disorganized crowds, then you would have found Woodstock a treat. For those of us who saw those things as a hassle, good music did not necessarily offset the discomfort. OK, for a lot of us who figured on buying tickets at the gate—and then arrived at the site to find that no box offices had been built—the fact that we got to hear top acts gratis was some compensation for the unpleasantness. And the spirit of the massive crowd, even if chemically mellowed by THC [an active chemical in marijuana] and other mood enhancers, was congenial, tolerant, and at times stoic. But in hindsight, what was Woodstock's bottom line? That 500,000 people jammed into in a mudhole didn't fight, riot, or annihilate each other? Is the fact that such a large crowd didn't become violent and start killing each other (albeit serenaded by sometimes brilliant musical performances) Woodstock's principal legacy? What's the big deal?

To be fair, maybe I was a bit too young for Woodstock, or what Woodstock turned out to be, though I probably shouldn't have been. A newly minted 17-year-old high-school graduate by August 1969, I nonetheless was a fairly accomplished patron of big-time pop or rock music events, having attended, *inter alia* [among other things], the American debut of Led Zeppelin at New York's Fillmore (they were the opening act for Iron Butterfly—*In-a-Gadda-Da-Vida, Baby*), a Newport Folk Festival (more of a rock event), and a Janis Joplin solo concert (the most memorable of the lot). The night before my high-school graduation party, I celebrated by watching *Hair* on Broadway. As the summer of '69 sweltered on, I scouted out additional entertainments, canceling one at the last minute due to fear of rain, only to find myself sitting at home watching the first men land on the moon.

For weeks, the organizers of Woodstock had been promoting their event with large ads (featuring the soon-to-be-immortal guitar logo) listing all the famous bands who were scheduled to play. Two of my closest high-school friends, with whom I had attended earlier events, suggested that we meet in New Jersey and drive up to Woodstock. We decided to travel the night before the festival was to begin because we hadn't bought tickets and figured that by arriving early, we not only might be able to get a choice parking spot, but also could avoid the massive ticket queues likely on the day the concert actually started. We did arrive in time to get a good parking spot in a forest clearing a few hundred yards from the stage. But the event was not quite the well-ordered megaconcert that had been advertised. No ticket gates, little food or other amenities, no fencing to separate the people who had paid from freeloaders like us—it was puzzling from the outset how the promoters were going to make back their investment, never mind deliver the scheduled performances.

By lunchtime the next day, we had staked out a small patch not far from the stage. Though prepared for the possibility of showers, we, like most of the rest of the growing crowd, were not prepared for torrential downpours. The rain threw off the concert schedule by hours and quickly began to turn the venue into a mud pit. To my surprise, the organizers did manage to produce the performers they had promised, even as we wondered whether the rain would cause them to electrocute themselves. But as helicopters swooped in and out taking rock stars to and from the scene while the rest of us soaked, I began to envy those privileged enough to merit air transport. The acts I remember—or at least think I remember, since memory can be a tricky business—seeing live on stage include Richie Havens, a group called Sweetwater, Sly and the Family Stone, and Country Joe and the Fish. I definitely did not see Jimi Hendrix play his trippy valedictory version of the "Star Spangled Banner." Actually, my clearest recollection of Woodstock had nothing to do with the music: during an interlude, I excused myself for a bathroom break. I'm still amazed that I managed to navigate myself to the portable toilets on the far outer perimeter, then back through a multitude of 300,000 to find my friends.

After an uncomfortable but dry night in a cramped car seat, I took a walking tour of the site and concluded that the crowd had grown too big for the venue. Concerned that I might not be able to escape for days, I decided to check out then and there. I grabbed a one-way bus that the promoters had organized for would-be refugees, and on a rural highway several miles away from the stage, I hitched a ride from a carful of disappointed concertgoers who had become frustrated with the regionwide traffic jam, and concerned about the radio bulletins warning hopeful attendees to stay away. When my new friends dropped me off near Grand Central Station, I was extremely grateful to return to civilization.

In hindsight, after spending 35 of the last 40 years as a professional journalist, Woodstock does not loom large in my consciousness when compared with some of the other major events I have been fortunate to witness. While the spectacle may have been tawdry, it seems to me that the uproar and congressional impeachment proceedings that resulted from revelations (by my *Newsweek* colleague Michael Isikoff) about President Clinton's relationship with Monica Lewinsky, at which I had a ringside seat for more than a year, had a far greater, if not necessarily beneficent, impact on politics and culture than Woodstock. As a cultural and political phenomenon, the anguish that swept the world and paralyzed Britain after the death of Princess Diana in a car crash was far more sweeping to my mind than any blip in the zeitgeist caused by Woodstock. Ultimately, a lasting and significant memory will probably be my presence last summer, with my teenage son, in Denver's Mile High Stadium when Barack Obama accepted his nomination as America's first African-American candidate for president. Maybe that's the kind of development for which Woodstock is supposed to have laid the groundwork, but I don't really see how you get from there to here.

Source

Hosenball, Mark. "I Was at Woodstock. And I Hated It." *Newsweek,* August 11, 2009. Retrieved from http://www.thedailybeast.com/newsweek/2009/08/11/i-was-at-woodstock-and-i-hated-it.html.

A Military Veteran Remembers the Festival

The Woodstock Music and Art Fair attracted all sorts of young people, including large numbers of young men and women who opposed American involvement in the war in Vietnam. One of these individuals was Edward D. Christensen, who had actually served in the U.S. Armed Forces in the mid-1960s before turning against the war when he went on to college. In the following essay, Christensen remembers the festival as an inspirational event that showcased the best aspects of human nature.

In the late 1960s young men were rightfully worried about being drafted and shipped off to Vietnam. I wasn't worried. My draft card read "4A, veteran." I'd joined the Navy in 1964, aged seventeen, believing media accounts of enemy gunboats attacking our ships in the Gulf of Tonkin. I served out my enlistment unaware that the entire story had been a hoax designed to increase troop levels. Still, I was one of the lucky ones. My time in the Navy amounted to a *get out of jail free* card from the draft. Plus, I got to go to college on the G.I. Bill.

Being in the military gives a young man a certain mindset. My ship docked in New York City in the spring of 1967. Before the crew went on liberty in the city, our officers told us we could ignore any "peaceniks and hippies" who attempted to harass us, because they weren't "men" like us. Once in college, however, I experienced a different point of view and soon let my hair grow and attended peace rallies, all while feeling a certain sense of detachment. After all, the draft couldn't get me. But of course I felt badly for anyone whose life was disrupted, or worse, as a result of Vietnam. My attitudes sound contradictory to me now, but those were contradictory times, and I was still a young man.

In 1969, my friend Frank and I were working second shift in a machine shop. About half the other guys in the shop were older World War II vets who considered us hippies. I wore bell-bottom jeans, never mind that they were uniform issue from my Navy days. When ads on the radio announced an Aquarian exposition to be held somewhere in upstate New York, Frank and I wanted to go, but my girlfriend, Lori, wanted to go too, and my tiny MG had only two seats. Luckily, my father was out of the country on business, and he had a big ol' Ford Galaxie. Frank and I quit the machine shop, and Lori quit her job at a bakery. We had to wait until Friday afternoon to get our last paycheck. When we left that night, it was already raining.

We reached our exit only to find road flares and barricades. Policemen in yellow rain slickers told us to go home, the roads were closed. We proceeded until we found an exit that wasn't blocked, and drove along back roads. It rained so hard the wipers couldn't keep up, and those back roads were blanketed in total darkness. It didn't matter. Our internal compasses were all pointing toward Woodstock. Around midnight exhaustion set in so I pulled off the road, and we slept in the car.

Saturday morning revealed that I had parked on a grassy strip beside a cornfield. I remember seeing a 1950s vintage ambulance converted to a hippie mobile, and an enormously fat local cop riding a Honda moped—so *Mayberry!* When two hippies dressed in ragged remnants of military uniforms drove by in a Cadillac convertible, I said, "The Army and the Navy are here."

We joined the migration, dozens of us, then hundreds, and by the time we were close to Yasgur's farm, thousands. Local citizens sat on their porches, watching this strange parade. All these years later, I remember a farmer in an old red pickup, milk cans of well water in the back, giving drinks to thirsty strangers, and handing out wax-paper-wrapped sandwiches to anyone who wanted one. I remember the feeling that was growing in me: that this was not just a concert; this was something more. Something important. And then word came back through the crowd, "the fences are down!" Not just the fences around a concert area, but all sorts of fences between people coming down.

Yeah, it rained, and yeah, it was muddy. Still, people were nice to one another, like you will notice sometimes when there's a snowstorm or a catastrophe—everyone helped everyone else. Half a million strangers recognized each other as brothers and sisters.

So many sights and sounds: the concert area at night, looking like the inside of a flying saucer with all the candles and lighters; the Santa-looking dude, complete with two pretty girl elves, who charged a "toll"—take a toke to pass—on the path up in the woods; the hole in the clouds that kept opening up right over us; and Jimi Hendrix at dawn on Monday. But what I remember most about Woodstock was the love. That sounds so foreign to us now, so foreign to a polarized nation. We act like it's never been that way in America, but it has. At Woodstock, we all proved that it's possible to come together, to take care of one another, and yes, to love each other. That's what I took away from

Woodstock, and what still matters the most to me now. We *can* love one another. We've done it before.

Source

Christensen, Edward D. "The Fences Are Down." In Reynolds, Susan, ed. *Woodstock Revisited.* Avon, MA: Adams Media, 2009, pp. 177-179.

The Saga of the *Woodstock* Port-O-San Man

One of the best-known scenes from the Woodstock documentary film is a brief interview with a middle-aged sanitation worker named Tom Taggert who is cheerfully cleaning out and disinfecting some of the festival's Port-O-San portable toilets. The encounter at first seems like an inconsequential one, and it might never have been included in the final version of the film. Just before leaving the toilet area, however, the worker volunteers that he has two sons—one who is enjoying the festival and another who is serving his country as a helicopter pilot in Vietnam. The filmmakers decided that this remark was both poignant and symbolic of the times, and they included the footage in the final version.

The scene made the "Port-O-San man" a sort of folk hero among the film's young fans, and the filmmakers insist that Taggert was initially proud of his part in the movie. The sanitation worker later claimed, however, that the filmmakers put him in the movie for cheap laughs at his expense. Citing feelings of humiliation and anger, he filed a lawsuit against the producers of the documentary. Taggert's suit was eventually dismissed. In the following excerpt from his book Woodstock: An Inside Look at the Movie That Shook Up the World and Defined a Generation, *associate producer Dale Bell provides his perspective on the Port-O-San man footage and the ensuing legal controversy.*

Saturday afternoon at the festival. Headquarters for Wadleigh-Maurice Productions, Ltd. at the festival was located on a couple of pieces of three-quarter plywood under a trailer to the left of the stage as you faced the audience pit. Our noses assured us that we were not far from a bank of Port-O-San toilets. Class act all around.

David Myers and his soundman, Charlie Pitts, had just returned to our headquarters that Saturday afternoon. As he was getting his gear together, picking up raw stock and audiotape for another run into the crowds, I noticed that a Port-O-San worker had just backed his truck in to clean the many toilets. He got out of the cab and moved to the rear of his truck to unhook the hose.

I approached him with my hand extended in typical Ivy League fashion. He took his glove off and we shook hands. I told him we were making a film, would he mind if we filmed him? No, was his reply. Through diligent training gained at NET on prior documentary shoots, I always knew it was best to ask permission of someone before you filmed them. It eased the relationship, broke the ice. I knew we were never going to get a signed release from all those whom we had filmed; my action was pure courtesy, an introduction on behalf of all of us to a stranger doing his work.

I backed out of the way to beckon in David and Charlie, who by that time had gotten their stuff together and were ready to shoot. David walked in, the red light on his camera indicating that he had begun to roll. Charlie was at his side with his microphone, alas, not pointed exactly where it should have been. Never at a loss for words, and one of the most innocent and engaging people in the world, David began his conversation with the Port-O-San man.

Should I say that the rest is history? Almost. As he had done so often before, and as he had always trained the rest of us neophytes, David Myers kept shooting, walking, talking, and moving his camera in and out, anticipating exactly where the image ought to be to coincide best with the words he was hearing or expected to hear. David, the cameraman with the best ears I had ever seen, delicately followed the unfurling of this little vignette, asking those pointed, *double-entrendre* questions with his wry sense of humor ever so slightly suppressed behind the constant twinkle in his eye. "Getting a little behind, aren't you?" was David's first little question which prompted all the rest of the quintessential sequence. Both were simply doing the job they came to the site to do: David to document, the Port-O-San man to clean toilets.

"No," the Port-O-San man replies, just as innocently. And as though it had been orchestrated, rehearsed, and now re-enacted, this *pas de deux,* this duet between David and the Port-O-San man, continues. Uninterrupted by the camera, the Port-O-San man keeps talking with the inquiring man who wants to know how being here, at this site, plays on the man with the long hose. As the Port-O-San man moves from one stall to another, David follows diligently, never losing sight of the overall narrative thread of this extraordinary man in his eyepiece.

Eternally youthful at the ripe age of 55, David was older than the man he was following with his camera. Though born at the outbreak of the First World War, David was far from a man of war. When it came time for him to serve in World War II, this warrior for peace filed with his draft board as a conscientious objector. To fulfill his obligation to his country, which as a New Englander he felt he must, he served as an aide in institutions and hospitals, then planted trees in the forest. He did not believe in killing, even for all the reasons millions went into the Second World War.

184

The Port-O-San man finishes his task. It hasn't taken him long. His training dictates that he rinse the seats of the stalls with disinfectant. Armed with a long handle, he brushes the liquid around the toilet seats. Now, they are clean enough for the next customer. He knows he will be back again tomorrow. And then, as though feeling the pulse of the multitude, he pauses and releases this simple sentiment born of the recesses of his soul: "*Happy to do this for these kids. I have one here, and one in Vietnam.*" Did he truly say that, unprompted, untutored? Did we get it right? Did no one write that for him to say?

I'm not sure, even as I write this 30 years after it actually happened and still feel the chill-bumps up my spine as I listen to the Port-O-San man's pronouncement echo in my mind, whether there is anything more profound in the entire movie. Does it compare to "One small step for man … " or "Ask not what your country can do for you … " or "Can't we all just learn to get along?" Was it to capture this essence that we decided to do the movie in the first place?

When this portrait arrived in the editing room, there was never a question that it would find its way into the documentary portion of the movie, virtually uncut. Yet it almost didn't make it, not because of the content but because of the sound.

Fast-forward to mid-February 1970. The Port-O-San sequence takes its turn on the dubbing stage, the place where all the sounds originally recorded on-site are processed, enhanced, equalized, tweaked, manipulated and/or otherwise balanced and modified to make them snap, crystal clear, out of the speakers. In spite of all the patching of cords, pushing of buttons, sliding of dials, opening and closing of pots, bouncing of VU meters, they could not isolate the dialogue of the scene from all the junk noise in the background. Time was pressing down on us. We tried every trick we had, but nothing seemed to be working.

Wads [director Michael Wadleigh] and I were pacing back and forth on the rug covering the floor of the dubbing stage. The big image was being projected above us. Even at this close proximity to the speakers, we were having extreme difficulty with intelligibility. Neither one of us wanted to lose this powerful piece, this symbol of the universality of humanity. But what to do?

Recalling our use of the bouncing ball over the lyrics in the Country Joe McDonald [Fish Song Cheer], I suggested that we use subtitles to allow the audience to read along while they listened to the words. The combination might make the audience hear better. We looked at each other. The mixers, the editors, all harkened to the idea. So off it went to the title company, preserved indelibly. But this was not the last we would hear or see of the Port-O-San man.

During the screening we had for Warner Brothers, where students and "suits" [studio executives] viewed our efforts for the first time one Sunday afternoon in March 1970, another spontaneous event occurred. Just after the Port-O-San man makes his pronouncement about his son on-site and the other son in Vietnam, the students (I didn't see any "suits" doing this!) leapt to their feet and cheered this man for what he stood for. He became an instant hero, a symbol for all caring individuals.

It was the first of many times this happened.

At the press screening in New York at the Trans-Lux Theater in late March 1970, he appeared in full life, dressed in a suit. A Warner staff person, at my instruction, had located the man (through Fred Dubetski at the Port-O-San company in New Jersey). With his wife and family surrounding him, he made his way into the theater, little knowing what to expect. He had been told simply that he was in the film. Period.

When the moment came for his sequence to appear, I moved from my spot at the back of the theater down the darkened aisle slightly behind him so that I could see his face bathed in the reflected light of the screen. As his story unfolded on the huge screen, I saw him clutch a family member close to him. I also think I saw a tear in his eye. But what remains forever imprinted in my memory is the thunderous cheer that erupted from that packed house as they celebrated his remarks. This warm crowd enveloped him in their arms, lauding his wisdom and compassion.

At the end of the screening, as the house lights were turned on, he was identified for the rest of the audience. Tom Taggert and his family. He stood proudly to receive their welcome once again.

To this day, wherever I have seen the movie, even in London at Leicester Square, the Port-O-San man received a standing ovation, so purely does he resonate. Yet sadly, even this is not the end of this noble story.

Several months after the movie opened across the country, presumably to similar responses, Warner Brothers, Wadleigh-Maurice Productions, Ltd., and exhibitors everywhere were served with a lawsuit pressed by attorneys representing the Port-O-San man and his family. We were charged with defamation of character, ridicule, libel, and he was seeking damages in the millions for what we had done to him before the world. Of course, we were astonished by his action. (It was one of half a dozen suits brought against *the film* for similar exposure or ridicule or whatever.) The suit charged that we had not obtained his permission in writing, that we had filmed him in a demeaning occupation, and that to add insult to injury, we had used subtitles to convey his words, as though he could not talk clearly and be understood.

Our hero had been ensnared by greedy attorneys, perhaps? Apparently, everyone in town knew he worked for the Port-O-San Corporation, but his job classification was labeled "sanitary engineer." No one had ever inquired about a job description, not even members of his family. Once the sequence in the film was exhibited across the country, the secret he had maintained from his family for all those years was now exposed. Apparently, his high school son was ribbed because of his dad's occupation. He was crestfallen; they were shocked that he performed liposuction on dozens of stalls a day. Friendly attorneys *must have* advised him to sue us.

I know I felt very sad at this development. None of us bore any hard feelings towards the Port-O-San man. Although we offered a settlement, they preferred to take the case to court, but they lost.

Other lawsuits were brought by people who thought they had been ridiculed by dint of being included in the movie (the man playing reveille on the bugle from the stage on Sunday morning), or caught unsuspectingly in embarrassing configurations (the man making love in the tall grasses who cocks his hat at a different angle once he has completed his session), yet none of them won.

I—we—regret any inconvenience we caused the Port-O-San man. To each one of us, he was a symbol of compassion and we wish him and his marvelous family well. I trust his son in Vietnam returned home safely, but I frankly do not know.

Source

"Dale Bell: The Port-O-San Sequence." In Bell, Dale, ed. *Woodstock: An Inside Look at the Movie That Shook Up the World and Defined a Generation.* Studio City, CA: Michael Wiese Productions, 1999, pp. 118-122.

Leaving Woodstock

By Sunday night, August 17, most of the massive crowd that had descended on Max Yasgur's farm for the Woodstock music festival had departed. By the time Jimi Hendrix capped the concert with his mid-morning performance on Monday, August 18, only a fraction of the record audience remained. The following news story, written by reporter Barnard L. Collier of the New York Times, *provides an account of the Sunday night exodus from the concert grounds, as well as a brief summary of some of the highs and lows of the weekend.*

W aves of weary youngsters streamed away from the Woodstock Music and Art Fair last night and early today as security officials reported at least two deaths and 4,000 people treated for injuries, illness and adverse drug reactions over the festival's three-day period.

However festival officials said the folk and rock music could go on until dawn, and most of the crowd was determined to stay on.

Campfires Burn

As the music wailed on into the early morning hours, more than 100 campfires—fed by fence-posts and any other wood the young people could lay their hands on—flickered around the hillside that formed a natural amphitheater for the festival.

By midnight nearly half of the 300,000 fans who had camped here for the weekend had left. A thunderstorm late yesterday afternoon provided the first big impetus to depart, and a steady stream continued to leave through the night.

Drugs and auto traffic continued to be the main headaches.

But the crowd itself was extremely well-behaved. As Dr. William Abruzzi, the festival's chief medical officer, put it: "There has been no violence whatsoever, which is remarkable for a crowd of this size. These people are really beautiful."

Months of Planning

Local merchants and residents eased the food shortage. Youths who endured drenching rain to hear such pop performers as Sly and the Family Stone and the Creedence Clearwater Revival overcame the water shortage by gulping down soft drinks and beer. And as the close of the festival approached, the spirits of the audience—mostly youths of 17 to 20—were high.

For many, the weekend had been the fulfillment of months of planning and hoping, not only to see and hear the biggest group of pop performers ever assembled, but also to capture the excitement of camping out with strangers, experimenting with drugs and sharing—as one youth put it—"an incredible unification."

The state police said last night that traffic was moving out of the area at a gradual and slow but steady pace. Throughout the weekend, parked and stalled cars had been stretched out on the roads in all directions.

The state police said they had about 150 men on duty to help deal with the traffic in a 20-mile radius. They were permitting no cars to enter the area.

Drugs Kill a Youth

Helicopters ferried out some youths who had fallen ill. About 100 people were treated yesterday for bad reactions to drugs, bringing to 400 the number of persons so treated during the three-day affair.

The pervasive use of drugs at the festival resulted in one death yesterday. The unidentified youth was taken to Horton Memorial Hospital in Middletown, N.Y., where officials said he failed to respond to treatment for what was believed to be an overdose of heroin.

Three young men were taken to the Middletown hospital yesterday in critical condition as a result of drug overdoses. One of them identified as George Xikis, 18 years old, of Astoria, Queens, also suffered a fractured skull when he fell from a car roof while under the influence of drugs, hospital officials said.

The two others in critical condition were identified as Anthony Gencarelli, 18, of Port Chester, N.Y., and Arkie Melunow, 22, of Franklin Township, N.J.

Despite the "bad trips" of many drug users at the festival, sales were made openly. Festival officials made periodic announcements from the stage that impure and harmful drugs were circulating in the crowd.

The use of heroin and LSD, popularly known as "acid" because of its chemical name, lysergic acid diethylamide, drew the public warnings. But marijuana was the most widely used drug, with many youths maintaining that practically everyone in the audience was smoking.

Only about 80 arrests were made on drug charges, a dozen inside the fair grounds. In addition to the death attributed to the overdose, one other youth was reported killed. The police identified him as Raymond R. Mizsak, 17, of Trenton, and said he had been run over by a tractor yesterday morning.

2 Babies Born

Dr. Abruzzi said yesterday that first-aid facilities were returning to normal after the arrival of medical supplies and a dozen doctors summoned as volunteers.

Dr. Abruzzi said two babies were born during the course of the festival, one in a car caught in traffic, on nearby Route 17B and the other in a hospital after a helicopter flight from the festival site. He said four miscarriages also were reported.

Though the festival was to end early today, there was no assurance that the crowds would vanish quickly. Anticipating massive traffic tie-ups in the area, many in the crowd said they would remain encamped for a day or two on the 600-acre farm of Max Yasgur that was rented for the event.

"Some of them might decide to live here permanently," one state trooper said.

Many of the fans, weary after listening to entertainment that started Saturday night and continued until 8 a.m. yesterday, slept late yesterday morning and into the afternoon. Most slept in the open and others in the thousands of tents surrounding the entertainment area.

Later, [the sun] brightened their outlook and began to dry the mud left by Friday night's heavy rains.

"The whole thing is a gas," said one long-haired young man, who identified himself as "Speed." "I dig it all," he said, "the mud, the rain, the music, the hassles."

When the rains came yesterday, however, the crowd began to break.

The storm, which struck at 4:30 p.m., after a sunny and breezy day, would have washed out any less-determined crowds. But at least 80,000 young people sat or stood in front of the stage and shouted obscenities at the darkened skies as trash rolled down the muddy hillside with the runoff of the rain. Others took shelter in dripping tents, lean-tos, cars and trucks.

The festival promoters decided to continue the show but also to try to persuade as much of the audience as possible to leave the area for their cars or some sort of shelter.

The problem was, however, that most of those who remained unsheltered had parked their cars many miles from festival grounds.

"It is really a problem because the kids are as wet as they can get already and they have miles to go before they can even hope to get dry," said Michael Lang, the executive producer at the festival.

The threat of bronchial disease and influenza was increased by the downpour, according to staff doctors here. Many boys and girls wandered through the storm nude, red mud clinging to their bodies.

When the storm struck, the performer on the stage, Joe Cocker, stopped playing and the hundreds of people on the plywood and steel structure scurried off for fear of its being toppled by winds, which were blowing in gusts estimated at up to 40 miles an hour.

Amplifiers and other electronic devices were covered to avoid damage, and recorded music was played for the crowd.

Naked Man Cheered

As performers wandered onto the stage to look at the crowd and to decide whether to play, they were greeted by loud cheering. One naked man also came up on stage and danced.

At 6:15 p.m. the sun broke through and spirits rose again.

Artie Cornfield [Kornfeld], a partner in the festival production company, said, "I guess this was meant to happen, and everybody is still with us. We're going to go on all night with the music."

Some Fans Reach Here

Young people straggling into the Port of New York Authority bus terminal at 41st Street and Eighth Avenue last night were damp, disheveled and given to such wild eccentricities of dress as the wearing of a battered top hat with grimy jersey, blue jeans and sandals.

They were, according to a driver, Richard Biccum, "good kids in disguise." Mr. Biccum, who is 26 years old, said: "I'll haul kids any day rather than commuters," because they were exceptionally polite and orderly.

Reginald Dorsey, a Short Line Bus System dispatcher, agreed that the youths were "beautiful people" who had caused no trouble.

Source:

Collier, Barnard L. "Tired Rock Fans Begin Exodus." *New York Times*, August 18, 1969. Retrieved from http://www.nytimes.com/learning/general/onthisday/big/0817.html#article.

Ayn Rand Denounces the "Phony" Values of Woodstock

After Woodstock was over, a heated debate broke out over the symbolic significance of the event. Many people hailed the festival as proof of the counterculture's genuine devotion to the principles of peace, love, and brotherhood. Many other people, though, saw the festival as a depressing spectacle that showed the most selfish, foolish, and irresponsible qualities of the young men and women growing up in the 1960s.

One of the most famous criticisms of Woodstock was penned by Russian-American novelist and philosopher Ayn Rand. Rand was a fierce advocate of individual rights, U.S.-style capitalism, and what she called "rational selfishness" until her death in 1982. Many of Rand's controversial works pivoted on her belief that societies harbor morally and intellectually superior citizens whose hard-earned gains and triumphs are under perpetual threat from their less gifted and less ambitious countrymen. In her 1969 essay "Apollo and Dionysus," excerpted below, Rand compares Woodstock Nation very unfavorably to the Americans who celebrated the 1969 Apollo 11 space flight to the moon.

On July 16, 1969, one million people, from all over the country, converged on Cape Kennedy, Florida, to witness the launching of *Apollo 11* that carried astronauts to the moon.

On August 15, 300,000 people, from all over the country, converged on Bethel, New York, near the town of Woodstock, to witness a rock music festival.

These two events were news, not philosophical theory. These were facts of our actual existence, the kinds of facts—according to both modern philosophers and practical businessmen—that philosophy has nothing to do with.

But if one cares to understand the meaning of these two events—to grasp their roots and their consequences—one will understand the power of philosophy and learn to recognize the specific forms in which philosophical abstractions appear in our actual existence.

The issue in this case is the alleged dichotomy of *reason versus emotion.*

This dichotomy has been presented in many variants in the history of philosophy, but its most colorfully eloquent statement was given by Friedrich Nietzsche. In *The Birth of Tragedy from the Spirit of Music*, Nietzsche claims that he observed two opposite elements in Greek tragedies, which he saw as metaphysical principles inherent in the nature of reality; he named them after two Greek gods: Apollo, the god of light, and Dionysus, the god of wine. Apollo, in Nietzsche's metaphysics, is the symbol of beauty, order, wisdom, efficacy (though Nietzsche equivocates about this last)—i.e., the symbol of reason. Dionysus is the symbol of drunkenness or, rather, Nietzsche cites drunkenness as his identification of what Dionysus stands for: wild, primeval feelings, orgiastic joy, the dark, the savage, the unintelligible element in man—i.e., the symbol of emotion....

Symbolic figures are a valuable adjunct to philosophy: they help men to integrate and bear in mind the essential meaning of complex issues. Apollo and Dionysus represent the fundamental conflict of our age. And for those who may regard them as floating abstractions, reality has offered two perfect, fiction-like dramatizations of these abstract symbols: at Cape Kennedy and at Woodstock. They were perfect in every respect demanded of serious fiction: they concretized the *essentials* of the two principles involved, in action, in a pure, extreme, isolated form. The fact that the spacecraft was called "Apollo" is merely a coincidence, but a helpful coincidence.

If you want to know fully what the conflict of reason versus irrational emotion means—in fact, in reality, on earth—keep these two events in mind: it means *Apollo 11* versus the Woodstock festival. Remember also that you are asked to make a choice between these two—and that the whole weight of today's culture is being used to push you to the side of and into Woodstock's mud.

In my article "Apollo 11" (*The Objectivist*, September 1969), I discussed the meaning and the greatness of the moon landing. To quote: "No one could doubt that we had seen an achievement of man in his capacity as a rational being—an achievement of reason, of logic, of mathematics, of total dedication to the absolutism of reality.... The most confirmed evader in the worldwide audience could not escape the fact that ... no feelings, wishes, urges, instincts or lucky 'conditioning' ... could have achieved this incomparable feat—that we were watching the embodied concretization of a single faculty of man: his rationality."

This was the meaning and motive of the overwhelming world-wide response to *Apollo 11*, whether the cheering crowds knew it consciously or not—and most of them did not. It was the response of people starved for the sight of an achievement, for a vision of man the hero.

This was the motive that drew one million people to Cape Kennedy for the launching. Those people were not a stampeding herd nor a manipulated mob;

they did not wreck the Florida communities, they did not devastate the countryside, they did not throw themselves, like whining thugs, at the mercy of their victims; they did not create any victims. They came as responsible individuals able to project the reality of two or three days ahead and to provide for their own needs. There were people of every age, creed, color, educational level and economic status. They lived and slept in tents or in their cars, some of them for several days, in great discomfort and unbearable heat; they did it gamely, cheerfully, gaily; they projected a general feeling of confident goodwill, the bond of a common enthusiasm; they created a public spectacle of responsible privacy—and they departed as they had come, without benefit of press agents.

The best account of the nature of that general feeling was given to me by an intelligent young woman of my acquaintance. She went to see the parade of the astronauts when they came to New York. For a few brief moments, she stood on a street corner and waved to them as they went by. "It was so wonderful," she told me. "People didn't want to leave after the parade had passed. They just stood there, talking about it—talking to strangers—smiling. It was so wonderful to feel, for once, that people aren't vicious, that one doesn't have to suspect them, that we have something good in common."

This is the essence of a genuine feeling of human brotherhood: the brotherhood of *values.* This is the only authentic form of unity among men—and only values can achieve it....

The "Woodstock Music and Art Fair" did not take place in Woodstock; like everything else about that event, its title was a phony, an attempt to cash in on the artistic reputation of the Woodstock community. The fair took place on an empty thousand-acre pasture leased by the promoters from a local farmer. In response to $200,000 worth of publicity and advertising, 300,000 hippies showed up for the occasion. (These figures are from the *New York Times;* some sources place the attendance estimate higher.)

According to *Newsweek* (August 25): "The three-day Woodstock fair was different from the usual pop festival from the outset. It was not just a concert but a tribal gathering, expressing all the ideas of the new generation: communal living away from the cities, getting high, digging arts, clothes and craft exhibits, and listening to the songs of revolution." The article quotes one of the promoters as declaring: "People will all be going into their own thing. This is not just music, but a conglomeration of everything involved in the new culture."

So it was.

194

No living, eating or sanitary facilities were provided; the promoters claimed that they had not expected so large a crowd. *Newsweek* describes the conditions as follows: "Festival food supplies were almost immediately exhausted ... and water coming from wells dug into the area stopped flowing or came up impure. A heavy rain Friday night turned the amphitheater into a quagmire and the concession area into a mudhole.... Throngs of wet, sick and wounded hippies trekked to impromptu hospital tents suffering from colds, sore throats, broken bones, barbed-wire cuts and nail-puncture wounds. Festival doctors called it a 'health emergency,' and 50 additional doctors were flown in from New York City to meet the crisis."

According to the *New York Times* (August 18), when the rainstorm came "at least 80,000 young people sat or stood in front of the stage and shouted obscenities at the darkened skies as trash rolled down the muddy hillside with the runoff of the rain. Others took shelter in dripping tents, lean-tos, cars and trucks.... Many boys and girls wandered through the storm nude, red mud clinging to their bodies."

Drugs were used, sold, shared or given away during the entire festival. Eyewitnesses claim that 99 percent of the crowd smoked marijuana; but heroin, hashish, LSD and other stronger drugs were peddled openly. The nightmare convulsions of so-called "bad trips" were a common occurrence. One young man died, apparently from an overdose of heroin.

The *Newsweek* report concludes with: "The promoters had hired members of the Hog Farm, a New Mexico hippie commune, to peacefully police the fair. At week's end near the Hog Farm campsite, a hard core of crazies barked like dogs and freaked out in a bizarre circle dance lit by flashing strobe lights. The songs seemed to sum up what the young Aquarians believed, despite all misadventures, the festival was all about: 'Now, now, now is all there is. Love is all there is. Love is. Love.'"

Who paid for this love-feast? Apparently, the unloved ones: those who know that there is more than the "now" for a human being—and that without it, even the "now" is not possible.

The citizens of Bethel, the nearest community, were the victims, abandoned by their law-enforcing agencies. These victims were neither bums nor millionaires; they were farmers and small businessmen, who worked hard to earn their living. Their stories, reported in the *New York Times* (August 20), sound like those of the survivors of a foreign invasion.

Richard C. Joyner, the operator of the local post office and general store on Route 17B, "said that the youngsters at the festival had virtually taken over his property—camping on his lawn, making fires on his patio and using the backyard as a latrine....

"Clarence W. Townsend, who runs a 150-acre dairy farm ... was shaken by the ordeal. 'We had thousands of cars all over our fields,' he said. 'There were kids all over the place. They made a human cesspool of our property and drove through the cornfields. There's not a fence left on the place. They just tore them up and used them for firewood.' ...

"'My pond is a swamp [said Royden Gabriele, another farmer]. I've got no fences and they used my field as a latrine. They picked corn and camped all over the place. They just landed wherever they could.... We pulled 30 of them out of the hay mow smoking pot.... If they come back next year I don't know what I'll do,' Mr. Gabriele said. 'If I can't sell, I'll just burn the place down.'"

No love—or thought—was given to these victims by the unsanitary apostles of love (and someday the world will discover that without thought there can be no love)....

The hippies are right in one respect: the culture of today's Establishment is done for, it is rotted through and through—and rebelling against it is like rebelling against a dead horse.

The hippies are wrong, however, when they fancy themselves to be rebels. They are the distilled essence of the Establishment's culture, they are the embodiment of its soul, they are the personified ideal of generations of crypto-Dionysians now leaping into the open.

Among the various types of today's younger generation, the hippies are the most docile conformists. Unable to generate a thought of their own, they have accepted the philosophical beliefs of their elders as unchallengeable dogma—as, in earlier generations, the weakest among the young conformed to the fundamentalist view of the Bible.

The hippies were taught by their parents, their neighbors, their tabloids and their college professors that faith, instinct and emotion are superior to reason—and they obeyed. They were taught that material concerns are evil, that the State or the Lord will provide, that the Lilies of the Field do not toil—and they obeyed. They were taught that love, indiscriminant love, for one's fellow-men is the highest virtue—and they obeyed. They were taught that the merging of one's self with a herd, a tribe or a community is the noblest way for men to live—and they obeyed.

There isn't a single basic principle of the Establishment which they do not share—there isn't a belief which they have not accepted.

When they discovered that this philosophy did not work—because, in fact, it cannot work—the hippies had neither the wit nor the courage to challenge it; they found, instead, an outlet for their impotent frustration by accusing their elders of hypocrisy—as if hypocrisy were the only obstacle to the realization of their ideals. And—left blindly, helplessly lobotomized in the face of an inexplicable reality that is not amenable to their feelings—they have no recourse but to the shouting of obscenities at anything that frustrates their whims, at men or at a rainy sky, indiscriminately, with no concept of the difference.

It is typical of today's culture that these exponents of seething, raging hostility are taken as advocates of love.

Avowed anti-materialists whose only manifestation of rebellion and of individualism takes the material form of the clothes they choose to wear, are a pretty ridiculous spectacle. Of any type of nonconformity, this is the easiest to practice, and the safest....

The hippies are a desperate herd looking for a master, to be taken over by anyone; anyone who would tell them how to live, without demanding the effort of thinking. Theirs is the mentality ready for a Führer.

The hippies are the living demonstration of what it means to give up reason and to rely on one's primeval "instincts," "urges," "intuitions"—and whims. With such tools, they are unable to grasp even what is needed to satisfy their wishes—for example, the wish to have a festival. Where would they be without the charity of the local "squares" who fed them? Where would they be without the fifty doctors, rushed from New York to save their lives—without the automobiles that brought them to the festival—without the soda pop and beer they substituted for water—without the helicopter that brought the entertainers—without all the achievements of the technological civilization they denounce? Left to their own devices, they literally didn't know enough to come in out of the rain....

I have mentioned the nature of the bond uniting the admirers of *Apollo 11*: the brotherhood of values. The hippies, too, have a brotherhood, but of a different kind: it is the brotherhood of fear.

It is fear that drives them to seek the warmth, the protection, the "safety" of a herd. When they speak of merging their selves into a "greater whole," it is their fear that they hope to drown in the undemanding waves of unfastidious human bodies. And what they hope to fish out of that pool is the momentary illusion of an unearned personal significance.

But all discussions or arguments about the hippies are almost superfluous in the face of one overwhelming fact: most of the hippies are drug addicts.

Is there any doubt that drug addiction is an escape from an unbearable inner state, from a reality one cannot deal with, from an atrophying mind one can never fully destroy? If Apollonian reason were unnatural to man, and Dionysian "intuition" brought him closer to nature and truth, the apostles of irrationality would not have to resort to drugs. Happy, self-confident men do not seek to get "stoned."

Drug addiction is the attempt to obliterate one's consciousness, the quest for a deliberately induced insanity. As such, it is so obscene an evil that any doubt about the moral character of its practitioners is itself an obscenity.

Such is the nature of the conflict of Apollo versus Dionysus.

You have all heard the old bromide to the effect that man has his eyes on the stars and his feet in the mud. It is usually taken to mean that man's reason and his physical senses are the element pulling him down to the mud, while his mystical, supra-rational emotions are the element that lifts him to the stars.

This is the grimmest inversion of many in the course of mankind's history. But, last summer, reality offered you a literal dramatization of the truth: it is man's irrational emotions that bring him down to the mud; it is man's reason that lifts him to the stars.

Source

Rand, Ayn. "Apollo and Dionysus." First published in *The Objectivist,* December 1969-January 1970. Reprinted in Schwartz, Peter, ed. *The Return of the Primitive*. New York: Penguin, 1999, pp. 99-118.

A Moment of Muddy Grace

In August 2009 many popular media outlets in America took note of the fortieth anniversary of Woodstock. Television and satellite radio programs, Internet sites, newspapers, and magazines all paused to remember the event and to offer perspectives on its impact on American culture. Following is a commentary from Jon Pareles, a respected veteran pop music critic who has written for such publications as Rolling Stone, Creem, *the* Village Voice, *and the* New York Times—*and a person who experienced Woodstock firsthand as a young man.*

Baby boomers won't let go of the Woodstock Festival. Why should we? It's one of the few defining events of the late 1960s that had a clear happy ending.

On Aug. 15 to 17, 1969, hundreds of thousands of people, me among them, gathered in a lovely natural amphitheater in Bethel (not Woodstock), N.Y. We listened to some of the best rock musicians of the era, enjoyed other legal and illegal pleasures, endured rain and mud and exhaustion and hunger pangs, felt like a giant community and dispersed, all without catastrophe.

A year after the riots at the Democratic convention in Chicago, expectations about large gatherings of young people were so low that this was considered a surprise. Although the festival didn't go exactly as planned, it was, as advertised, three days of peace and music. That made Woodstock an idyll, particularly in retrospect, even though it was declared a state disaster area at the time.

"Not withstanding their personality, their dress and their ideas, they were and they are the most courteous, considerate and well-behaved group of kids I have ever been in contact with in my 24 years of police work," Lou Yank, the chief of police in nearby Monticello, told the *New York Times*.

Yet for all the benign memories, Woodstock also set in motion other, more crass impulses. While its immediate aftermath was amazement and relief, the festival's full legacy had as much to do with excess as with idealism. As the decades roll by, the festival seems more than ever like a fluke: a moment of muddy, disheveled, incredulous grace. It was as much an endpoint as a beginning, a holiday of naïveté and dumb luck before the realities of capitalism resumed. Woodstock's young, left-of-center crowd—nice kids, including students, artists, workers and politicos, as well as full-fledged L.S.D.-popping hippies—was quickly recognized as a potential army of consumers that mainstream merchants would not underestimate again. There was more to sell them than rolling papers and LPs.

With the 40th anniversary of Woodstock looming—so soon?—the commemorative machinery is clanking into place, and the nostalgia is strong. There's a Woodstock Festival museum now at the Bethel Woods Center for the Arts and a recently built concert hall at what was the concert site, Max Yasgur's farm (though the original Woodstock hillside has been left undeveloped).

A new, much expanded anthology of music recorded at the 1969 festival has been issued: the six-CD "Woodstock 40 Years On: Back to Yasgur's Farm" (Rhino). Complete Woodstock performances by Sly and the Family Stone, Santana, Janis Joplin and others have been released by Sony Legacy. Cable and public television channels have their Woodstock specials scheduled, and there's yet another batch of commemorative books, including "The Road to Woodstock" (Ecco) by the festival's instigator, Michael Lang, which includes tidbits like how much the bands were paid. "Taking Woodstock," a comedy directed by Ang Lee, is due for release this month.

A summer package tour, Heroes of Woodstock, features musicians who appeared at Woodstock—including Jefferson Starship (playing Jefferson Airplane songs), Levon Helm from the Band, Tom Constanten from the Grateful Dead, Ten Years After, Canned Heat and Country Joe McDonald. It arrives at Bethel Woods precisely on Aug. 15.

Unlike previous anniversaries in 1994 and 1999, however, there's no big festival this year bearing the Woodstock name—reflecting, perhaps, the dismal memories of Woodstock '99 in Rome, N.Y., where a hot, pent-up audience, angry at high vendor prices, set fires and looted and vandalized the site.

While the original Woodstock showed how much discomfort an audience would put up with for the sake of sharing an event—something promoters were happy to learn—Woodstock '99 breached the limit of fan exploitation.

Yet the original Woodstock still has a rosy glow. It was finite and all smiles—far different from the Vietnam War, the racial tensions and the much-discussed generation gap of the same era. Woodstock became free in both senses of the word: free as in liberated (from drug laws and dress codes) and free as in gratis, not collecting tickets and handing out, as Wavy Gravy said, "breakfast in bed for 400,000."

A cynic might see the festival as a prime example of how coddled the baby boomers were in an economy of abundance. The Woodstock crowd, which arrived with more drugs than camping supplies, got itself a free concert, and when the people responsible could no longer handle the logistics, the government bailed them out. Some people took it upon themselves to help others; many just freeloaded.

Still, Woodstock gave virtually everyone involved—ticketholders, gate crashers, musicians, doctors, the police—a sense of shared humanity and cooperation. Trying to get through the weekend, people played nice with one another, which was only sensible. Musicians performed for the biggest audience of their lives. Townspeople and the National Guard pitched in to keep people fed and healthy. No one, the *New York Times* reported, called the cops "pigs."

One lunatic with a gun could have changed everything. The Altamont Festival, marred all day by violence, took place only four months later. Miraculously, at Woodstock, there was none.

Seemingly within minutes after it ended Woodstock was the stuff of legend: a spirit, a nation, an ideal, amorphous but vivid, with an Oscar-winning documentary film, the 1970 "Woodstock," to prove it wasn't all a hallucination. (The film was also an early lesson in how profitable ancillary rights could be; the festival itself lost money, but the film recouped it many times over.)

Sheer size made Woodstock consequential. It was huge. The Beatles had played to 55,000 people at Shea Stadium; the 1965 Newport Folk Festival spread about 71,000 people over four days. Had Woodstock drawn the 100,000 to 150,000 people that its promoters planned for, it would simply have been one in a string of big rock festivals dating back to Monterey Pop in 1967, which had an estimated total of 200,000 people over three days.

After Woodstock gave up on collecting tickets—abandoning flimsy fences and declaring itself a free festival—it grew to what was variously estimated as 300,000 or 400,000 people, more than double the attendance of previous rock festivals. That number would have been considerably higher if traffic problems hadn't turned some away; many people walked for miles to the site.

When the hippie subculture surfaced en masse at Woodstock, two years after the Summer of Love, it was still largely self-invented and isolated. There were pockets of freaks in cities and handfuls of them in smaller towns, nearly all feeling like outsiders. For many people at the festival, just seeing and joining that gigantic crowd was more of a revelation than anything that happened onstage. It proved that they were not some negligible minority but members of a larger culture—or, to use that sweetly dated term, a counterculture.

At Woodstock hippiedom simultaneously reached its public peak and opened itself to imitation and trivialization—one more glimmer of rebellion to be deflated into a style statement.

For true believers Woodstock was about cooperation and mutual aid, and about making love, not war. (At a time when Vietnam had divided America into hawks and doves, that was a peace dove sitting on the guitar in the festival logo.) But Woodstock was also a whole lot of people getting stoned at a rock concert, which was much easier than working to change the world.

Politicos like Abbie Hoffman, who is widely credited with coining the phrase Woodstock Nation, wanted to claim Woodstock as a symbol of resistance to repression. But Pete Townshend batted Hoffman off the stage with a guitar when Hoffman interrupted the Who's set to protest the imprisonment, for drug possession, of a fellow activist, John Sinclair.

There was antiwar fervor in some songs, like Richie Havens's "Handsome Johnny" and McDonald's "I-Feel-Like-I'm-Fixin'-To-Die Rag." Joan Baez spoke about her husband, in jail for draft dodging, and sang "We Shall Overcome." There was also, in much of the music, that particular late-1960s aura of imminent doom or enlightenment, in songs like "Wooden Ships" (performed by both Jefferson Airplane and Crosby, Stills, Nash and Young) and the Who's "Amazing Journey." And there was Jimi Hendrix's "Star-Spangled Banner," with its screams of feedback and its divebombing glissandos, brash and dire, angry and insistently American. But Woodstock was no earnest rally; it had love songs, blues and extended guitar jams.

After the buzz wore off, the utopian communal aura of a Woodstock Nation gave way, almost immediately, to the reality of a Woodstock Market: a demographic target group about to have its dreams stripped of radical purpose and turned into commodities. A wider audience realized it was possible to enjoy the music, drugs and fun without the ideological trappings. Soon enough everyone was a quasi-hippie; long hair on men no longer signaled anything about what they stood for. FM radio, which was the pipeline for underground rock, traded quirky, exploratory disc jockeys for consistent formats that advertisers could depend on. Now that it was clear how large an audience was at stake—that it wasn't just a few freaks—professionals were back in charge.

Woodstock and other late-1960s festivals changed the scale of rock concerts. Bands eagerly moved up to arenas from theaters; a week before Woodstock, for example, two of its acts, the Jefferson Airplane and Joe Cocker, shared a bill at the Fillmore East, which had all of 2,700 seats. Music soon expanded, or bloated, to fill its newfound arenas. The early 1970s were the era of noodling jams and 10-minute drum solos that would have to be torpedoed, a few years later, by punk-rock.

Larger gatherings followed Woodstock. An estimated 600,000 people showed up at both the Isle of Wight Festival in 1970 and at the one-day Summer Jam at Watkins Glen, N.Y., in 1973. But those were merely concerts, not cultural symbols. Appropriately or not, Woodstock is still invoked when describing latter-day festivals, although they are considerably smaller, better organized and more comfortable than Woodstock was. None of them tolerate gate crashers.

Since Woodstock I've been to more rock festivals than I can easily remember. Most, sooner or later, involve mud. Some have simply been like extremely long standing-room concerts; some have the comforting familiarity of ritual, like the annual New Orleans Jazz and Heritage Festival (which dates back almost as far as Woodstock; it had its 40th edition this year).

A few, like Coachella and Bonnaroo, run in stretches like a smart disc-jockey set, segueing neatly through various bands. And a handful have felt like generational statements: the first Lollapalooza (in 1991) and Lilith Fair (in 1997) and, surprisingly, Woodstock '94 (in Saugerties, N.Y.), which juxtaposed performers from the original Woodstock Festival with more contemporary bands, creating what was probably the only mosh pit ever to greet Crosby, Stills and Nash. But all of them have been consumer experiences: a planned entertainment package of scheduled music and convenient vendors.

Woodstock was different. It was, particularly for a sheltered teenager, an adventure: sloppy, chaotic, bewildering, drenched, uncertain, sometimes excruciating, sometimes ecstatic. Although I was drug free, I had the feeling that the crowd was more than just an audience at a show, that something major was at stake, that Woodstock would prove something to the world. What it proved—that for at least one weekend, hippies meant what they said about peace and love—was fleeting and all too innocent; it couldn't stand up to everyday human nature or to the pragmatic workings of the market. But 40 years later the sensation lingers.

Source

Pareles, Jon. "Woodstock: A Moment of Muddy Grace." *New York Times,* August 5, 2009. Retrieved from http://www.nytimes.com/2009/08/09/arts/music/09pare.html?ref=woodstockmusicfestivals.

IMPORTANT PEOPLE, PLACES, AND TERMS

Acid rock

A type of rock music with elements of folk rock, blues, and pop that glorified recreational drug use, sexual freedom, and individuality; also known as psychedelic rock.

Baby boomer

Person born in the United States during the postwar "baby boom," a sustained period of high birth rates usually defined as the years between 1946 and 1964.

Baez, Joan (1941-)

Folksinger and political activist who headlined the first night of Woodstock.

Beat movement

A cultural movement of the 1950s that rejected American "middle-class" values and traditional institutions of authority and emphasized the importance of individual choice and freedom.

Communism

A political system in which the state controls all economic activity, distributes resources evenly among the populace, and exerts significant control over citizens' rights and freedoms.

Counterculture

A cultural movement of the 1960s that centered around sexual freedom, recreational drug use, a return to "natural" living, and the rejection of middle-class America's emphasis on acquiring money and consumer products.

Dylan, Bob (1941-)

Folksinger-turned-rock star whose lyrics and attitude hugely influenced rock and roll during the 1960s.

Headliner
A performer who receives top billing at a concert event.

Hendrix, Jimi (1942-1970)
Electric guitarist whose most famous concert performance came at Woodstock.

Hog Farm
Hippie commune that distributed food and provided other services at Woodstock.

Kornfeld, Artie (1942-)
Woodstock promoter and recording industry executive.

Lang, Michael (1944-)
Concert promoter and co-founder of the Woodstock Music and Art Fair.

LSD
Lysergic acid diethylamide, a hallucinogenic drug that was enormously popular in the American counterculture, both before and after it was made illegal in 1966.

McCarthyism
The leveling of false or unfounded accusations of disloyalty or Communist sympathies against American individuals or groups with differing political or cultural views.

McCarthyites
Followers of Senator Joseph McCarthy or proponents of his brand of Cold War political warfare, known as McCarthyism.

Psychedelic rock
A type of rock music with elements of folk rock, blues, and pop that glorified recreational drug use, sexual freedom, and individuality; also known as acid rock.

Roberts, John (1945-2001)
Woodstock promoter and business entrepreneur who provided most of the funding for the festival.

Romney, Hugh "Wavy Gravy" (1936-)
Leader of the Hog Farm commune and social activist.

Rosenman, Joel (1942-)

Woodstock promoter and business entrepreneur.

Set

A live performance of a group of songs by a single band or musician.

Underground press

Small, independently owned and operated newspapers, magazines, and other media, usually associated with the counterculture. In some countries, the term refers to illegally published newspapers and magazines.

Wadleigh, Michael (1942-)

Documentary filmmaker who directed *Woodstock*.

Woodstock Nation

A term used to refer both to attendees of the Woodstock festival and to the youth-led counterculture of the late 1960s.

Yasgur, Max (1919-1973)

Dairy farm owner who leased his property for the Woodstock Festival.

CHRONOLOGY

1945

World War II draws to a close and the United States begins an extended period of strong economic growth. *See p. 7.*

1954

The U.S. Supreme Court hands down its *Brown v. Board of Education* decision, which outlaws segregation in American public schools. *See p. 8.*

Vietnam successfully pushes longtime colonial ruler France out of the country. Terms of the peace agreement call for the temporary partition of Vietnam into northern and southern halves. *See p. 12.*

1956

The United States derails elections designed to reunite Vietnam under a single government. Instead, it lends its support to the creation of an independent South Vietnam. Communist leaders in North Vietnam and Communist rebels in South Vietnam take up arms in a bid to force reunification. *See p. 12.*

Elvis Presley's "Heartbreak Hotel" becomes his first Number One single on the U.S. pop charts. *See p. 24.*

1957

The Philadelphia-based *American Bandstand* becomes a nationally syndicated music show. *See p. 25.*

1959

An airplane crash claims the lives of Buddy Holly, Richie Valens and J. P. "Big Bopper" Richardson. *See p. 24.*

1961

The United States begins sending military advisors and supplies to South Vietnam to support the pro-American government against the Communist threat. *See p. 12.*

1963

February 19 – Betty Friedan's *The Feminist Mystique* is published in the United States. *See p. 16.*

May 27 – *The Freewheelin' Bob Dylan* is released. *See p. 25.*

August 28 – The famous March on Washington civil rights event takes place in Washington, D.C. *See p. 11.*

November 22 – President John F. Kennedy is assassinated in Dallas, Texas, and Vice President Lyndon B. Johnson is sworn in to replace him. *See p. 11.*

1964

July 2 – President Johnson signs the Civil Rights Act of 1964 into law. *See p. 11.*

August 7 – U.S. Congress passes the Tonkin Gulf Resolution, empowering President Johnson to dramatically increase American military involvement in the Vietnam War. *See p. 12.*

1965

March 8 – The first U.S. ground troops are deployed in Vietnam. *See p. 13.*

July 25 – Bob Dylan "goes electric" at the Newport Folk Festival. *See p. 28.*

August 6 – President Johnson signs the Voting Rights Act of 1965 into law. *See p. 11.*

December 3 – The Beatles release *Rubber Soul. See p. 28.*

1966

May – Dylan's *Blonde on Blonde* is released. *See p. 27.*

June – The National Organization for Women (NOW) is founded. *See p. 16.*

1967

May 16-18 – The Monterey Pop Festival takes place and features breakout performances from Jimi Hendrix and Janis Joplin. *See p. 33.*

June-August – The so-called Summer of Love unfolds in San Francisco's Haight-Ashbury District. *See p. 32.*

July 23 – A destructive and deadly race riot breaks out in Detroit.

October 21 – An antiwar protest in Washington, D.C., draws as many as 250,000 supporters.

December – U.S. troop levels in Vietnam increase to 485,000.

1968

January 30-31 – North Vietnam and the Viet Cong launch the Tet Offensive, which dramatically changes public opinion in America about the war. *See p. 19.*

March 31 – President Johnson announces that he will not seek re-election. *See p. 19.*

April 4 – Civil rights leader Martin Luther King Jr. is assassinated in Memphis, Tennessee. *See p. 19.*

April 5-14 – Riots break out in more than 100 American cities in the days following King's death. *See p. 19.*

June 6 – Democratic presidential candidate Robert F. Kennedy is assassinated in Los Angeles, California. *See p. 20.*

August 26-29 – The Democratic National Convention in Chicago is marred by repeated clashes between city police and antiwar demonstrators. *See p. 21.*

1969

February – Michael Lang, Artie Kornfeld, John Roberts, and Joel Rosenman agree to form a partnership called Woodstock Ventures for the purpose of organizing a multi-day rock festival. *See p. 39.*

July 15 – The town of Wallkill, New York, reneges on its agreement to host the Woodstock festival. *See p. 43.*

July 16 – Michael Lang visits Max Yasgur's farm in Bethel, New York; Yasgur subsequently agrees to lease a portion of his property for the Woodstock festival. *See p. 45.*

July 21 – Officials in Bethel approve all the local permits needed for Woodstock to take place on the Yasgur farm. *See p. 47.*

August 9-10 – A murderous cult led by Charles Manson goes on a killing spree in southern California. *See p. 89.*

August 11 – Concertgoers begin arriving at Woodstock, prompting an even more frenzied drive to prepare the grounds for the upcoming festival. *See p. 51.*

August 15 – The Woodstock Music and Art Fair officially opens. *See p. 54.*

August 16 – The second day of the Woodstock festival is held. *See p. 58.*

August 17 – The third day of the Woodstock festival takes place. *See p. 65.*

August 18 – The multi-day concert finally draws to a close with a morning performance by Jimi Hendrix; the gargantuan task of post-concert clean-up begins. *See pp. 66 and 84.*

August 19 – The *New York Times* backtracks on its earlier criticisms of the festival and publishes a pro-Woodstock editorial titled "Morning After at Bethel." *See p. 88.*

December 6 – A rock and roll festival at Altamont Speedway in Livermore, California, becomes infamous after members of the Hell's Angeles motorcycle gang murder a concertgoer in front of the stage during the Rolling Stones' set. *See p. 89.*

1970

March – A film documentary of the Woodstock festival called *Woodstock: 3 Days of Peace and Music* is released. *See p. 93.*

September 18 – Jimi Hendrix is found dead of a drug overdose. *See p. 96.*

October 4 – Janis Joplin is found dead of a heroin overdose. *See p. 96.*

1973

March – After years of withdrawals, the last American troops leave Vietnam. *See p. 110.*

1975

South Vietnam falls to Communist forces, bringing the Vietnam War to an end. *See p. 110.*

1994

 August 12-14 – A twenty-fifth anniversary Woodstock concert is held in Saugerties, New York. *See p. 104.*

1999

 July 23-25 – The Woodstock '99 festival, held in upstate New York's Mohawk Valley, is marred by violence and vandalism. *See p. 105.*

SOURCES FOR FURTHER STUDY

DeCurtis, Anthony, James Henke, and Holly George-Warren, eds. *The Rolling Stone Illustrated History of Rock & Roll: The Definitive History of the Most Important Artists and Their Music.* New York: Random House, 1992. This oversized, richly illustrated general history of rock-and-roll music provides comprehensive coverage of giants of the 1960s such as Bob Dylan, the Beatles, the Rolling Stones, the Who, and Jimi Hendrix. It also makes an effort to place the work of these and other artists within the context of their times. The book's opinionated coverage of the value of various performers, though, reflects the stance of *Rolling Stone* magazine alone, and not necessarily that of the wider world of rock-and-roll criticism.

George-Warren, Holly. *The Rock and Roll Hall of Fame: The First 25 Years.* New York: Harper-Collins, 2009. This heavily illustrated resource provides in-depth biographical portraits of every inductee into the Rock and Roll Hall of Fame in its first quarter-century of existence. Each profile, whether on a musician, band, or producer, blends Hall of Fame memorabilia, photographs from various points in the individual's career, quotes and anecdotes, biographical background, and lists of top-selling records, hits, and awards.

Get Up, Stand Up: The Story of Pop and Protest. PBS, 2005. This two-hour documentary explores the history of protest songs in American history from the early twentieth century to the present. It pays particular attention to protest music of the 1960s, when civil rights, the Vietnam War, and black nationalism all sparked the creation of culturally significant new songs. The film, which is hosted by Chuck D, cofounder of the rap group Public Enemy, combines historical footage with commentary from some of leading musical artists and music critics from the 1990s and 2000s.

Lang, Michael, with Holly George-Warren. *The Road to Woodstock: From the Man Behind the Legendary Festival.* New York: Ecco, 2009. An entertaining and fast-paced account of the creation and production of the Woodstock Music and Art Fair from Lang, the most visible member of the Woodstock Ventures partnership.

Makower, Joel. *Woodstock: The Oral History.* New York: Doubleday, 1989. This fascinating work stitches together interviews from dozens of people involved with Woodstock to tell the story of the festival and its various triumphs and tribulations.

"Protest Songs," *Lift Every Voice: Music in American Life.* University of Virginia Library, 2009 [last updated]. Retrieved from http://www2.lib.virginia.edu/exhibits/music/protest.html.

This section of the *Lift Every Voice* online project provides a broad overview of the history of protest music in American culture. Lyrics are provided for some featured songs, and the site features audio clips of notable protest songs by performers like Bob Dylan and the Beatles.

"The 200 Greatest Songs of the Sixties," *Pitchfork.com,* 2006. Retrieved from http://pitchfork .com/features/staff-lists/6400-the-200-greatest-songs-of-the-1960s/. Rock-and-roll fans will argue endlessly about these rankings, but many great and enduring songs are featured, and rock legends like the Rolling Stones, the Beach Boys, the Beatles, Bob Dylan, and Jimi Hendrix pop up again and again. Each song listed is accompanied by a paragraph or two of commentary.

BIBLIOGRAPHY

Books

Bell, Dale, ed. *Woodstock: An Inside Look at the Movie That Shook Up the World and Defined a Generation*. Studio City, CA: Michael Wiese, 1999.

Brokaw, Tom. *Boom! Voices of the Sixties, Personal Reflections on the '60s and Today*. New York: Random House, 2007.

Cleveland, Les. *Dark Laughter: War in Song and Popular Culture*. Westport, CT: Praeger, 1994.

Curry, Jack. *Woodstock: The Summer of Our Lives*. New York: Weidenfeld and Nicolson, 1989.

Editors of Time-Life Books. *Turbulent Years: The 60s*. Alexandria, VA: Time-Life Books, 1998.

Evans, Mike, and Paul Kingsbury, eds. *Woodstock: Three Days That Rocked the World*. New York: Sterling, 2009.

Fornatale, Pete. *Back to the Garden: The Story of Woodstock*. New York: Touchstone, 2009.

George, Nelson. *Where Did Our Love Go? The Rise and Fall of the Motown Sound*. Champaign: University of Illinois Press, 2007.

Lang, Michael, with Holly George-Warren. *The Road to Woodstock: From the Man Behind the Legendary Festival*. New York: Ecco, 2009.

Makower, Joel. *Woodstock: The Oral History*. New York: Doubleday, 1989.

Miller, James. *Flowers in the Dustbin: The Rise of Rock and Roll, 1947-1977*. New York: Simon and Schuster, 1999.

Palmer, Robert. *Rock and Roll: An Unruly History*. New York: Harmony Books, 1995.

Perone, James E. *Woodstock: An Encyclopedia of the Music and Art Fair*. Westport, CT: Greenwood Press, 2005.

Pielke, Robert G. *You Say You Want a Revolution: Rock Music in American Culture*. Chicago: Nelson-Hall, 1986.

Roberts, John, Joel Rosenman, and Robert Pilpel. *Young Men with Unlimited Capital: The Story of Woodstock*. New York: Harcourt, Brace & Jovanovich, 1974.

Spitz, Robert Stephen. *Barefoot in Babylon: The Creation of the Woodstock Music Festival*. New York: Viking Press, 1979.

Szatmary, David P. *Rockin' in Time: A Social History of Rock-and-Roll.* Upper Saddle River, NJ: Prentice Hall, 2009.

Tiber, Elliot, with Tom Monte. *Taking Woodstock: A True Story of a Riot, a Concert, and a Life.* Garden City Park, NY: Square One, 2009.

Unterberger, Richie. *Eight Miles High: Folk Rock's Flight from Haight-Ashbury to Woodstock.* San Francisco: Backbeat Books, 2003.

Wilentz, Sean. *Bob Dylan in America.* New York: Doubleday, 2010.

Online Resources

The Rock and Roll Hall of Fame and Museum, *Rockhall.com*, n.d. Retrieved from http://rock hall.com/.

"The Sixties: The Years That Shaped a Generation," *PBS.org*, 2005. Retrieved from http://www .pbs.org/opb/thesixties/.

"The Woodstock Festivals," *Woodstock.com.* n.d. Retrieved from http://www.woodstock.com/ themusic.php.

DVD/Blu-Ray

Woodstock: 3 Days of Peace and Music (The Director's Cut). Warner Home Video, 1997.

Woodstock: 3 Days of Peace and Music, The Director's Cut (40th Anniversary Ultimate Collectors' Edition). Warner Home Video, 2009.

Woodstock '99. Sony, 2000.

PHOTO AND ILLUSTRATION CREDITS

Cover and Title Page: PRNewsFoto/Signatures Network, Henry Diltz via AP Photo.

Chapter One: AP Photo/Bill Hudson, File (p. 10); LBJ Library photo by Frank Wolfe (p. 14); AP Photo (p. 16); ©Lisa Law (p. 18); ©Topham/The Image Works (p. 20).

Chapter Two: Michael Ochs Archives/Getty Images (p. 24); Photofest (p. 27); ©CBS/Photofest (p. 29); Album cover: FILLMORE WEST 1969/The Grateful Dead. Label GDP/Grateful Dead Production/WEA (p. 31); AP Photo (p. 33).

Chapter Three: ©John Dominis/The Image Works (p. 38); ©Warner Bros/Photofest (p. 41); John Duprey/NY Daily News Archive via Getty Images (p. 45); DVD/Movie still: WOODSTOCK: THREE DAYS OF PEACE & MUSIC. Photo ©1969 Michael Lang/ Henry Diltz. ©Warner Home Video (p. 47); AP Photo (p. 51).

Chapter Four: ©Elliott Landy/The Image Works (p. 55); Bill Hanley, Woodstock 1969 - Photo by David Marks (3rd Ear Music/Hidden Years Music Archive, South Africa: www.3rd earmusic; e-mail: thirdear@iafrica.com) (p. 57); ©Elliott Landy/The Image Works (p. 62); ©Warner Bros/Photofest (p. 65); Henry Diltz/AFP/Getty Images/Newscom (p. 66).

Chapter Five: ©Warner Bros/Photofest (p. 70); ©Peter Menzel/HIP/The Image Works (p. 73); ©Warner Bros/Photofest (p. 75); ©John Dominis/The Image Works (p. 77); ©Elliott Landy/The Image Works (p. 80).

Chapter Six: AP Photo (p. 85); ©John Dominis/The Image Works (p. 87); AP Photo (p. 90); ©Warner Bros/Photofest (p. 92); ©Warner Bros. Pictures/Photofest (p. 95).

Chapter Seven: Wikimedia Commons (//commons.wikimedia.org/wiki/File:20090811_ Lol lapalooza.jpg). Author: LaCabeza Grande. Originally posted to Flickr (http://flickr .com/photos/28146866@N00/3812730832) (p. 101); Cambria Harkey/Lollapalooza (http://www.lollapalooza.com) (p. 103); Lucas Jackson/Reuters/Newscom (p. 104); Photo courtesy of Bethel Woods Center for the Arts (p. 106); Photo courtesy of Bethel Woods Center for the Arts (p. 109).

Biographies: Courtesy National Archives, photo no. 306-SSM-4C(53)3. Rowland Scherman, Photographer. (p. 115); David Gahr/Getty Images (p. 119); Photofest (p. 124); Gary Coronado/The Palm Beach Post via Zuma Press/Newscom (p. 128); ©Henry Diltz/The Image Works (p. 131); Evelyn Straus/New York Daily News Archive via Getty Images

INDEX

X-Y-Z